Praise for *The Social Organization*

'This book is a must-read for anyone responsible for driving the performance and culture of an organization, whether CEO or HR practitioner. Grounded in theory and practice, it shows how to evolve a people strategy, with rich, illustrative case studies from a variety of industry sectors. These lead to a diagnostic tool and a robust organizational prioritization model. A book that unlocks tremendous value for academics, HR practitioners and business leaders alike.' **James Cullens, Executive Director, Group HR and Marcomms, WS Atkins plc**

'This is the book that has been missing for social enterprise practitioners of any function – HR, IT, Operations or... Quality. Bringing together multiple disciplines, it provides compelling insights about how to make an organization greater than the sum of its parts. A must-read.' **Céline Schillinger, Head, Quality Innovation and Engagement, Sanofi Pasteur**

'This is a fantastic book for all strategic organization development practitioners. It provides best-practice guidance supported by sound underlying principles and excellent case studies. The reader will be challenged to reconsider their own assumptions and attitudes towards organization development and this makes the book particularly valuable.' **David Frost, Organizational Development Director, Total Produce plc**

'If you are going to take networks seriously – and after reading this book you will understand why you must – then you need to learn how to better manage them. Taking an organization development perspective, *The Social Organization* shows how social capital helps organizations create value, compete and collaborate.' **Paul Sparrow, Emeritus Professor of International HRM, Lancaster University Management School**

'Jon Ingham provides an important contribution to ensuring that in future we develop more successful organizations, that make the most of people, not only individually but in how they work effectively together in teams, networks and communities. A must-read for helping to ensure the future of Good Work for many and not just a privileged few.' **Lesley Giles, Director, The Work Foundation**

'Jon Ingham draws on his rich experience as both HR Director and consultant, providing key insights from academia matched with great case stories. He extracts the essentials of what must be addressed for an organization to perform to its full potential. Highly readable and highly recommendable.' **Bjarte Bogsnes, Vice President, Performance Management Development, Statoil, and Chairman, Beyond Budgeting Roundtable**

'I would love to see our HR decision makers reading Jon Ingham's great food for thought – rooted in many very relevant case studies and references... The author's analytic approach, staying close to the facts and studies, makes this book a sound base for his conclusions – it is mind-opening on the basis of great observations. After reading it, I felt empowered and engaged to drive my own social/digital/organizational transformation.' **Harald Schirmer, Manager, Digital Transformation and Change, Continental**

'This book is a compendium of concepts and thoughts enabling understanding of the evolution and functioning of organizations. It combines a theoretical background with practical examples from leading companies. What makes it particularly interesting is the combination of different viewpoints, through the lens of many different disciplines. I enjoyed reading and learning.' **Dr Hans-Juergen Sturm, Head of Collaboration, Content and Portals, Amadeus IT Group**

'The building blocks of how people deliver value have changed fundamentally with the advent of social technologies. Jon Ingham brings his years of experience and offers a treasure trove of useful insights to build social capital within organizations and weave an ecosystem of high performance.' **Tanmay Vora, Country Head and Director (R&D), Basware, author and blogger**

'In *The Social Organization*, Jon Ingham takes an insightful look at organizations from a social perspective. He reminds us what we already know but tend to forget – that organizations are social communities of people and that to understand and manage them well we need to pay attention to human disciplines such as psychology, sociology, anthropology and neuroscience.' **David Gurteen, Director, Gurteen Knowledge**

'This book is the guide to understanding the social organization, with a cross-disciplinary point of view focusing on how it creates value. Ingham presents a model to make this happen. He provides readers with new and relevant perspectives on people and organization development approaches and on how these create important outcomes.' **Nicolas Rolland, Head of Engie University, Engie**

'Through a very complete and engaging journey in the "The Social Organization" dimension, Jon Ingham is shifting our focus out of the traditional boundaries and usual management approaches. He is helping us to discover, to design and to manage what will be the future and how to get the best from our people capabilities by creating a unique, successful organizational and social system dynamic.' **Philippe Bonnet, Vice President, Human Resources, Global Head, Learning and Development, Essilor International SA**

'This book is a must for public sector HR professionals. It captures the essence of good practice, is full of creative but sensible thinking and opens up the mind to what is possible. Our people are not just assets, they are a precious resource and implementing even a fraction of what is in here will make a difference to them and to your business.' **Sue Evans, former Head of HR and Organizational Development, Warwickshire County Council, and President 2016–2017, Public Sector People Managers Association (PPMA)**

'I define good organization as "capable people working well together". Jon Ingham takes the idea of relationships much further. Social capital, he argues, is enhanced by good organization design and by other design choices, such as the use of technology. While Jon likes to position people management as the most important activity of all (his organization value chain), he takes a business rather than an HR view.' **Andrew Campbell, Ashridge Executive Education, and co-author of** *Designing Effective Organizations* **and** *Operating Model Canvas*

'Organization Design, as a discipline, is frequently dominated by strategy, structure and fitting people into roles. In this book, Jon Ingham takes the discipline beyond that, highlighting that designers should think more completely about how processes and technology tools enable an organization to leverage employee knowledge through collaboration. In my experience, employees crave the opportunity to collaborate, and if the organization doesn't enable that, they are missing out.' **Tim Gardner, Director, Organizational Effectiveness, Kimberly-Clark**

'*The Social Organization* is a well-supported study, examining human capital and the activities necessary to increase business performance. The chapter on "Designing the workplace" is spot on as an enabler for increasing employee satisfaction and productivity.' **Gene Carr, Global Workplace Strategy Lead, The Kellogg Company**

'I found the concepts that Jon Ingham outlines extremely helpful in bridging the gap between traditional HR models and new ways of thinking about how sustainable value can be created through organization. The ideas he takes the reader through are both stimulating and challenging, which in turn makes them invaluable to anyone grappling with some of the most pressing issues that confront organizations today.' **Geoff Lloyd, Group Human Resource Director, Serco**

'It is indisputable that we are better as a team than as a collection of individuals. Collaboration is at the heart of most successes. Yet traditional HR has often led to organizations which suppress, or at best ignore, rather than nurture this key asset. Work and the workplace today are dramatically different from how they were at the turn of the millennium, and in a competitive knowledge-based economy being successful requires an agile HR with a new focus. This book offers precisely that.' **James Purvis, HR Department Head, CERN**

The Social Organization

Developing employee connections
and relationships for improved
business performance

Jon Ingham

Anton,

Best wishes,

Jon.

First published in Great Britain and the United States in 2017 by Kogan Page Limited

2nd Floor, 45 Gee Street	c/o Martin P Hill Consulting	4737/23 Ansari Road
London	122 W 27th St, 10th Floor	Daryaganj
EC1V 3RS	New York NY 10001	New Delhi 110002
United Kingdom	USA	India

www.koganpage.com

© Jon Ingham, 2017

The right of Jon Ingham to be identified as the author of this work has been asserted by him in accordance with the Copyright, Designs and Patents Act 1988.

ISBN   978 0 7494 8011 0
E-ISBN   978 0 7494 8012 7

British Library Cataloguing-in-Publication Data

A CIP record for this book is available from the British Library.

Library of Congress Cataloging-in-Publication Data

Names: Ingham, Jon (Independent consultant) author.
Title: The social organization : developing employee connections and
   relationships for improved business performance / Jon Ingham.
Description: 1st Edition. | New York : Kogan Page Ltd, [2017] | Includes
   bibliographical references and index.
Identifiers: LCCN 2017014122 (print) | LCCN 2017020985 (ebook) | ISBN
   9780749480127 (ebook) | ISBN 9780749480110 (alk. paper) | ISBN 9780749480127
   (ebook)
Subjects: LCSH: Personnel management. | Interpersonal relations. | Strategic
   planning. | Social capital (Sociology) | Corporate culture.
Classification: LCC HF5549 (ebook) | LCC HF5549 .I56325 2017 (print) | DDC
   658.3/145--dc23

Typeset by Integra Software Services, Pondicherry
Print production managed by Jellyfish
Printed and bound by CPI Group (UK) Ltd, Croydon, CR0 4YY

CONTENTS

13   Using social technologies and analytics 280

ABOUT THE AUTHOR

Jon Ingham is a researcher, writer, speaker, trainer and consultant in strategic people and organizational management. He currently runs his own company, Strategic Dynamics. Prior to this he worked as Director of Human Capital Consulting, Europe for Buck Consultants/ACS (now Conduent); Head of HR Consulting for Penna (now part of Adecco/Lee Hecht Harrison); and HR Director for Ernst & Young (now EY), working first in the UK and then based in Moscow, covering the former USSR. Before this he worked as an IT/change management consultant for Andersen Consulting (now Accenture).

He is the author of a previous book on strategic human capital management and a well-known blog, Strategic HCM. He has also contributed chapters to several other books and has published dozens of articles, including 'Building better HR departments', which he co-authored with Dave Ulrich in 2016.

Jon has lectured on Executive MBA courses in strategic management, HR management and change management. He speaks at many leading HR, IT, property and other business conferences around the world and trains several hundred HR practitioners in small group sessions each year. He also partners with Glassdoor to provide UK media commentary on the world of work, and has recently appeared on the Radio 4 *Today* programme, *BBC Breakfast*, *BBC World Business* and *Sky Breakfast*.

Jon has a BA in psychology, a master's degree in engineering and an MBA. He is a Fellow of the Chartered Institute of Personnel and Development (CIPD). He is married to Sandra who is a marketing consultant and town/borough councillor, as well as their business's company secretary, and was also chief indexer for this book. They have two daughters, Elena and Kamila, and a cat, Amba. Jon's interests include sailing, travel and gaining new skills and experiences – he is currently trying to learn Japanese and also continues to try to stay on top of new developments in technology. You can often find him on Twitter, in the Social HR 'community' in Google Plus and the Art of HR group in LinkedIn. His main website for this book is http://www.organization.social.

FOREWORD

It is an honour to write a foreword to a book of outstanding ideas by my colleague Jon Ingham. It is easy to write since I agree with most of the ideas. But it is important to clarify what ideas have the most impact and why and how these ideas impact key stakeholders. One of Jon's obvious strengths is his eclectic thinking and ability to access an inordinate number of theories, frameworks, tools and examples. I will select only a few that illustrate the quality of this work.

What ideas have impact and why

Organization matters

In a world of individuation and decomposition of organizations, many deny or misunderstand the power of organizations. Organizations make the whole better than the individual parts. Effective organizations create more economic success and personal well-being than people working alone. Organizations turn strategic aspirations into sustainable actions leading to results. These results come from strategic maps (Chapter 1) that create financial, customer, operational and organizational value chains. These value chains enable organizations to compete in their market. In my consulting work I often ask executives to divide 100 points among strategic, financial, operational and organizational capabilities required for their organization to compete in their marketplace. Inevitably, 'organization' gets 30–40 per cent of these votes. By focusing on value created (Chapter 2), organizations matter because they serve others. In recent work (set out in the book I co-authored, *Victory through Organization*), we found that the organization has four times the impact on business performance than the skills of individuals.

In addition, the social relationships within an organization help define the organization's capabilities as well as its ability to be effective (Chapter 4). Organizations provide a setting for individuals to learn, grow and develop their talents. Human neurology teaches us to avoid threat and seek opportunity by managing issues of status, certainty, autonomy, relatedness and fairness (see *Handbook of NeuroLeadership* (2013) by David Rock and Al Ringleb). Organizations are settings where relationship issues can be managed to improve personal well-being. I have spent much of my professional life helping people to find meaning from the organizations where they work, live and play (see *Why of Work* (2010) co-authored with Wendy Ulrich).

Organizations are measured by the value they create

Organizations exist and survive when they create value for others. Rather than measuring activities that occur within an organization, it is important to focus on the outcomes of these activities (Chapter 2). These outcomes include employee well-being or strategy execution inside the organization as well as customers and investors outside the organization. The focus on outcomes of organization human resource (HR) work has been a driving premise of our work for 30 years. We have focused on how leaders turn customer promises into employee actions (Ulrich, *Leadership Brand*, 2007), how culture is less about values and more about firm identity in the marketplace made real to employees, and how leaders can deliver shareholder value (Ulrich, *Leadership Capital Index*, 2015).

Organizations may be defined as capabilities more than hierarchies

Rather than just looking at an organization as a hierarchy with roles and rules, this book looks at an organization as a bundle of capabilities focused on identity, core strengths and processes that can be leveraged to create value (Chapters 2, 6 and 7). It identifies emerging capabilities of accountability, talent, collaboration and agility. The network organization (Chapter 8) interprets how people create social relationships through their organization that enable them to be personally effective and for the organization to succeed. The network organization suggested offers insights into how social relationships can be connected together within an organization through various types of communities (Chapter 8). The book then shows how HR practices can enable these communities (Chapter 9) and change the nature of the workplace (Chapter 10). It offers innovative HR practices to make this new organization happen (Chapter 11).

When we wrote *Organizational Capability* in 1990 we were generally ignored. Organization models focused on right sizing, delayering, re-engineering and role clarity. In the ensuing years, the concept of organization as capability has increased attention on culture, systems thinking and the power of organizations.

In my recent work with Arthur Yeung, we are defining the market-based network organization where platforms of capabilities can be used to shape new market opportunities. These new organizations move quickly to create new opportunities. Platforms of capabilities embedded in market networks may be the next extension of the organization capability logic.

Organization understanding requires multidisciplinary views

To understand how organizations operate requires insights from many disciplines. In this book Jon does an outstanding job drawing on theory and research from multiple disciplines to define an organization, including: psychology, sociology, anthropology, neuroscience, behavioural economics and strategy. Each of these disciplines offers insights into how organizations operate by creating a social organization. This social organization can then be architected (Chapter 6) to deliver sustainable value. Through his 'organization prioritization model' (OPM), Jon evolves how to diagnose and improve social organizations. The OPM extends traditional organization diagnoses by including organization enablers, but also relationship elements, and key organization capability outcomes. He also suggests the innovative use of managing groups (Chapter 12) and technology and analytics to embed the organization (Chapter 13).

Again, the above are only a small set of the many ideas proposed in this book. Collectively, they evolve how various stakeholders define and improve organizations.

How these ideas impact key stakeholders

HR professionals who want to deliver value can better do so by understanding and creating the right organization capabilities. Because of Jon's deep background in HR, he is able in every chapter to offer insights on the evolving HR profession. He talks about how HR can link to strategy through capabilities (Chapters 1 and 2); and how to innovate HR practices in engagement, recruiting, careers, performance management, rewards, diversity and development (Chapter 3). He also shows that integration of these HR practices can be used to deliver the right organization capabilities required to win. HR is not about HR, but about the value that HR creates for the business and its stakeholders. HR analytics (Chapter 13) should evolve from scorecards and insights to business impact. Jon offers not only ideas, but tools and examples of leading companies such as Zappos, HCL, IBM, Cisco, Xerox, Morning Star, Spotify, Whole Foods and many others.

In particular, his ideas benefit organization development experts who operate at the intersection of business strategy, personal and organizational change, HR systems and information. He extends traditional models of organization diagnosis (eg 7S, STAR) by focusing on delivering capabilities of innovation, talent, change and collaboration. He also offers innovative tools (eg gamification and hackathons in Chapter 6) to perform organization diagnosis. His OPM model offers those charged with designing organizations a more robust framework for doing so.

His ideas can be adapted to other staff functions, including real estate, facilities management, information technology and finance. To be effective, these functions require understanding of the social organization Jon proposes and they, like HR, can be transformed to deliver more through applying his organization principles.

Ultimately, line managers have accountability and responsibility for social organizations. The ideas and tools throughout this book will help line managers to move beyond maxims about people (as our most important asset) to real actions that deliver value.

Conclusion

This outstanding compendium of ideas evolves traditional thinking about organizations. It captures the latest thinking and articulates the next thinking on how people come together into social organizations to create value. For the last 100 years, organizations have been primary producers of economic wealth and social well-being. With thinkers like Jon, the next 100 years may be just as propitious.

Dave Ulrich
Rensis Likert Professor of Business,
University of Michigan
Partner, RBL Group

PREFACE

I started my career working in chemical engineering before moving into IT, and then, fairly accidentally, into what was a very new discipline of change management. That led to taking on an HR Director job to undertake a change management role. Moving into HR without really knowing anything about the function enabled me to ask the sort of seemingly stupid questions that become more difficult with increasing experience. One of the questions I asked was why, if the point of performance in business is increasingly the team, did so much of what we focused on in HR concern the performance of individuals? A related question was how, if we needed to change our people practices to focus more on teams, could we best achieve this?

These questions have been at the back of my mind for most of my subsequent career. Ten years ago I wrote a book on managing people to create human capital, which I defined as the value created for an organization by its people (Ingham, 2007). One of the case studies this book referred to was a leadership development programme led by people development consultant Nigel Paine whilst he was Head of Learning at the BBC. This involved the early use of social media in the form of a wiki used to share insights between participants on the programme. The case study stimulated my own interest in social media, and encouraged by other learning leaders like Donald Taylor, Charles Jennings and the late Jay Cross, I set up my own blog, Strategic HCM. To the extent that I am known in and beyond HR this blog is probably the main reason why.

My blog acts as the top of my business development funnel, providing a pull- rather than push-based approach to doing business. However, it also acts as an accelerator for my own learning. I am, I think, one of the very few people who have actually used a learning log. I used to complete this on the way home after work but gave up after leaving it on the train! But then I realized I could keep a blog as a learning log. A blog is in the cloud so I never lose it, I can access it anywhere I go, and it is social – people can comment on my posts and their comments then trigger another whole round of learning. This is therefore informal learning but social learning too. And after 10 years of posting, my blog is almost becoming my second brain. I often find I forget about some previous learning I have had but I can generally remember that I posted on it, so I just go to my blog and remind myself of the insight. It is the nearest thing to Neo learning to fly a helicopter in *The Matrix* that I, at least, have ever been involved with.

Although my last book concentrated on managing people for human capital I did also mention that an even more important organizational quality is social capital – the value of the social relationships, teaming and collaboration between the people working in an organization. Back in 2007 I also set up a blog called The New Social Business.

I find blogging relatively easy but writing books enormously hard. So it has been a while, but a decade after my first book this new one is a result of my subsequent experiences, conversations, reflections and blogging on these reflections, leading to further conversation and reflections. It is also in fact an attempt, finally, to answer the two questions I posed at the start of my career in HR (or perhaps a rather broader discipline covering people, organization and relationships), which I noted above.

Providing answers to the questions is now much more important than it was back then. Businesses are now much more complex, not just relying on teams but also on communities, networks and cooperation across the whole organization. In some ways it is also somewhat easier – through social media in particular, things that were very difficult to do are now extremely simple. At the same time, in some ways it is now much harder too, particularly given the amount and pace of transformation already under way in organizations. I remember presenting at an HR conference about 10 years ago where the chairperson suggested that there was really nothing new that organizations could do, that the key need was just to do simple, obvious things well. Thankfully, I do not hear that said any more! Changes in technology, society, business and other areas are leading to profound change within organizations too. In fact in many areas of people and organizational management there has been so much change there is almost no comparison between the way things are done now and how they were performed 10 years ago.

So, for example, if you look at recruitment there is almost no similarity between the post-and-pray job advertising we used to focus on 10 years ago and the conversational, community-based and technology-enabled approaches used by many employers today. Similarly, learning has been through profound change, moving from traditional, sage-on-a-stage training to informal, conversational and again technology-based approaches. This includes the use of virtual conferences and massively open online courses (MOOCs). Internal communication has changed from a top-down, time-consuming cascade to an ongoing conversation between people operating across the organization. Even performance management, which however obviously broken, seemed for a long time immune from change, is now going through a major transformation. Many companies are now moving to simpler, ongoing, more conversational approaches, often dropping reviews and ratings in the process. It is only really the reward part of the employee life cycle that now remains unchanged – but possibly not for much longer, particularly as companies that have dropped performance ratings realize they need to find another way of differentiating pay.

Changes are also extending into the design of our organizations. People now talk about the future of work being flat, self-managing, democratic, emergent etc. I think these would all be largely positive, socially oriented attributes, although as yet there are a relatively low number of maverick organizations embracing them. However, a broader proportion of organizations are reducing layers, changing the role of the line manager, empowering employees, and experimenting with networks and communities.

A common theme behind a lot of these changes is the use of social media. However, this is not the only enabler. The last 10 years in particular has seen huge advances in our understanding of organization design, workplace design, HR practices, teaming, organization development, social network analysis and other areas, including the workings of the human brain. You may notice that even though these changes extend beyond social media there is still often something about 'social', ie people's relationships, which connects them. However, despite this commonality these different socially based developments are often not that well integrated. In many organizations I find excellent work being undertaken in HR, property, IT and other disciplines but these areas are often not talking to each other about these separate changes, or even if they are, often do not have a common perspective on what they are trying to achieve.

In addition, the changes I have listed are all potentially positive but in some cases I worry that firms are making changes just because it seems to be the new thing to do. Performance management is a particularly good example. There is so much encouragement to drop reviews and ratings that organizations run the risk of doing this just because it seems to be the new standard approach, not actually because there is a business rationale for doing so. But it is important that organizations change for a purpose, not just for the sake of change. Disputing things just for the sake of disruption is just a disruption. And just replacing one set of best practices with another set is unlikely to produce much positive benefit. Instead, what is needed is a shift from best practice to best fit, where firms tailor and align their organizational changes according to their own individual needs.

This implies that companies cannot follow a single path, often expressed as a maturity curve. The journey cannot be as simple as moving from one state of maturity to another, however compelling these future states may sound. Plus I think that organizations struggle to weigh up the benefits of becoming more mature, eg in moving from achievement-orange to evolutionary-teal (Laloux, 2014) or level 4 (collaborative) to level 5 (unbounded) (Hlupic, 2014). This means many organizations fail to develop the sort of mature approaches that would actually be useful for them. Instead of this, organizations need to figure out what makes most sense for them at a particular point in time.

Social capital provides a means of responding to these problems by providing a focal point for social innovation. If organizations have not been thinking about outcomes like social capital then they should start to do so. If they have only been planning to create human capital they can shift their attention to social capital, or broaden their focus to incorporate both of these qualities. Once they have done this, it generally becomes clear that the people and organizational activities they are undertaking will need to be changed. The difference here is that all these changes in activity are changes for a purpose. That is, they are the actions that are required to keep aligned with the organizational outcomes that a particular business needs. The approach encourages employers to invest appropriately in their people and the relationships between these people as drivers of business performance.

In addition, this approach provides a basis to select the activities that will have the greatest impact on a company's social outcomes, regardless of the functional areas they are from. It contrasts with investing in social media, or any other areas, just because these seem to be the right, or the popular, things to do. Companies that follow this approach are the social organizations that are the focus of this book.

There are, unfortunately, a few issues associated with the use of the word 'social'. The first is that the word has alternative meanings relating to leisure and recreation (social clubs) and the external community and environment (social responsibility). In particular, people also use the term social enterprise or social business in this second alternative context where it refers to a cause-driven, not-for-profit business (Yunus, 2011). This has little to do with the social organization of this book other than, first, that it indicates the growing desire for business to have values that are people-centred and connected to what is going on around them. Second, there also is increasing evidence that social capital is a major driver of sustainable development and economic success.

Social business is also already used in the context of people's relationships. However, most of the time it refers more specifically to the way organizations are using social media. It also tends to focus on the external use of this technology to enhance the conversations that firms have with their customers and other external stakeholders. This book, and the idea of the social organization, is part of an attempt to rebalance the agenda by focusing on the internal relationships between the people working for a business. This does not mean that external relationships are not important – clearly they are. I also appreciate the trend for organizational boundaries to become more permeable, meaning that there is increasingly less difference between what is internal and external. However, there is still enormous value in understanding and acting on the potential and the opportunity to improve internal relationships. In particular this book argues that external relationships can only be effective when internal relationships have been developed first. Social business rides on the back of the social organization.

There is also a second challenge, which is that 'social' is becoming, or possibly has already become, a rather hackneyed term. After all, I, and others, have been suggesting that the social adoption curve may have reached its peak since the early 2010s (Donkin, 2011). However, that really only applies to the use of social media. The transformation of businesses into true social organizations that focus on their people's relationships has only just begun. In particular, despite the long-standing interest and focus on human capital within the HR area, firms are still struggling to develop this effectively. There has been very little interest or focus on social capital. The result of this is that whilst social may be much more important than human capital, it is generally much less well developed. In fact, for me at least, moving HR's focus onto the outcomes of teaming and collaboration – ie the improved relationships/social capital in our businesses – is the most important opportunity the discipline faces to improve its contribution, impact and credibility.

So, yes, organizations can do a lot to improve relationships without using the word 'social'. However, if organizations want to become truly social – ie to maximize the value they can gain from their people's relationships – then they really need to be able to use the word! So let's call the social organization what it is, and embrace rather than avoid the word, and idea, of being social.

The social organization also lies behind a lot of the other changes being prioritized within businesses today. As an example, globalization continues to be a disruptive force impacting many organizations, and a key requirement and enabler in global businesses is managing the relationships between people coming from different national cultures.

The need for innovation is another key requirement. Businesses need to focus on exploring new opportunities through networks of people who have time and space to think creatively. In tandem with this, they need to manage traditional functions and efficient, standardized processes focusing on exploiting existing current revenue streams. The new networks also build particularly heavily on relationships and social capital.

Technology is a bigger disrupter still, with many firms seeking to become digital businesses. But at the heart of digital is usually an enterprise social network, and at the heart of this social technology are people's relationships. Digital is also leading to the introduction of platforms that are supplementing an existing increase in the use of the contingent workforce. Contractors, consultants and others now make up a large proportion of organizations. In the United States these groups already account for 34 per cent of the workforce (Frey and Osborne, 2016). These groups all contribute to an organization's human and social capital, though often not as simply as in a traditional workforce. The rise of platforms and the sharing economy mean that many organizations are now also augmenting or replacing their internal traditional and contingent workforces with supposedly external, independent gig workers.

These people can also contribute to an organization's human and social capital but their main role is to perform separate business activities outside the firm, which are accessed through market mechanisms rather than organizational ones. A gig-economy business competes through its agility and scalability, and often the way it can circumvent employment legislation. The use of gig workers could therefore be a fairly short-term phenomenon as governments seek to extend employment legislation to cover these self-employed individuals. In the meantime, however, it is even more important that traditional organizations do find and use the value of their social capital as one of their few remaining ways to compete against their new and often nimbler competitors.

Many of the roles that lend themselves to the gig economy are also the same ones that can be easily automated and are therefore some of the most likely to be replaced by artificial intelligence and robotic technology. In total, 35 per cent of all jobs in the United Kingdom and 47 per cent of those in the United States are at risk of this. In terms of knowledge management work, management thinker Tammy Erickson's analysis suggests that a range of basic to intermediate tasks – including using, creating, categorizing, assessing, making recommendations, deciding and innovating – can all now be performed by computers. The only areas in which people retain an edge are in relational tasks to do with connecting, sharing and empathizing; decisions involving values and morals, and things to do with change (Ingham, 2015). This provides further reinforcement of the need for organizations to think about the relational aspects of their people. Even if organizations do shrink down to a smaller core, with an increasing proportion of their work being outsourced over digital platforms or undertaken via technology, the small core will be even more focused on relationships than it is now.

But personally, I am not convinced that these predicted changes will take place, at least not for some time to come, or to the extent that is often suggested. My belief is that lots of people will continue to work in lots of medium- to large-sized businesses for several decades at least. This book focuses on how we can make these organizations and the work of these people as effective as possible.

For these organizations this new book should be very helpful as, despite the importance of organizational relationships, few other business books explain how organizations can develop social capital and the benefits of doing this. I would point to *Hot Spots* (Gratton, 2007), *A Bigger Prize* (Heffernan, 2015a), *Beyond Measure* (Heffernan, 2015b), *Team of Teams* (McChrystal *et al*, 2015), *11 Rules for Creating Value in the Social Era* (Merchant 2012) and *The Silo Effect* (Tett, 2015) as a few of the books that do. However, I would still suggest that even these texts lack clear advice on actions that can be used to develop relationships at this strategic level. This is therefore what *The Social Organization* tries to do. That is, that since the point of performance in business is now even more definitely the team, and other forms of group, the book explains how we need to change our people and management practices to become more social too. I hope the book will be useful to you in doing this.

References

Donkin, R (2011) [accessed 1 January 2017] The pros and cons of networking, *Financial Times*, Special Report: New World of Work, 7/12 [Online] https://www.ft.com/content/e47c7546-1b67-11e1-8b11-00144feabdc0

Frey, CB and Osborne, M (2016) *Technology at Work v2.0: The future is not what it used to be*, Oxford Martin School, University of Oxford, Oxford

Gratton, L (2007) *Hot Spots: Why some companies buzz with energy and innovation – and others don't*, Financial Times Prentice Hall, Harlow

Heffernan, M (2015a) *A Bigger Prize: When no one wins unless everyone wins*, Simon & Schuster, London

Heffernan, M (2015b) *Beyond Measure: The big impact of small changes*, Simon & Schuster, London

Hlupic, V (2014) *The Management Shift: How to harness the power of people and transform your organization for sustainable success*, Palgrave Macmillan, Basingstoke

Ingham, J (2007) *Strategic Human Capital Management: Creating value through people*, Butterworth Heinemann, Oxford

Ingham, J (2015) [accessed 1 January 2017] Managing in the Digital Age [Blog] Symposium, 6/11 [Online] http://www.symposium.co.uk/managing-in-the-digital-age/

Laloux, F (2014) *Reinventing Organizations: A guide to creating organizations inspired by the next stage in human consciousness*, Nelson Parker, Brussels

McChrystal, S, Collins, T, Silverman, D and Fussell, C (2015) *Team of Teams: New rules of engagement for a complex world*, Penguin Books, London

Merchant, N (2012) *11 Rules for Creating Value in the Social Era*, Harvard Business Review Press, Boston

Tett, G (2015) *The Silo Effect: The peril of expertise and the promise of breaking down barriers*, Simon & Schuster, New York

Yunus, M (2011) *Building Social Business: The new kind of capitalism that serves humanity's most pressing needs*, Public Affairs, New York

ACKNOWLEDGEMENTS

Few books contain the ideas of just one person, and that applies particularly strongly to those emphasizing the importance of connection and collaboration. I think this is partly because authors want to role-model the behaviours they are writing about, and also because they tend to be quite collaborative individuals themselves. However, for me at least, it is also because the topic is quite vast and it would be very difficult to be expert in all of its manifestations.

Therefore, although I hope and believe that I am providing new insights and provocations in quite a few areas, in quite a lot of the topics I am really just reporting on other people's earlier findings and conclusions. I still hope that I have bridged between some of these ideas quite nicely. However, I would like to thank the writers of the other books and case studies I have referenced, and also everyone who talked to me about their own cases. Thank you to each one of you.

My own insights have often originated from my consulting projects. Unfortunately, I have not been able to include any in-depth client case studies. I find these days that the first question new clients ask me is 'Are you happy to sign a non-disclosure agreement (NDA)?' Of course I always say yes, so I am not able to write about these projects. Though interestingly, the second question many clients ask is 'Can you tell me about work you have done with other organizations?' This, of course, I often cannot, as they will have made me sign NDAs too. Something to think about perhaps? Anyway, thanks at least to Ernst & Young (EY) for allowing me to write about my experience there as HR Director. This experience is somewhat dated now but still illustrates some of my points very nicely. And my more recent consulting work is still included in the book, but as part of broader and more generic discussion points rather than as specific case studies. So thank you to all my clients for stimulating these ideas too.

I also get a lot of learning from my training sessions and the conferences where I have been speaking, blogging or simply listening and usually tweeting. I am not the sort of speaker who arrives at a conference late, delivers a speech without taking any questions, and then leaves again immediately afterwards. I value what I learn from others as much, if not more, than the opportunity to explore with others what I think. I would therefore like to thank all the conference organizers who have invited me to speak or otherwise participate in their events, as well as the various training providers I have worked with, especially Symposium in the UK and Lighthouse in Singapore.

In terms of conferences I would also like to acknowledge the many inputs from other speakers, bloggers, tweeters and other attendees who have entertained and provoked me over the years. This includes conferences in HR but also Enterprise 2.0/social business, social media, digital technologies, workplace design, innovation and other areas. That is a lot of people! I am not going to be able to list everyone here, or even remember everyone. Plus of course there will be others in my broader social network who I may not even be aware of having influenced me. But listing some and not others would go against the idea of fairness that is so core to the social organization. Therefore, I would just like to repeat my thanks to everyone who has informed my thinking that has led to this book. Some of you at least will know who you are.

I will, however, make one small but important exception to thank Dave Ulrich for his extensive contributions to people and organizational management and leadership, for his generous personal support on several occasions, and especially for providing the foreword for this book.

My final thanks should go to Lucy, Amy, Sophia, Philippa, Amanda and Megan at Kogan Page. Thank you all for making the whole book possible and for the ongoing guidance, support and encouragement that has been so important in helping me put it all together.

To the three women in my life, my wife Sandra, and my daughters, Elena and Kamila, who form what will always be my most important social organization.

Introduction

One of the main reasons that so few other books address organizational social capital effectively is that so much thinking about social organizations is compartmentalized within individual disciplines. This book will review and provide new ideas and case studies from within people management and development, organization design and development, community management, leadership, enterprise social networking, knowledge management, workplace design, social network analysis and other disciplines. But many of these cases and their practices are little known outside of their own areas. Even when disciplines acknowledge the role of other areas they tend to give these other disciplines less attention and make them subservient to their own. Probably the best example of this is technology professor Andrew McAfee's suggestion that Enterprise 2.0 (which can be loosely defined as social business/organization enabled by enterprise social networking technologies) is 'not not' about the technology – ie that it is mainly about technology (McAfee, 2009).

The result of this lack of integration is that there are many organizations that exhibit aspects of a social organization – ie they are doing great things in one or two areas, whether these are HR, organization design, team development, social technologies or social workplace design etc. But there are very few that are working effectively in all these areas, or at least all of the areas in which it would be useful for them to work. Many times, approaches in these areas look disjointed and their impacts suboptimal.

This book collects together the different opportunities and places them on a more equal basis by focusing them on the social outcomes that a particular firm is trying to create. It should therefore appeal and apply fairly equally to senior, strategically focused professionals working in any of the disciplines listed above, including HR, organization design, organization development, internal communication, learning and development, reward, recruitment, IT, knowledge management, and corporate real estate/property and facilities.

The other key discipline that I hope will be interested in the book is strategy. The social organization is not just about a better way to manage people, property and technology. It also provides a new basis for competitive success. This is the focus of Part 1 of the book. Chapters 1 and 2 outline this new basis for strategic management, which uses the outcomes of people and organizational management to both add and create value – and without getting bogged down in concerns about culture. Chapter 3 develops the approach to describe how organizations can create human and organization capital and Chapter 4 extends this to social capital. Chapter 5 describes the overall approach that can be used to identify the particular activities, from all the different disciplines that have been described, which will best meet the social capital requirements of a particular business.

Within Part 1, it is only Chapter 4 that focuses heavily on social capital and this chapter also explains some of the evidence from psychology, sociology, anthropology, neuroscience, behavioural economics and other areas that reinforce the need to focus on social relationships. The other chapters (1, 2, 3 and 5) are relatively generic in that the strategic approach they outline can also be applied to other types of people and organizational management, ie to ones emphasizing human or organization capital. However, the contrast between the strategic approach and traditional approaches will be greatest when focusing on creating social capital. Explaining the approach in the context of the social organization therefore reinforces its value. Given the lack of investment in social capital in most firms this also will be the main opportunity to apply this strategic approach in many organizations.

Taking this relatively generic stance also means that the book will be useful for those companies wanting to develop social relationships but where the strategic opportunity is to create human or organization capital, rather than to emphasize social capital to the extent of the fully fledged social organization. This may be because these organizations just want to develop better relationships to support other ways of competing, or because they want to develop some social capital as part of a broader organizational capability, which might be expressed less formally as developing a more social culture.

Organization design practitioners should find the book useful too, as much of it deals with needs relating to this discipline. I had in fact thought of just writing a book on organization design and a separate one on becoming more social – however, my main point about designing an organization is that it needs to be contextual. Therefore, I actually think it works better to describe how design can work by explaining how it enables a particular outcome, in this case, social capital, than writing about it more generally. I also think that social capital is a more urgent and important requirement in many organizations today than organization capital, which is what most organization design work focuses on.

Part 2 of the book responds to these needs by presenting and building upon a new organization model called the organization prioritization model (OPM). This is introduced in Chapter 6 and then explained further in

Chapters 7–10. These chapters explain how the model can be used to create a 'social architecture' that provides a sound basis for developing people and their relationships.

Chapter 8 will also explain why the preferred option for a social organization is the network form. However, I also recognize that the main structure used by most businesses, even true social organizations, now and probably for a considerable time to come, is a functional or divisional one. Social organization designers therefore still need to understand a number of key things that are all described within the book. These include, first, the main pros and cons of all the different options. Second, how to use, tailor and adopt a functional form to support social outcomes. And third, whether changing from a functional to a network form will achieve greater or lesser alignment and benefit than doing something else. However, most of the ideas in Part 2 and the OPM model itself can be applied to any other organization design challenge too.

This book should also be useful for corporate real estate and facilities management professionals who want to help their organizations become more social. It will particularly help those who understand the need to integrate with other functions and approaches. Chapter 10 actually proposes that organizations consider the workplace as an important strand of their organization architectures and the workplace is therefore considered a key element in the OPM.

I should be clear, however, that most of the content of the book focuses on people management and therefore on HR. Social relationships are about people and therefore whilst IT, property and other disciplines need to play an important role in creating a social organization, the central focus and driver for it should generally be HR. This is not the same as saying that the social organization is 'not not' about HR (in the same way that Andrew McAfee referred to Enterprise 2.0, described in the first paragraph of this chapter). I am not suggesting HR is the most important activity, I am explaining that if the outcomes we are interested in are human and social capital then the discipline most closely connected to these is probably HR.

This is not a normal HR book either though, because it focuses on social outcomes rather than HR activities. This means that the HR activities it does explore are quite different from those used in most organizations. They fall instead into what might be called social HR. Again, however, this term is often used to refer to social media-based HR processes rather than in the way it is used here. This is to mean practices that focus on relationships rather than simply on people, and that are applied to groups rather than just individuals. These activities are described in Chapter 11, which is the first chapter in Part 3 of the book and focuses more directly on people and their relationships.

Organization development practitioners should definitely be interested in this book. In fact in one way, which will be described, the whole book is about organization development. But Chapter 12 focuses specifically on facilitating teams and other groups as well as creating a broader 'organization society' in which relationships are managed strategically across the whole organization. This includes the new, artful and important role of the community manager.

IT practitioners should also benefit from reading the book. Technology is not the single driving force behind social organization but it is definitely a hugely important enabler. The specific role of social technologies within the social organization is described in the first half of Chapter 13. However, most of the approaches described earlier on can also be enabled through smart technology. The issue is that they do not need to be. The social organization is not dependent on technology and it will often make sense to review what activities need to be undertaken before considering which of these can be automated, rather than simply thinking about what can be done through IT.

Analytics is another important enabler in the social organization, just as it is for other areas of business and organizational management. Again, however, opportunities like social network analysis should not be the first things organizations focus on but can be very useful once main opportunities have been had. This important supporting role is described in the second half of Chapter 13.

The book will also be useful for line managers, business leaders and other people working in non-functional process and project teams, service pods, communities, networks and other organizational units described within the book. And it will obviously be particularly relevant to social organization designers charged with creating this type of organization. Perhaps I should just write that it will be useful for anyone working in an organization that wants to be more social. After all, creating a social organization will need a social, collaborative and participative approach for both its design and its implementation.

Once again, though, I should note my own bias is towards HR. This is partly due to my own background, which has been mainly in HR consulting, and as an HR director, though I have worked in other functions, especially IT. Therefore, I frequently use HR to explain the changes required within social organizations. And I sometimes use HR as a simple shorthand for people and organizational management. But when I do this I really do mean anyone – in any function or line management – concerned with the effectiveness of people and their organization and especially, of course, the relationships between the people in an organization.

This is a bigger, more inclusive HR, perhaps better termed Human Relationships, than the department that exists in most organizations today. And as you will see, it is also this discipline that will increasingly become the central focus of a successful business.

Reference

McAfee, A (2009) *Enterprise 2.0: How to manage social technologies to transform your organization*, Harvard Business Press, Boston

PART ONE
Strategic management of people, organization and relationships

Locating the value in people management

01

Introduction

In Part 1 of this book I will introduce you to the nature and importance of social relationships. Parts 2 and 3 will then describe how organizations can enable and develop these relationships. First, however, I need to clarify how the management of people in an organization, including the development of the relationships between these people, really works – where the value gets created.

Therefore, in this chapter I outline a value chain that can be used to describe all organizational and people management activities within a business, as well as to link these activities to the outcomes they create. This organization value chain helps explain why people and people's relationships are as important as they are, and why we need to focus on the outcomes we create via this chain. It also helps distinguish the social outcomes that need to be created by a social organization.

Value chains are important and popular tools already used in many businesses and so I first want to set the scene by explaining a couple of other value chains that you or your business colleagues may be familiar with and might be using. I can then explain the organization value chain in the context of these other models. I think it is really important to understand this value chain, so please do read on.

The business strategy map

The easiest way for me to introduce this section is to refer you to the most prevalent planning tool used in business, which is Robert Kaplan and David Norton's business strategy map, built upon their even more commonly used measurement tool, the balanced business scorecard (Kaplan and Norton, 2004). This suggests that there are four perspectives that each need to be incorporated into a business strategy. These are usually identified as learning and growth, business operations, customers and financials.

The idea is to identify a roughly equal, or balanced, number of objectives in each of these perspectives, and also to describe the flow through them, ie how what a business does in learning and growth informs what it can achieve in operations, which leads on to its success with customers and finally on to its financial results. The learning and growth perspective includes anything that needs to be put in place before a business can perform its operations effectively. This includes all the people and relationships objectives this book is going to focus on. In fact many organizations simply label the learning and growth perspective as people.

The business strategy map also gets referred to as a value chain – the top-level process of any business. It suggests that what a business does is to use people to perform operations so it can satisfy customers, because doing this produces financial results. It is important to note that there are a number of variants around this model, particularly in the public and voluntary sectors. Here, for example, stakeholders can replace customers; mission can replace financials; or the order of customers and financials can be swapped around. This indicates that financial success is important but only to the extent that it enables an organization to service and satisfy customers.

With these few broad variations, this value chain sounds like it could apply to just about any business. It is also very high level, which is why it can be applied so broadly. But there are also a number of more detailed or specific value chain models, which all look a bit like the model in Figure 1.1.

Figure 1.1   Generic value chain model

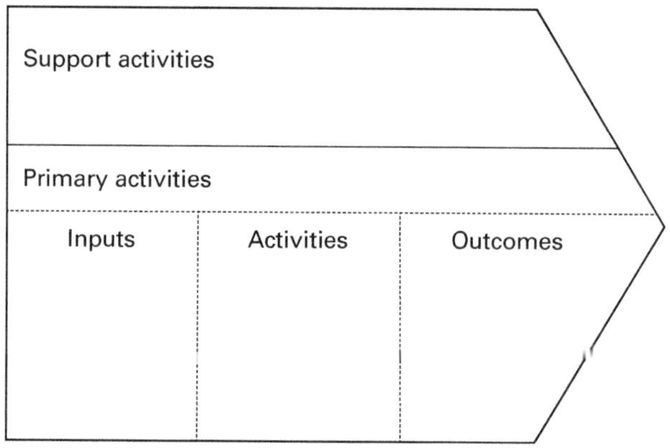

The financial value chain

The best well known of these more specific models is management guru Michael Porter's business or financial value chain (Porter, 1985). This suggests that there are a number of primary activities that lead directly to margin, profitability and growth. For a traditional manufacturing company these primary activities might be procurement; manufacturing; distribution; sales; and customer service. Other sectors will have substantially different value chains. Even companies within the same sector will have different value chains that reflect their own particular business strategies.

To help companies align their value chains with their business strategies Porter suggests businesses need to choose between a couple of generic strategies: niche or differentiation, and cost leadership. These are about the products or services offered by a firm. Differentiation is about providing a product or service with a unique feature. Not all potential customers will want this feature, but enough will and those who do will be prepared to pay extra for it. This means that every time the product or service is sold the firm makes more margin, hence is more profitable and can grow more quickly, eventually taking over its rivals and becoming a monopoly. Cost leadership is about providing the same product or service as everyone else but doing so more cheaply, which also leads to higher margin, profitability and growth.

There are also a number of secondary activities in the value chain. These do not contribute directly to margin but support the effectiveness of the primary activities in doing this. One of these secondary – or support – activities is people management, or HR. A company that only uses Porter's approach, therefore, defines people management as a support activity, and HR as a support function.

Porter suggests that the only way a company can gain competitive advantage (or for organizations in the public/voluntary sectors to transform the type and level of services that are provided) is to use his value chain. However, there are already other value chain models available too.

The customer value chain

A particularly important alternative or addition to Porter's model is the customer value chain. This focuses on attracting and retaining customers and building more business from their custom. Marketing professor Francis Buttle (2003) proposes that this consists of customer portfolio analysis; customer intimacy; network development; value proposition development; and managing the customer life cycle.

You can see why this chain is important through a profitability analysis, shown in Figure 1.2. A business can increase profits by increasing prices and therefore revenue or by reducing fixed and/or variable costs. Or it can increase turnover to shift the point at which margin is calculated over to the right. It can do this either by increasing the number of its customers, or by increasing loyalty and encouraging each customer to spend more. This is an approach followed by firms such as Apple, Marriott and Southwest Airlines. The strategy makes good sense, given that analysis completed by Bain's Frederick Reichheld, which led to the development of the Net Promoter Score, suggests that a 10 per cent increase in customer retention can count for a 125 per cent increase in customer value (Reichheld, 2003).

Figure 1.2   Customer profitability analysis

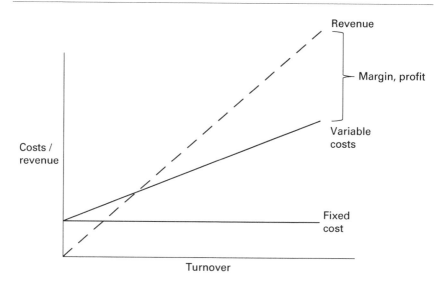

This model is a value chain. But unlike Porter's model it does not deal with building products or services. Instead it deals with maximizing customer spend when they then buy the products. The customer value chain happens before the financial one. In fact it applies to the customer perspective in Kaplan and Norton's strategy map, whereas Porter's value chain covers the financial perspective in the strategy map.

The operations value chain

There is another value chain in the operations perspective of the strategy map as well. This deals with improving the way the business works, leading to a fit-for-purpose business model, and in particular the quality, alignment and effectiveness of its business processes. It is not about executing these – that is included in the customer and financial value chains – it is about improving them in advance of their execution.

You can also think about the outputs of the operations value chain as core competencies. These are bundles of business processes plus supporting technologies and intellectual capital (patents and knowledge) that enable a business to do certain things well. Authors Gary Hamel and CK Prahalad (1996) write about US manufacturing company 3M as an example of this type of approach. 3M has well-developed and aligned business processes, technologies and intellectual capital in glues, substrates and adhesives and competes largely on developing these core competencies through the operations value chain rather than the customer or financial ones.

The activities included within this value chain focus on improving process quality and alignment across the organization. A good example is the use of six sigma techniques to reduce process variance. It is these types of activities that are the main focus of quality and business excellence award programmes such as the Malcolm Baldrige National Quality Award (particularly the operations focus) and the EFQM Excellence Model (particularly the processes perspective).

Linking value chains

Finally, or firstly if looking at the value chains in a sequential order, there is the organization value chain. This corresponds to Kaplan and Norton's (2004) learning and growth perspective. I want to spend a little longer describing this particular value chain, given that it will now be the focus for the rest of the book. However, before I do this I would like to tease out eight key points relating to the overall strategy map and the four constituent value chains:

1 Each of the four value chains I have described link to a particular perspective in Kaplan and Norton's (2004) strategy map.

2 The primary steps in each value chain consist of inputs (bringing new raw materials, potential customers or other resources into a business); a set of activities (transforming these inputs in some way); and some outputs and outcomes (for me, outcomes are simply the most important outputs).

3 Each value chain also has a number of secondary – or support – activities, which will generally include people management (though not in the organization value chain).

4 The outcomes from each value chain are a form of capital, or some store of value. The capitals I have described so far are financial capital (the pool of funds available to a business); customer, brand or relationship capital (the value of a business's relationships with its customers); and business excellence, core competencies or business process capital (the value provided by the quality and alignment of a business's operations). I will go on to introduce organizational capability as the outcome of the organization value chain.

5 All four value chains are about differentiation or cost leadership. I referred to these options in the section on Porter's financial value chain and they apply just as strongly to the other three chains too. Business success is not just about having the best products or services, customer service, business processes or people management activities – but the right ones!

6 The inputs to each value chain include the outcomes from the previous value chain (the one to the left of it – see Figure 1.3). So brand capital is an input or enabler to the financial value chain; business excellence is an input to the customer value chain and organizational capability is an input to the operations value chain. This is shown in Figure 1.3.

Figure 1.3   Links between value chains

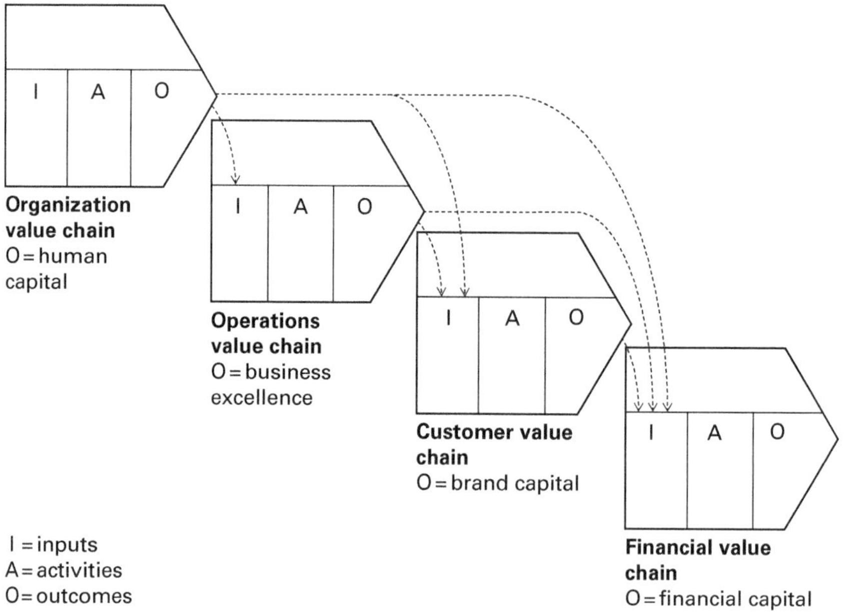

Organization
value chain
O = human
capital

Operations
value chain
O = business
excellence

Customer value
chain
O = brand capital

Financial value
chain
O = financial capital

I = inputs
A = activities
O = outcomes

7 This means that the value chains towards the start or the left-hand side of the strategy map have the potential to make the greatest contribution to business success, as they perform an important role in their own right

and also inform all the other value chains that follow. An action in the organization value chain will have an impact on organizational capability but also benefits from a multiplier effect on the other three value chains too.

8 Because Porter's value chain is the best known of these models, people often assume that the value provided by people management is described adequately by its role as a support activity within this value chain. Nothing could be further from the truth. People management does support the three most right-hand value chains, but it has the greatest impact and performs its most strategic role in the organization value chain.

The organization value chain

The organization value chain describes the inputs, activities and outcomes that relate to the management of people within an organization. I call this the organization value chain because it applies more broadly than people management as it also includes how people are organized and how their relationships are developed and maintained. I also use the word 'organization' when focusing on the activities within the organization value chain, whereas I use the word 'business' to refer to activities in the operations, customer and financial value chains. This applies to commercial businesses and to non-commercial 'businesses' in the public and voluntary sector that might normally consider themselves organizations rather than businesses.

The organization value chain is a little harder to understand than the three I have already described as so much of what we create in and around people is intangible. It is for this reason that the organization value chain is often equated to a black box, and developing an understanding of how it works is likened to opening the box's lid and peering inside. Nevertheless, our understanding of what is in the black box dates back until at least 1984 when Michael Beer at Harvard developed what is called the Harvard Model (Beer *et al*, 1984). This suggested that human resource management (HRM) policy choices (activities) have value by aligning to stakeholder interests and situational factors (both inputs) to produce HR outcomes – commitment, competence, congruence and cost effectiveness. It is these outcomes that then enable the rest of the business to produce long-term consequences, including financial results.

More recently David Guest at Birkbeck College, London, as part of his work on the future of work, has proposed that HR practices (activities) need to be aligned with business and HR strategies (inputs) and then cascaded through an effective HR function to produce outcomes – employee competence, commitment and flexibility. These then lead on to the quality of goods and services, productivity and financial performance (Guest *et al*, 2001).

More recently still, John Purcell and colleagues at University of Bath concluded that HRM activities produce organizational levels of ability, motivation and, most importantly, opportunity to participate (outcomes). They place an emphasis on the last of these ability, motivation and opportunity (AMO) factors to note that we often employ relatively able and reasonably committed people and then put them in dysfunctional organizations that stop them contributing! The three outcomes are cascaded through an individual line manager's style to produce employee commitment, motivation and job satisfaction. These lead to the delivery of discretionary occupational citizenship behaviour, ie whether people do the right thing when no one is looking (Purcell *et al*, 2003).

All three research findings, and other studies, all say much the same thing, which is shown in Figure 1.4. People management in the organization value chain is about using inputs to perform activities leading to outcomes.

Figure 1.4   The organization value chain

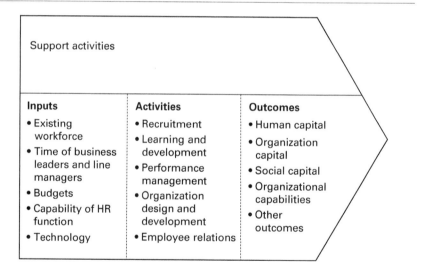

Inputs

Inputs include the initial states of people and the organization before we take action to change these states. Inputs also include the resources we need to have in place before we take these actions. That is, inputs are anything we need to have or do before we perform our activities, and which inform these activities. Examples include a budget, management time, sponsorship of business leaders, capable HR professionals, good HR technology and so on. Inputs can also be processes (see below).

An interesting example of an input is an employer brand – which we need to have in place before we implement a recruitment process, or an internal engagement process. This has always been important to our effectiveness in these process areas but changes in the way we manage people are making it even more important too. Examples of this are included throughout the book.

Activities

Activities are the actual things we do, building on these inputs and leading to the creation of outcomes. They include the HR processes and practices spanning across the employee life cycle. They are also the organization design changes and the organization development interventions we undertake.

One way to categorize these activities is by using the McKinsey 7S organization model. This is the most popular holistic model of an organization used within organization design. The model is popular partly because it originated with the management consulting firm McKinsey and also because Tom Peters and his consultancy colleagues were quite clever in picking seven levers available within an organization that all begin with the letter 'S'. These levers include the 'hard triangle' of strategy, structure and systems (meaning processes, including IT systems), and the 'soft square' of staff, skills, style and – in the centre of the model – shared values (or superordinate goals). The 7S model is used primarily for change management not organizational effectiveness, so each 'S' refers to change activities not just to the results of the changes within that area. For example, the staff element can focus on activities such as implementing new management development programmes as well as describing the actual quality of the people working in the organization (Waterman, Peters and Phillips, 1980).

Outcomes

Outcomes are what we create using the above activities. They are the qualities we develop in our people and organizations such as competence, commitment and opportunity to participate. They are also what the rest of a business uses to create business success in the other value chains, culminating in the financial results.

There are three types of outcome or aspects of organizational capability that are produced in the organization value chain. These are human capital, organization capital and social capital. The inclusion of human capital is why I sometimes refer to the organization value chain as the human capital management (HCM) value chain. However, it is important to remember each of the three types of capital produced in this value chain as they are each quite different from the other.

First, human capital is the value organization's gain from their people's own resources or capabilities (their own individual human capital), including their abilities, level of engagement, wellness etc. It is also based on the level of diversity across the workforce.

Whilst human capital is formed out of the qualities people own inside them it is not just another name for people – it is the value these people provide. For example, you could imagine there might be a group of people who could offer substantial amounts of human capital to one organization that needs the skills these people could provide. But the same group of people might provide no human capital at all to an organization down the road if this second firm does not need the skills these people can provide.

Second, organization capital is the value of the way people are organized to get work done, including their alignment and enablement. It is based mainly on the harder, more tangible aspects of an organization, particularly its structure and systems/processes.

It is useful to understand that processes can form part of organization capital or other outcomes, but they can also be inputs or activities leading to these outcomes. Which exactly depends on their relationship to organizational and business outcomes. If a process leads directly to the production of business results in the operations, customer or financial value chains then it is an outcome in the organization value chain. An organizational budgeting process would be an example of this. If, however, a process leads to an organizational outcome then it is an activity. A recruitment process that provides people and human capital is an example of this. If it does not even lead directly to an outcome – if it only supports another process – then it is an input. An example of an input process might be leadership development which in one context might not create outcomes by itself. Instead, it might be used so that leaders and managers become more competent in their roles, helping them to maximize other processes such as performance management. It is the performance management process that is an activity. This is because this is the process that creates a useful outcome in terms of better skilled and managed people working in the business.

Designing the right organization may not always be as important as getting the right people (hence the old adage, 'the right people in the wrong organization will still get the job done but the wrong people in the right organization won't'). However, even then the organization can still have a large impact on business performance.

Finally, social capital is the value provided by the connections, relationships and conversations taking place within the organization. This is based on the way people work with each other and the effectiveness of teams, networks and communities. It is often the most important basis for the way people work in an organization, the beliefs they live by and the values they demonstrate. Social capital is also what people often mean when they talk about culture.

It is important to note that the words 'value' and 'capital' do not imply a direct financial worth. They simply mean that we are interested in the aspects of people and organization that are important to a particular firm. However, all three capitals do lead on to financial value through their impact on and through the other three value chains. Therefore, they have an indirect impact on financial value rather than a direct financial value of their own.

It can also be useful to think about organizational capabilities. These are the few, differentiated outcomes at the top level of the organization that will be strategically useful in creating competitive advantage. Capabilities are similar but also different to the core competencies produced in the operations value chain. Using the analogy of an individual working in an organization, the person's leadership abilities will be broadly similar to organizational capabilities, while their functional or technical competences will be more like the organization's core competencies.

Capabilities will generally include a combination of human, organization and social capital, though they will also sometimes focus predominantly on just one or two of these sources of value. The social organization focuses on the creation of social capital as the most important aspect of organizational capability.

The differences between outcomes, capital and capabilities are summarized below:

- Outcomes are important outputs in any of the four value chains. People and organizational improvements are outcomes. Other benefits obtained within the organization value chain (for example, revenues from having other organizations attend an internal training course) may be outputs but are not outcomes.

- Capital relates to outcomes that investors or other stakeholders care about, generally because they are either large scale or are particularly important.

- Capabilities consist of instances or combinations of the three capitals that contribute to the strategic success of a business.

We will probe further into the outcomes of the organization value chain in Chapters 3–4 and the rest of the book will then focus on the development of social capital.

The need to shift focus from activities to outcomes

Hopefully this value chain, building on inputs and activities to create outcomes, will resonate for you, as it is what all organizations do. However, it is not how we usually think. I see this whenever I work with business executives on their business strategy maps. When I look into the learning and growth perspective I will always find plenty of objectives for activities but very rarely anything for inputs or outcomes. Similarly, when working with HR or others on people management strategies I will find the same focus on activities and a similar absence of objectives for inputs and outcomes.

There is a reason for this, which is that in our psychology we pay more attention to things that we can see, touch and describe – things that are tangible – than things we cannot as they are intangible. This is part of the halo/horns effect, which explains the way that our perceptions about people and things are framed by the most readily available information on them (Rosenzweig, 2007). Many of the outcomes of people and organizational activities are intangible so we tend to pay more attention to the tangibles (ie the activities) than the intangibles (ie the outcomes). But doing that is a mistake.

We need to have a more balanced approach to setting objectives, including targets for inputs and outcomes as well as activities. Shifting focus from activities to outcomes is particularly important as it provides three important benefits – becoming more strategic, being seen as more credible and creating value – as set out below.

Becoming more strategic

First, focusing on outcomes tends to make HR and people management more strategic. The outcomes in the organization value chain are our deliverables. It makes no sense to ignore them. Doing so is a bit like a car manufacturer paying all their attention to their engineering and manufacturing operations but not bothering to check on the finished vehicles.

In addition, if we focus on activities we tend just to do more of these activities. (If you have a hammer every problem seems to become a nail.) My best example of this comes from my time working as HR Director at Ernst & Young (now EY) in the UK when the international firm announced that 90 per cent of its development activities would in future be provided by e-learning. In my view, doing this was a mistake, contributing to lots of fairly boring e-learning (a common experience back then and which still puts many people off e-learning even today, despite how far this technology and the solutions that are available have improved). The problem occurred simply because we were developing strategy by looking at the activity of learning, not the outcomes we needed to achieve.

The common alternative to just focusing on activities is to try to connect activities and business results, ie to miss the outcome step in the organization value chain. Unfortunately this tends not to work that well either. It is actually quite hard to look at the business objectives of a firm and then identify what HR activities will support these objectives. It is a lot easier, and results in better alignment, to ask what organizational outcomes will support and enable these business objectives, and then what activities will create those outcomes.

I like to explain this by looking at performance management. I do not particularly like competency frameworks but I think one benefit they provide is helping to connect performance objectives and training needs. So, if a manager and employee sit down at the start of the year and the performance management system asks a manager to identify six specific and measurable objectives, most managers can give this a decent go. However, if the next page of the form or system asks them to identify the training that will help that person to achieve their objectives, many managers will struggle – and the person does not get any training.

It is easier if the second page of the system asks what competencies will help the person to achieve their objectives. Most managers can do this. And then if the third page asks what training does the person need to develop these competencies they can do that too. Result – the person gets more training to support their competencies to achieve their objectives. These two systems are asking the same thing, but without the use of competencies there is just too big a conceptual jump between what the person needs to do and the training they need in order to do it. Competencies help cut down the time and distance between the work and training objectives and make each question smaller, making them easier to answer and providing greater alignment too. It is the same with the organization value chain. It is actually quite hard to look at the business objectives and then say what HR activities will support these objectives. It is a lot easier, and results in better alignment, to ask what outcomes will support and enable these business objectives, and then what activities will create those outcomes.

Aligning activities with outcomes also helps ensure that these activities are best fit, rather than simply best practice. This means that they are designed to be appropriate for a particular organization, its strategy and context etc, rather than just copied from what other organizations are doing. This is particularly important as many of our current best practices are not even that good, never mind best! But there is also a growing amount of evidence that what is important to organizational success is best fit, not just best practice.

My favourite example of this comes from John Boudreau and Ed Lawler at the University of South California (Lawler and Boudreau, 2015). Their research into global trends in HR suggests that the effectiveness of HR activities depends upon the business strategies that are being followed. A very relevant example for the social organization is that a business following a strategy focused on innovation would seem to benefit strongly from investments in social networking activities and systems (correlation coefficient r = 0.33). However, investments in employee relations correlates in reduced performance for these same innovation-focused businesses (r = −0.16). That is not an issue with employee relations – other businesses, for example those using a sustainability-based strategy, would seem to benefit from investments in this practice area (r = 0.16). The research indicates that what matters is not best practice, it is best fit.

Being seen as more credible

As well as making us more strategic, focusing on outcomes makes those of us who focus on people management, eg in the HR department, seem more credible. People who create something are always seen as more valuable than people who just do something. For example, HR practitioners will be seen as more impactful if they talk about raising commitment or the skills of the salesforce rather than if they talk about running communications briefings or delivering training courses.

In addition, one of the major challenges faced by many HR practitioners in raising their credibility is showing that they are accountable for something important in the organization. In fact many business leaders question whether HR is accountable for anything at all, and if they are not accountable, whether the function can be abolished.

It is easy to see how we have got to this situation – HR is obviously accountable for the design of the quality and effectiveness of HR processes but no one cares very much about that. More important is the use of these processes, but it needs to be line managers who are accountable for the bulk of this as they are the people who implement the processes. It is important to remember this point. When HR tries to be accountable for delivery of activities we end up taking a policing role, which can substantially interfere with our desire to be strategic. There is also a need in most businesses to strengthen line managers' accountability for the operation of these processes, which often makes HR wary of taking accountability in case this further reduces the accountability that line managers are taking.

HR is also clearly not accountable for business results (though we do play a role as a support function in helping to produce them). So if we only focus on organizational activities and the broader business objectives we very naturally end up not taking accountability for anything important. Outcomes give us a way to square the circle – to take accountability for something that is absolutely critical to business performance – the outcomes in the organization value chain. This is not about accountability at the individual team or department level. It still needs to be team leaders, line managers and business leaders who take accountability for the people in their teams and units. But we can take accountability for the outcomes we develop across the whole organization. For things like the overall levels of skills, engagement and people's propensity to collaborate. And if we do not do this, who will?

Note that I am not suggesting HR should take more responsibility for delivering people management activities. But HR can, and I strongly believe should, take accountability for providing the capabilities our organizations need to be strategically successful. Therefore, the HR practitioners in my earlier example will be seen as even more credible if, as well as talking about the increase in sales skills, they put their jobs on the line and accept there will be consequences if they do not succeed in ensuring that this change is delivered. We need to focus on outcomes because that makes it more likely that we will talk about, and take accountability for, these outcomes too.

Creating value

Finally, outcomes provide the most important basis to create value through people, which will be the focus of Chapter 2.

The changing nature of competitive success

The fact that each of the four value chains I have described correspond to a step or perspective in Kaplan and Norton's (2004) strategy map can be considered to mean that these are simply more detailed processes operating at the next level down below the top-level process provided by the strategy map. However, the four value chains can also be seen as alternative top-level options that each stress different sources of competitive value.

Traditionally, companies have competed through Porter's generic strategies in the financial value chain. However, if you review the literature on strategic management my suggestion would be that we have developed three other main schools of thought about strategic success since Porter's model was developed. This does not mean that Porter has become any less popular. One of the best-selling business books since the start of the new millennium has been W Chan Kim and Renée Mauborgne's *Blue Ocean Strategy*, which largely restates the case for Porter's competitive positioning (Kim and Mauborgne, 2005). However, this is no longer the single model for competitive strategy.

The first alternative basis for strategy to become popular was customer first. As shown by the customer value chain this approach is much more significant than simply pushing customers to buy more product in the financial value chain. It is about investing in customers, growing their number and their loyalty in terms of the percentage of the lifetime spend provided to the company. Some companies prefer to put their focus here rather than focusing too much on the products they are selling. Of course the financial value chain is still important, but for many companies following this strategy there is a belief that if they get close enough to their customers then these businesses or individuals will help them develop the products that they need.

The second alternative approach to competitive success is internal resource-based strategy, and in particular development of the resources called core competencies promoted by business thinkers Gary Hamel and CK Prahalad, as well as others. As described earlier, core competencies are bundles or clusters of business processes, technologies and intellectual capital that are created in the operations value chain. A little like my description of the customer-first approach, the idea is that if you create the right core competencies the more the financial value chain starts to take care of itself.

So, for example, 3M marketers and researchers do not worry too much about studying the types of glues made by their competitors, or trying to find a new niche. They just focus on innovating and experimenting with different types of glue and glue-making processes, believing that if they do this they will develop the products that their customers need. This of course actually happened with Post-it notes, which were developed when 3M found a clever and profitable use for a glue that did not stick.

Hamel suggests that given the rate of change in business, competitive positioning is no longer a sustainable basis for competitive advantage. Competitors can copy your differentiated or cost-leading products or services, but they will find it much harder to copy your business processes and technology or core competencies.

The last alternative approach is the development of organizational capabilities, which I have also referred to previously and will return to again in Chapter 2. Capabilities are based on the value provided by people and their organization. Although there may be some overlap between organizational capabilities and core competencies, capabilities have a clear bias towards the organization value chain whereas core competencies focus much more on the operations value chain.

The concept was first introduced by Igor Ansoff (1965). Whilst best known for his product-market grid, his contingency model also refers to firm-level capabilities, which includes organization values, managerial competencies, organization structure, processes and technology. More recently, most of the thinking around capabilities has taken place in HR. HR's chief guru, Dave Ulrich, suggests that capabilities are things an organization knows how to do well. For any organization to compete successfully in today's market, it must focus on building not only from the outside but from the inside too (Ulrich and Lake, 1990).

These days, however, the idea is also gaining a lot of traction in businesses and strategy consultancies too. The consultancy BCG suggest that lasting transformation hinges on capabilities. These capabilities sound quite a lot like core competencies but they also suggest that at the core of the capabilities are behaviours: 'the activities, interactions, and decisions made by a set of individuals in a company who exemplify that capability' (Hemerling *et al*, 2016). PwC's Strategy& consulting arm have a similar perspective, focusing on superior, distinctive and reinforcing capabilities that overlap with core competencies but that also extend to take in culture (Leinwand and Mainardi, 2016).

But the best example of a business strategy consultancy's focus on organizational capabilities comes from McKinsey. This firm calls their version of capabilities 'organizational health'. McKinsey consultants Scott Keller and Colin Price, writing in their book *Beyond Performance* (2011), note the increasing pace of change within business making it easier to copy a competitor's competitive advantage. However, 'what can't be so easily replicated is the ability to grow from within through better ideas and better execution, ie better health'.

Keller and Price explain the difference between the traditional basis for business performance and organizational health: 'Performance is very much about our strategy, the big goal we're going for that we can measure in financial terms, the set of initiatives we're going to go after, the salesforce stimulation programme, the lean production programme, whatever bundle of things they're going to do in order to get to those numbers. The health side is very much about me – how well do we align people on where we want to go, how efficiently do we execute against that, and how effectively, and how do we renew ourselves along the way, keep our energy up and be able to continue once we even get to that target' (Mlabvideo, 2011).

That sounds to me a lot like activities in the organization value chain! By the way, it is also interesting to note that McKinsey has also switched its focus from activities (the 7S model) to outcomes (organizational capabilities/ health), reinforcing the need for us to put more focus on outcomes within our organizations too.

Looking at these four different approaches to business strategy and their evolution over time there has been a clear shift from an external to an internal perspective on strategy development – from the right-hand to the left-hand side of the business strategy map; from the financial to the organization value chain.

Today, the organization value chain is not only important because of its multiplicative effect on the other value chains but because it is now the most sustainable basis for competitive success. Because, do you know what? Given the rate of change in the business environment your competitors can copy your core competencies just like they can copy your competitive positioning too. The only thing they cannot easily copy is your people and organization and the alignment between these (which is commonly referred to as an organization's culture).

You can also see this change in the increasing proportion of market value that is based on intangibles. Sometimes people try to show this by looking at the growth in firms' market values compared to the growth in their fixed assets. For example, one analysis of Standard & Poor's 500 index (Ocean Tomo, 2015) suggests that the proportion of market value that cannot be accounted for by tangible assets has grown from 17 per cent in 1975 to 84 per cent in 2015 (with a big dip around the global financial crisis in 2007). Other analyses subtract Interbrand or EquiTrend estimates of brand values from the remaining intangibles to try to get a better estimate of human, organiza- tion and social capital. Unfortunately this is not really the way that a firm's market value is set. Investors do not make a direct valuation of a company's human, organization and social capital. They pay a particular amount for a company because they expect a certain level of future profitability. The grow- ing market value of companies is simply an indication that investors expect them to make greater profits in future. But they do clearly understand that most of this growth is due to the importance of intangibles, ie they have at least some understanding of the flow of value through the four value chains.

This is also the reason why analysts and others are trying to get a better understanding of the value of these forms of capital. For example, the International Integrated Reporting Council (IIRC) has proposed that firms report on six forms of capital – human, social and relationship, intellectual (organization/core competency) as well as natural, manufactured and financial (from the financial value chain). This is not about putting these capitals on the balance sheet but about understanding the flows between them. In fact the IIRC's model also uses a value chain based on inputs, activities, outputs and outcomes (The IIRC, 2013).

None of this discounts from other changes in strategy development, including this being increasingly unplanned and emergent, but where formal or informal strategy formulation does take place it should increasingly focus on the organization.

Summary and additional comments

1 Inputs, activities and outcomes – the key elements of the four value chains I have reviewed – are often referred to in descriptions of processes and business transformations. For example, one common approach to defining processes uses the acronym SIPOC – suppliers, inputs, process, outputs, customers. It makes a lot of sense to describe our top-level people and organizational management process in the same way.

2 Understanding that the source of value in people management lies in the organization value chain is important. It means that people and relationships are not just a means of supporting the creation of margin in the financial value chain. They are now the basis for important outcomes in their own right.

3 In addition, given the changes in the world of business it is these outcomes from the organization value chain that offer a business its most important and most sustainable basis for competitive success.

4 This also means that people management is a primary business activity, and that HR needs to be seen as a business function with a direct role in creating competitive success.

5 HR functions wanting to contribute strategically should focus on the organization value chain. This is where the opportunity lies to be a strategic driver of success rather than just a support function. I will describe this opportunity further in Chapter 2.

6 Even if your business thinks its business strategy is based on competitive positioning, you can still focus on capabilities as well. Your business colleagues are probably wrong, and you can offer them the required capabilities even if they do not realize how important these are.

7 Even if the business really does need a differentiated competitive positioning, it will still benefit from supporting this with useful capabilities too. The link works both ways. If you compete on capabilities, this will help you to develop existing and new core competencies and competitive positions. If you compete on positioning, this will be enabled by aligned core competencies and capabilities as well.

8 Although it is not the subject of this book it is worth recognizing that organizational capabilities are increasingly being informed by new technologies operating alongside people and their organization. This includes the role of robots and artificial intelligence which can sometimes reduce the need for people. There are also a range of human augmentation and enhancement technologies which help people increase their impact in an organization.

References

Ansoff, HI (1965) *Strategic Management*, Palgrave Macmillan, Basingstoke

Beer, M, Spector, B, Lawrence, PR and Mills, DQ (1984) *Managing Human Assets: The groundbreaking Harvard Business School program*, Free Press, New York

Buttle, F (2003) *Customer Relationships Management*, Butterworth-Heinemann, Oxford

Guest, D, Michie, J, Sheehan, M and Conway, N (2001) Getting inside the HRM – performance relationship, ESRC future of work programme, working paper, 8

Hamel, G and Prahalad, CK (1996) *Competing for the Future*, Harvard Business School Press, Boston

Hemerling, J, Bhalla, V, Dosik, D and Hurder, S (2016) [accessed 12 January 2017] Building Capabilities for Transformation that Lasts, *BCG Perspectives*, (7 June) [Online] https://www.bcgperspectives.com/content/articles/transformation-large-scale-change-people-organization-building-capabilities-transformation-that-lasts/?chapter=3

Kaplan, RS and Norton, DP (2004) *Strategy Maps: Converting intangible assets into tangible outcomes*, Harvard Business School Press, Boston

Keller, S and Price, C (2011) *Beyond Performance: How great organizations build ultimate competitive advantage*, John Wiley & Sons, New York

Kim, WC and Mauborgne, R (2005) *Blue Ocean Strategy*, Harvard Business School Press, Boston

Lawler, EE III and Boudreau, JW (2015) *Global Trends in Human Resource Management*, Stanford University Press, California

Leinwand, P and Mainardi, C (2016) *Strategy that Works: How winning companies close the strategy-to-execution gap*, Harvard Business Review Press, Boston

Mlabvideo (2011) [accessed 12 January 2017] Beyond Performance: Changing How Managers Think About Health, *Management Innovation Exchange* [Online] https://www.youtube.com/watch?v=iexD_Mo-xuU

Ocean Tomo (2015) [accessed 12 January 2017] Annual Study of Intangible Asset Market Value, *Ocean Tomo LLC* [Online] http://www.oceantomo.com/2015/03/04/2015-intangible-asset-market-value-study/

Porter, M (1985) *Competitive Advantage: Creating and sustaining superior performance*, Free Press, New York

Purcell, J, Kinnie, N, Hutchinson, S, Rayton, B and Swart, J (2003) *Understanding the People and Performance Link: Unlocking the black box*, CIPD, London

Reichheld, F (2003) The one number you need to grow, *Harvard Business Review*, (December)

Rosenzweig, P (2007) *The Halo Effect... and the Eight Other Business Delusions that Deceive Managers*, Free Press, New York

The IIRC (2013) [accessed 12 January 2017] Get to Grips with the Six Capitals, *International Integrated Reporting Council* [Online] http://integratedreporting.org/what-the-tool-for-better-reporting/get-to-grips-with-the-six-capitals/

Ulrich, D and Lake, DG (1990) *Organizational Capability: Competing from the inside out*, John Wiley & Sons, New York

Waterman, RH Jr, Peters, TJ and Phillips, JR (1980) Structure is not organization, *Business Horizons*, **23** (3), pp 14–26

Adding and creating more value

02

Introduction

We now understand that the greatest value provided by our management of people, including development of the relationships between them, occurs in the organization value chain. However, it is also important to understand the nature of the value that is developed. Most of the outcomes in the organization value chain are intangible. They are things we cannot see or even describe and certainly cannot assess that easily. Think about someone's skills, their motivation, the quality of their relationship with the person sitting next to them, or the ease with which someone can communicate with another person they do not work with regularly. All of these qualities are highly important but are internal to the person or the working of the organization.

Intangibles apply to other value chains as well. Core competencies (particularly the intellectual capital part) and customer relationships are intangible too. But the extent of this is vastly increased when focusing on people, and particularly on the relationships between the people, working within an organization.

The intangibility of organization value is important. Intangibles behave very differently to tangible resources. For one thing they do not get used up. A tangible quality such as someone's availability reduces as they do more work. An intangible such as the quality of their relationships tends to increase the more work they do. Working with someone builds trust, and increased trust makes it more likely that people will do further work together. As I explain within this chapter, this means it is possible to create as well as add value to the outcomes in the organization value chain. The role and differences between these two types of value can be best explained by using a model called the value triangle.

The value triangle

The value triangle, shown in Figure 2.1, defines the value that can be provided through the management of any intangible and, in particular, from people management. The idea of the model being a triangle, or a pyramid, is that it builds up from lower value at the base of the triangle to higher value towards the apex at the top. This build upwards is important – if HR and people leaders do not provide basic value at the bottom of the triangle it will be much more difficult to provide value higher up. For example, if we fail to pay people properly no one is going to want to hear about our talent management programmes. However, if HR only provides value at the bottom of the triangle then it has largely missed the point as the real value it can provide is at the top.

Figure 2.1   The value triangle

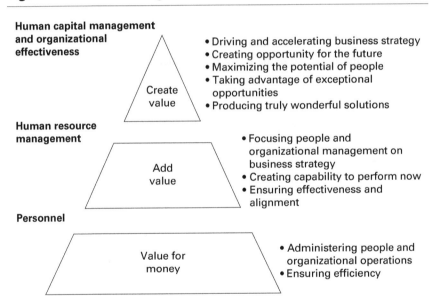

You can think of the bottom two levels of the triangle as being related to efficiency and effectiveness, though I am going to define them a little differently to these too. Creating value will then be a new way of thinking about organizational management for many people.

Value for money

The bottom level of the triangle is called value for money. This refers to basic, largely tangible value that is useful but is not necessarily about meeting business objectives or providing customer satisfaction. It includes delivering people management as a secondary, supporting activity in the financial, customer or operations value chains. This is why I link value for money to the personnel department – in the days when we had personnel functions, value for money was as much as these functions ever even intended to deliver. No more was required. As long as the personnel department delivered support in health and welfare, often supported by a dollop of tea and sympathy, everyone was happy.

A relevant example for the social organization might be removing the source of conflict from a team. More broadly, value-for-money activities may include any of the following:

- Providing increased efficiency through time or cost savings.
- Making incremental improvements in effectiveness, eg by using best practices.
- Making improvements in high-volume operational processes that are not changing substantially, but which, given the amount of time or energy they take up, may still demand significant attention.
- Achieving better usability – reducing frustrations with processes or systems.
- Meeting legislative requirements within a particular country or region.
- Meeting other compliance requirements, eg applied by regulators within a sector.
- Applying requirements imposed by other stakeholders, eg being cascaded from head office (things that are strategically important for the whole company but may not be that important for a local operation).
- Maintaining other basic standards, eg implementing actions to retain a quality award.
- Undertaking basic, operational risk management activities.
- Supporting sustainability – caring for the environment, the local community or the organization's reputation.

Value for money is important, and we still need to ensure it is undertaken both well and efficiently (possibly without the tea and sympathy). But we can also do much more. The first higher-value opportunity is adding value.

Adding value

Adding value is really the opposite to the above. It is about meeting business objectives. It does this by aligning everything we do in people and organizational management with the business results that are required. This ensures that all of the activities and outcomes in the organization value chain support existing business plans in the operations, customer and/or financial value chains.

Adding value is generated by focusing on the business. This is why I link adding value to human resource management (HRM), which is all about aligning HR with the rest of the business. It is also why HR people often talk about the need to get closer to the business and to talk the language of business (ie finance – currently, at least). There is even a fairly new ambition that is being worn almost as a badge of honour by some HR directors, about being a business person first and an HR person second. (I will have more to say about the language of business and being a business person first later on in this chapter!) Dave Ulrich's perspective on 'outside in' fits in here too. This idea suggests that HR needs to go beyond the boundaries of the business to understand the needs of its customers, investors and the local communities the business works within (Ulrich *et al*, 2009).

Having this deep understanding of a business means that whereas value-for-money activities are always at risk of being automated or outsourced, added-value activities are a useful focus for an organization's effort because the people working in the organization understand its needs better than any outsourcer. Business requirements can then be translated back up the organization value chain – identifying outcomes that will support these requirements, and activities that will create the required outcomes. An example of adding value might be coaching a team to perform to help them achieve their performance goals.

Adding value around people management in the organization value chain is really important and most businesses and HR teams could add significantly more value than they currently do. But I worry that many HR practitioners and teams see this as the end of the journey – that once they add as much value as they possibly can this will mean that HR will have fully developed its role within a business. I do not believe that this will be the case. In fact there is a whole new, even more important, level of value that exists beyond and above adding value.

Creating value

Creating value is in many ways the opposite to adding value. This level of value comes from focusing on people and the organization, finding new possibilities based on an understanding of what these can or could do. This might be about leveraging the existing capabilities and engagement of the workforce, which could help the business to achieve even more. Or it could be about investing in the hidden or unrealized potential of people in order to create new capabilities that might then be used in the future. Creating value still acts within the context of the mission and purpose of an organization and its people's roles – it is a very commercial and businesslike approach. But it recognizes that many workforces and organizations could achieve much more then they currently do and that this is unlikely to be realized simply by focusing ever more directly on the business. Continuous improvements are no longer enough – created value is needed to surprise competitors and change the nature of the competition. This level of value is, therefore, hugely important to most businesses, which increasingly need to maximize every opportunity to differentiate and renew themselves wherever they can find them.

The direct objective of creating value is, therefore, to optimize the contribution of people and their organization. The indirect objective is to help a business succeed. Business results become a supplementary, or oblique, impact of focusing on people, their relationships and the organization. These results may be about achieving more of the organization's existing business objectives; accelerating how quickly these objectives can be met; setting new or more stretching business goals; or even sometimes completely transforming the way the business works to create new opportunities for competitive advantage.

So, creating value is about reversing the order of our thinking about the business strategy map, explained in Chapter 1. *Adding value* was about understanding the needs in the rest of the business and then aligning people and organizational outcomes and activities in the organization value chain with these needs. *Creating value* builds upon the capabilities or potential of people working in an organization and the way they are organized to do their work. It focuses on developing better outcomes around these people and their organization and then looks down the strategy map, in the other three value chains, to identify the additional business impacts these outcomes could provide. This is shown in Figure 2.2.

Creating value is also about doing things differently so no one approach to it will have universal application. However, an example could be transferring people between two teams in a way that ignites the potential of both groups. Some firms are creating value through their reward strategies, using reward decisions to inform financial budgets rather than waiting for finance to provide HR with recommendations for annual adjustments. Another good example of creating value comes from my own experience as an HR director at EY, where the firm thought very seriously about the

Figure 2.2 Order of thinking in creating versus adding value

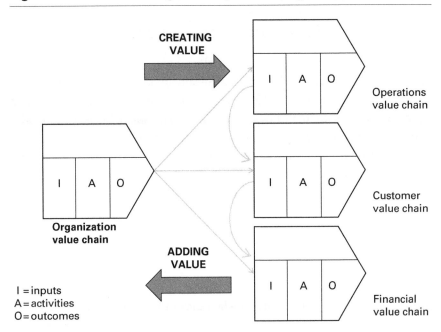

type of work it was taking on, not just in terms of a project's revenues and margin, but also the type of work it offered to its people. The firm wanted to be a global employer of choice for the people it chose, and realized that if it offered these people boring work, however profitable, this strategy would break down.

It is also worth noting that creating value does not always need to act at this strategic, organizational level. It could also relate more simply to developing a truly wonderful solution through a deep knowledge and understanding of people and the organization, or taking advantage of a once-in-a-blue-moon opportunity that happens to come along. So, for example, you might be mapping out the employment market for a particular role and come across someone in a different area who you think would have a tremendous impact on your organization. Even if there is no vacancy they would fit against, you might still be able to see – based on your knowledge of the business and the people it requires – how much difference having this person on board would make. So you make a case for bringing them into your business. That would be created value too.

However, the biggest opportunity for many businesses to create value will be in the provision of organizational capabilities.

Organizational capabilities

Organizational capabilities and culture

I have already referred to organizational capabilities in Chapter 1, where I defined them as outcomes that are strategically important and suggested that they provide an alternative and equivalent basis for competitive advantage to core competencies, brand capital and financial capital. To be strategically important, outcomes will generally need to be based on creating value. Adding value can produce useful resources from people and organizational management but these resources tend not to be strategically important in their own right. They do not need to be – in adding value strategic importance resides in the rest of the business. Therefore, capabilities tend to be a major product of creating value and are largely limited to this level of value too.

Capabilities are constituted by important factors relating to people, their relationships and the organization – aspects of human, social and organization capital. Capabilities (particularly the social capital parts) are also what people are often really referring to when they talk about culture.

Ulrich (2015) provides a good explanation of this, suggesting that capabilities are analogous to an individual's personality. This aspect of someone's character and the way they think can be described and measured in standardized ways, eg by using the 'big five' scales of openness, conscientiousness, extraversion, agreeableness, and neuroticism. In a similar way, organizational capabilities describe how an organization plans and responds to its environment based upon what it sees as important. They can be described by looking at the different aspects of capability, eg human, organization and social capital.

Culture's human analogy is the habits and routines that inform a large proportion of how we behave, which determines our lifestyle and supports our personal identity. Looking back at an organization, culture refers to the patterns and events in how an organization works, which help support its identity too (Ulrich, 2015). Figure 2.3 provides my summary of these analogies and their linkages.

Basically, in people, our habits are a consequence of our personality and in an organization, culture is a result of capabilities. The analogy is not perfect, of course. Personality cascades into habits very easily and naturally. Defined capabilities do not necessarily impact, never mind become, the culture. But this is really just about implementation of the capabilities, and particularly whether people are aware of them, believe in them and act in a way that is aligned with them.

Figure 2.3 Analogies explaining capabilities and culture

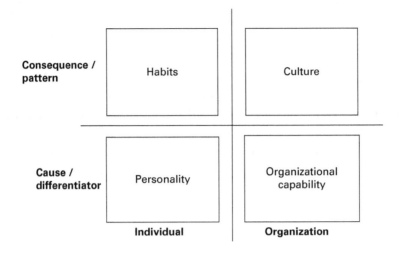

	Individual	Organization
Consequence / pattern	Habits	Culture
Cause / differentiator	Personality	Organizational capability

The real issue is that personality and capabilities are both relatively easily categorized, measured and assessed. Habits and culture are emergent and nebulous. Just like our own habits, organizational culture is hugely important, which is why so much time gets devoted to it – but again, like our own habits it is relatively difficult to describe or change.

I have been working with culture since 1993 when I was working in IT consulting with Andersen Consulting (now Accenture), which had decided at that point that change management was going to be a thing. The firm then created a change management services group of 300 people, which I somehow ended up being part of. And in my early years working in that group I used to find culture an enormously helpful concept to express what is important in an organization. But because it is so nebulous, and also because these days the term is so overused, misused and abused, I no longer find it helpful.

This is different to the use of the term in anthropology, eg in reference to a national or group culture, since there is no organizational intent behind this and it is important to simply explain the way things are. In organizations we are not just interested in why things are as they are but also how to change them. We are not just leaving an organization to its own devices, we are trying to steer and shape it. This is not the same as in a traditional community, eg a village. Capability provides a better basis than culture for thinking about, and in particular for changing, organizations.

Seen as complex adaptive, living systems (see Chapter 5), organizations do have emergent properties that are not exhibited in their constituent parts, such as the processes, structures, people, and people's relationships with other people. But even when using this perspective to think about organizations I generally find concepts such as shared consciousness are more helpful than culture.

Therefore, these days, if someone talks to me about their culture I will ask them what they are really talking about – is it their people's values or attitudes, their behaviours, the alignment of their organization's HR processes, the stories people tell themselves or what else? Often, of course, it is a combination of these things, but that is fine – we simply address each one together. But quite often I find that the different strands of culture do not correspond with one another. For example, it is quite possible for individuals in an organization to value something like intrapreneurship whilst acting in a constrained, traditional manner because that is what their processes make them do. Plus, as Marcus Buckingham points out, there often is no one single culture – this varies dramatically when looking from team to team (Labarre, 2001). This, once again, is down to differences in the extent and way in which capabilities are implemented. These points also make it difficult to talk about culture as a single thing.

It is also particularly irksome to talk about culture when referring to social capital. Culture can be seen to relate to the activities that create social capital, to the social capital itself, and to the whole system that creates the social capital, including both the activities and outcomes. So people end up talking about using culture to create culture in the context of the culture. It really is not a helpful term. Because of this I try not to talk about organizational culture much at all. In fact apart from when I am making reference to my or other people's use of the term, this will be the last but one time I use the word in this book. For me, capabilities provide a much more useful focus. They are easier to describe and understand. They are also easier to change. And they inform all the other things that we see as important. This is not a denial of the importance of culture – it is a desire to express something that is so critically important in a way that better enables us to deal with it.

Categorizing capabilities

As suggested previously, capabilities are not about having the best people or the perfect organization, they are about making the right choices for a particular firm. Just like competitive positioning and other sources of strategic advantage, capabilities need to be differentiated or to provide cost leadership. Deciding what particular capabilities are required depends upon the requirements of the business strategy, the context of the organization, the people who are employed, their skills, experience and expectations, and lots of other factors besides. I will provide a recommended approach to doing this in Chapter 5.

Gaining cost leadership would require the same sorts of capabilities as a competitor, but with the ability to develop these more cheaply than this other organization. This might involve a fairly harsh approach to employment in order to save costs. Two examples of companies reported to have used this approach are Amazon's order fulfilment centre division (Kantor and Streitfeld, 2015) and, in the UK, Sports Direct (Vandevelde, 2016). It is a strategy that can work – if only for as long as there are sufficient numbers of people prepared to work for this type of employer and insufficiently strong employee representative groups or employment legislation in place to stop it happening. Cost leadership may also be something that is open to employers using a more humanistic approach to management if they find a way to apply this approach particularly cost effectively. This may be something that will become more feasible as new technologies such as digital platforms continue to distinguish the digitally enabled from other organizations that do not have the same IT fire power.

However, the main option for most organizations will be differentiation. This is about creating the right set of capabilities that will transform and drive a business forwards. These capabilities could be about anything, as long as these things are really important for the particular organization. The critical requirement is to focus on the key few things that will make a real difference to the business. Less is more. Having too many capabilities makes it really difficult to truly differentiate any one of them. Focusing on a small number provides a much better opportunity to make a real difference within these most important areas.

Ulrich suggests having about three or four capabilities and provides the following examples of commonly used capabilities: learning, shared mindset, accountability, talent, collaboration, speed and leadership (Ulrich and Lake, 1990). More recently he has added to this list customer connection, innovation, strategic unity, efficiency, social responsibility, risk management, simplicity, connection and agility (Ulrich *et al*, 2009). I provide a short review of four of these capabilities – accountability, talent, collaboration and agility – below.

Accountability

Accountability provides a good example of how having a capability in place can generate improved business results. This capability is about having a deep sense of ownership for achieving business results. I have already described how HR functions can take accountability for their outcomes, and similar approaches can help other areas of business to become more accountable for their own results too.

My favourite example of an organization stressing this capability is alcoholic beverages company Diageo. Rather than asking people to agree to performance objectives or goals, the company asks people to make a performance promise. The company believes that promises are more psychologically meaningful than objectives and therefore have more impact on the people making them. They also help people to work with each other effectively. People's promises are also supported by HR processes that reinforce the importance of delivering on commitments, reviewing promises made versus promises kept. This approach has given Diageo the ability to develop a strategy and know it will be able to execute it. That has provided the company with a huge competitive advantage. As is often the case, the devil is in the detail and the implementation of any idea, so a company looking to go down this route would need to ensure that the focus on promises didn't become so strong that employees became reluctant to promise anything substantial.

Accountability requires a combination of human, organization and social capital. Many other capabilities have a leaning towards one particular capital rather than the other two. This is the case in the capabilities described below.

Talent

Some capabilities are very focused on human capital. For example, a capability in talent is simply about having the best people in a particular skill area. A good example of a company with this capability is technology business Microsoft. This firm has a very sophisticated sourcing strategy, developing relationships with the best IT-oriented universities and business schools around the world, and then with the best students at these universities. I have even heard that this approach sometimes extends down to the feeder schools for these key universities as well. Microsoft aims to have such good relationships with the best students that they will have already mentally committed to join by the time they graduate. The company also uses a creating value job-design technique called job sculpting, or job crafting, which contrasts with the traditional approach of designing a job and then recruiting someone to fill it (Wrzesniewski, Berg and Dutton, 2010). Job sculpting looks for the best person who can be found within an area, recruits them, and then looks to design the best role for that person. This role would be designed to ensure the individual can best use their skills, and will find the role motivating, and hence will be encouraged to maximize the contribution they make to their new employer.

Collaboration

The capability of talent contrasts with the capability of collaboration. This suggests that what really matters is great teams not just great people. This is a social capital-oriented capability and is a prime example of a capability demonstrated by the social organization. It is a capability that seems, until recently, to have been lacking within Microsoft, which is an interesting absence because collaboration is particularly prized by most technology companies. The modules used within IT systems need to work in tandem with each other but there is a suggestion, known as 'Conway's Law', that software vendors will be constrained to design products that resemble their organization structures (Brooks, 1995). Firms that are organized into separate departments will therefore produce compartmentalized software.

In fact it has been argued that Microsoft lost its leadership position in the technology sector because its people were not sufficiently united (Brass, 2010; Thompson, 2013). Margaret Heffernan (2015) suggests it used to be 'super chicken central' (super chickens are enhanced chickens that outcompete more normal ones by pecking them to death). Improving collaboration has therefore been the focus of a lot of Microsoft's recent activities – including work on organization design (see Chapter 6) and performance management (see Chapter 11).

Organizations, just like individuals, find it much easier to develop existing strengths than to turn a weakness into a strength. In addition, the company needs to be careful that its increasing focus on collaboration does not detract from its existing differentiation in talent. There is a very useful idea called trade-offs, introduced by Michael Porter (1995) for use in competitive positioning but which can be applied to the other types of competitive strategy too. This suggests that there are a limited number of things a company can do well as these take resources, time and energy to do. Therefore, as well as deciding what a company is going to differentiate around, it is useful to consider what it is not going to see as important. The suggestion is that reducing focus in these other areas means it can move resources into those areas it does care about. Deciding what not to do can be a really difficult question to answer. It can therefore be an even more important decision to make than the one about the positive differentiation. For me, Microsoft had made a trade-off between talent and collaboration. Purely tactical actions to improve collaboration may therefore backfire. Fortunately I think Microsoft is making its changes as part of a strategic, prioritized and integrated programme of activities.

Agility

Agility is an example of a capability that is based mainly on organization capital. The term originates in agile software development (Beck *et al*, 2001), where it focuses on iterative product development delivering working software, initially through a minimum viable product. This is followed by frequent updates keeping up with changing user requirements. These are produced in short blasts of work, which in the scrum approach are referred to as sprints. Doing this requires people to have freedom to do what is most useful rather than just what is in the process and also to be able to make improvements to the process. The approach contrasts with the traditional 'waterfall' approach to project management in which there is a long sequence of tasks that flow from start to finish like a cascade of water. However, the broader ideas around flexibility and speed, as well as some of the specifics like sprints and scrums have been extended into many other areas. As an example, some organization designers are talking about minimum viable structures as a way of promoting simplicity, adaptability and agility. For me it is about making change fast. At its most developed, it can even be about having the capability to quickly develop new capabilities.

Developing agility is not just about organization capital, it does require appropriate human capital and social capital too. Indeed the inclusion of people and the development of self-organizing teams are two key tenets of an agile approach. However, it is still the organization capital that is the most critical aspect of the capability. A good example of a company with capability in agility, which illustrates this organizational basis, is – or was – the mobile-phone business Nokia. It may seem odd to include within this book an example of a business that largely failed – however, before being sold to Microsoft the firm was doing some leading work to develop its organization as well as the relationships between its people. In particular it had a very agile structure, supported by key business processes and the use of social technologies. HR professor Lynda Gratton describes one particular restructuring in which nine divisions were restructured into four business units, supported by three horizontal operations and support groups. This major change only required 100 people to change jobs and was fully implemented in just one week. Nokia's modular design meant that the rest of the company's people and teams could simply be cut and pasted into new parts of the organization (Gratton and Casse, 2010).

The example demonstrates that great organizations can exist within failing businesses and this is why I am not going to worry too much about whether my case studies have great or not-so-great business performance.

Producing the right organizational capabilities in the organization value chain will enable performance in the three later business value chains (for operations, customers and financials). Capabilities can therefore be used to stack the odds in favour of a particular business. However, organizational capabilities cannot guarantee business success. Of course you would hope that having the right people and organization would lead to changes in its business model, but organizations can experience powerful forces that stop this happening too. Nokia probably needed another capability in emotionally rich decision making (Vuori and Huy, 2016), supported by processes in zero-based strategic planning, in order to dig itself out of its fairly terminal situation.

50 shades of capabilities

Chapters 3 to 5 will review examples of activities that can be undertaken to create capabilities, based on human, social or organization capital, or on combinations of these. This includes capabilities such as accountability, talent, collaboration and agility, which have been reviewed above. However, I would like to reinforce again that a capability can be anything. That is, it can be about whatever aspect of people and organization that is going to be useful and important in transforming a company's success. For example, in my earlier book on human capital management I provided a case study of a project I had worked on with BT, focused on creating a capability of performance (Ingham, 2007). Through a concerted effort to improve execution of its approach to managing performance, the company largely succeeded in maximizing the performance of each of its employees and teams. This had a dramatic effect on business performance, for the short term at least.

Within any particular capability there are lots of potential arrangements of people, relationships and organizational archictectures. Two companies both with capabilities of collaboration could still have two very different approaches to gaining strategic success. Chapter 5 will look further at developing the right capabilities, particularly focused on the social organization.

A note on terminology

I referred earlier to my aversion to the word 'culture'. Words are important, particularly when referring to social capital. I have already defined this as the value of people's connections, relationships and conversations. This means that the words we use inform the social capital we produce. Social organization designers therefore need to choose their words carefully. In this book I use a lot of specific language, and I will define each of the terms that might otherwise be misunderstood. And if I cannot define something, like culture, then I will try not to use it.

I have also hinted that I think we need to change the language of business to be less financially and more people oriented. This links to suggestions from innovation professor Gary Hamel that the stale, bland language we use in organizations contributes to stale, bland environments and the low levels of engagement we find around the world. This language includes the use of terms such as value, quality, growth, leadership, differentiation, excellence, superiority, service and focus (Hamel and Breen, 2007). There is nothing wrong with any of these words. Indeed they are all highly important. But we should also recognize that they are not innately compelling for most people. Hamel notes that no soldiers ever went 'over the top' in the name of efficiency. (It may be worth noting that although we met Hamel in connection to core competencies and the operations value chain, I would suggest his latest thinking is very firmly anchored in the organizational space.)

Responding to both these points requires a balance between being specific whilst remaining as human as possible. A good example of this is the use of terms like human and social capital, and human capital management (HCM), which I discuss in Chapter 3. Seeing people as providers of human or social capital rather than just human resources is an enabling idea. However, it is important to understand that HCM is managing people for human capital, not managing people as human capital – indeed the need to place people at the centre of creating value makes it even more important that HCM treats employees as fully rounded people. We should therefore refer to people as people, and not just as employees, talent, learners or recruits, and particularly not as seats, users or nodes! (See Chapter 10 on workplace design and Chapter 13 on technology and social network analysis.)

However, I recognize that I do use a fair amount of stale, bland language in this book. That is not wonderful but it is probably appropriate. I write mainly for those readers who care enough about the social organization to want a full, rather than just a partial or high-level understanding of the topic. This requires use of specific terminology. My hope is that you will be sufficiently interested in the ideas and approaches I am writing about to cover for the rather dry nature of much of the writing. As you now know, I started my career with Andersen Consulting and although I work mainly in emergent, complex environments these days my earlier training on disciplined, standardized approaches still informs a lot of the way I think and communicate. Still I wish I could entertain you with plenty of interesting stories but that is not my style either, and I really do not have the space to do so!

But it is terminology that I am using, not jargon. It would be jargon if I used some of the same terms when speaking with a broad group of people working in your organization. (And, of course, I would not do that – I would find looser but more resonant terms to get my main ideas across.) However, to give you a full understanding of the social organization, and therefore a full appreciation of the benefits it provides, we need to use specific words, even if that makes them less compelling. I will still do what I can to make things as easy as possible for you. We are going to be spending a lot of time focusing on social capital. But most of the time I will use the looser but less ugly word 'relationships'. We still know what we mean. Even so, I am sure I will still get some criticism for using 'HR-speak'. And if you want to take this perspective then Figure 2.4 provides a set of words you can use to play buzzword bingo as you read through the book – have fun!

Figure 2.4   HR buzzword bingo

B	U Z Z W O R D			
B	I	N	G	O
organizational capability	meaning	accountability	trust	holistic
bottom up	re-engineering	human capital	agile	big data
third place	complexity	gamification	serendipity	engagement
paradigm	buzzword bingo	gig economy	employee experience	differentiation
predictive analytics	emergence	Zappos	collaboration	self-organization

Why is it, though, that no one criticizes the use of terms such as revenues, costs, net present value and economic value added, or attempts to develop understanding the company's balance sheet as finance-speak? Clearly these are important terms that help us to understand our success in the financial value chain. Similarly, when we talk about the marketing value chain we use words such as segmentation, market penetration, brand and Net Promoter Score (NPS). When using the operations value chain we refer to systems, supply chain management, quality and excellence. We need to use a language focused on people and organization when we talk about the organization value chain too. For example, Hamel suggests that increasing focus on people means we need a new corporate language that includes the type of words that have inspired humanity to great deeds over the centuries. Words like joy, truth, honour, fidelity, equality, wisdom, beauty, justice and love. I will have more to say about love in Chapter 12.

If we want to move to a future position but we use words associated with where we have been in the past rather than where we want to go in the future, we will make moving between the two states harder than it would otherwise have been. If we want to emphasize the organization value chain rather than the other chains within a business then we need to prioritize the use of words associated with the former rather than the latter.

I think this is important as I see HR spending lots of time challenging itself to speak the language of business. This is useful and important but only to an extent. It is a feature of adding value. What we need to focus on even more is creating value by building an environment where we are better able to extract value from people and their organizations. So actually rather than us speaking the language of business it is even more important that we get the whole business speaking the language of people. It is why I worry about being a 'business person first, HR person second'. Yes this can help build our credibility but it is not going to help us become more strategic and build better organizations for our people. We actually need more focus on people, and more people in business focused on people management, not less. So HR and other business leaders need to be able to use HR-, people- or relationship-oriented terminology without being criticized for this.

There is a great case study from Stanford that relates to this (Hoyt and Rao, 2007). This describes the personal transformation of a former chief financial officer (CFO) at technology firm Infosys, who was moved over to take up the leadership of HR. The new head of HR explains that whilst in finance he used to think about people in terms of their net present value but since moving into HR had learnt to see them as bundles of emotions and aspirations. Infosys is a successful and well-led organization that the case likens to a human capital supply chain company. But surely it would be even more successful if its CFO and other business leaders had this more progressive approach to people, and without them all having to take a job in HR?

HR functions in some organizations are so focused on their businesses that they can sometimes seem to be forgetting about the people who make businesses work. And bizarrely, they are doing this at just the point at which many businesses are finally starting to get more interested in their people. I sometimes worry that if HR carries on in this direction it will pass the rest of the business leadership community like ships in the night – HR will have all of its science and data, but it will be the finance department that is being held accountable for love, empathy, passion and everything that is important in an organization. I think you can see some of this in Ram Charan's suggestion that the finance department should take over HR's strategic role for developing leadership and organization (Charan, 2014).

I do not mean any disrespect to finance by these comments – however, the fact is that the days when finance was king are long behind us. These days, HR is king – or certainly should be. I explain more on this in the next section.

The consequences of a creating-value perspective

People-centricity

Creating value must not be something that only concerns HR or social organization strategists. Everyone working in an organization needs to put other people at the centre of their thinking. There are three reasons for suggesting this. The first is that we should always think about others and treat people well. Acting decently towards people is part of what it is to be human. As the word suggests, when we act inhumanely we act as not human (see Chapter 4 on our social brains). We should care for each other in business as well as elsewhere. The problem, described further in Chapter 4, is that business can become so task-focused that people do not always act in the way they would do outside of work. That needs to change.

The second reason we need to be more people-centric is that it is people who do work, acting as the main resources to deliver business strategy. This is just repeating the point that many chief executives themselves use – that 'people are our most important asset'. It is also reinforced by my suggestions in Chapter 1 to focus on the organization value chain, and to add value through this value chain, the reasons for which have been explained above. Actually this is the bit that most managers do understand and remember. Business managers know that it is not enough to develop a great strategy, they need to be able to deliver it too. And they know that execution of these plans is increasingly difficult. So they do generally recognize the need to engage and involve their people. Unfortunately, seeing people as resources does not always produce the desired behaviours either.

The third point, which I do not think is always understood, is that people can be central to the identification and development of strategy as well as its implementation. Think about the other sources of competitive advantage: financial capital, customer capital and business excellence. When these were the most important assets, businesses did not just think about using them to implement existing business strategies. These other assets were used to develop new business strategies supported by activities that would have been impossible without the assets being in place. So why do we think about people management simply as something that will ease implementation of existing business strategies?

It is an important distinction. Focusing just on implementation sees people as cogs in a well-oiled machine. But people are not just an important part of the machine, they also provide its design and therefore inform what it produces. We therefore need to treat people as the central asset in a business, developing and investing in them for the future of the business. We also need to create people-centred business strategy in the organization value chain, which can then influence and inform plans in the other three chains.

One great example of people-centricity was the behaviour of Campbell Soup's former chief executive, Doug Conant. He used what he called 'touch-points' – simple exchanges like meetings, e-mails and chance encounters in the corridor – to provide often-overlooked opportunities to influence people towards better performance. One particular habit was sending out 10–20 personal thank-you cards each day. That amounted to 30,000 cards during his tenure as CEO. It is this type of behaviour, and other similarly people-centric activities, which can get people truly engaged, aligned to what is important and committed to applying their own potential for the success of the business they work within.

This need for more people-centric management lies behind much of the rest of the book. Its suggestion is that investing in people and relationships is the most profitable and effective way to run a business. To some people that will sound rather disingenuous. And in fact I would love to think companies would invest in their people simply because they care about them and understand that this is the right thing to do. However, the evidence is that many and probably most businesses do not do this currently and therefore will probably not do so in the future either. To a large extent it does not matter why people invest in their people as long as they do.

In addition, new ideas based solely on humanistic ideologies are unlikely to be implemented. For example, a number of people are very excited about the potential for completely flat, self-managing organizations but few businesses are implementing these designs. The social organization provides a compelling argument for change, which should result in more organizations radically transforming – the supplementary benefit of which is that we will get more human organizations.

Changing HR into a driver of strategic success

As I suggested in Chapter 1, creating value also implies a more strategic role for the HR function. Becoming more strategic has been the big agenda item in HR for the last 20 years or more. The issue is that if a business is competing purely on Porter's competitive positioning then HR is, by definition, a support function. A lot of what is discussed elsewhere in terms of HR's strategic role is really just about it being more proactive. For example, much of it concerns the need for HR to be at 'the table', being consulted early about important business changes. However, the focus is still on strategic opportunities and challenges occurring in the rest of the business, and HR supporting these. The difference is often just how quickly it provides this support.

For HR to have a strategic role it needs to focus on the organization value chain. However, this is still not enough. It also needs to ensure its thinking across the business strategy map moves from left to right as well as right to left, ie that it is focusing on creating as well as adding value. This is because adding value still assumes that strategy is taking place in the rest of the business. This is why, when I defined adding value, I explained that it ensures organizational activities and outcomes support the needs of a business. And what do we call a function that supports the business? Obviously we call it a support function.

If HR really wants to be strategic, it has got to create value, by providing new people-oriented opportunities to a business. And it is going to have to do this by creating people-centred business strategy through its actions in the organization value chain. Creating value rests on an understanding of people and organizations and so the key skills come from psychology, sociology and anthropology as well as neuroscience and behavioural economics. It does not come from even tighter focus on business needs. This is necessary but not sufficient for creating value. HR practitioners often feel a tension between being strategic and focusing on people. But actually these are the same thing. It is by focusing on people that we become strategic and it is when we focus purely on the business that we act as a support function.

HR also needs to be more confident about its strategic contribution. Too many HR people are apologetic about their roles and often try to suggest the things they are working on are business projects not HR initiatives. This may have some short-term benefit for these individual projects, but at some point HR practitioners need to face the real issue – which is why they feel the need to dress everything up as business rather than HR. People management is important, and it needs to be understood as such. HR will only be able to truly maximize its impact when it can say something is an HR initiative and everyone understands this means that it is important and they need to pay attention to it.

Summary and additional comments

1 Adding value supports businesses to gain competitive advantage through the operations, customer or financial value chains. Creating value provides competitive success from the outcomes, especially organizational capabilities, produced within the organization value chain.

2 Creating value is of course an additional reason why we should focus on organizational outcomes – if we only think about activities and business impacts it is going to be much harder to be able to spot or take advantage of the additional value that people and organizational management can provide.

3 Whilst the steps in the organization value chain are very clearly distinguished, the levels in the value triangle are much more blurred. It is often difficult to be clear whether something is adding value or creating value, and it is generally not that important either. The critical thing is that each HR function, practitioner and people leader always thinks about how they can generate more value within what we do. For example, if we are asked to do something that is value for money we should look at how we can add some value too. Or if we need to undertake an adding-value activity, we need to ask ourselves how we can do that and create some value at the same time.

References

Beck, K *et al* (2001) [accessed 12 January 2017] Manifesto for Agile Software Development, *The Agile Alliance* [Online] http://agilemanifesto.org/

Brass, D (2010) [accessed 12 January 2017] Microsoft's Creative Destruction, *New York Times*, 4 February [Online] http://www.nytimes.com/2010/02/04/opinion/04brass.html

Brooks, FP Jr (1995) *The Mythical Man Month: Essays on software engineering*, Addison Wesley, Boston

Charan, R (2014) It's time to split HR, *Harvard Business Review*, July–August, pp 63–71

Gratton, L and Casse, J (2010) [accessed 12 January 2017] Inside the Nokia Booster Programme, *London Business School* [Online] https://www.london.edu/news-and-events/news/inside-the-nokia-booster-programme

Hamel, G and Breen, B (2007) *The Future of Management*, Harvard Business School Press, Boston

Heffernan, M (2015) [accessed 12 January 2017] Forget the Pecking Order at Work, *TED* [Online] http://www.ted.com/talks/margaret_heffernan_why_it_s_time_to_forget_the_pecking_order_at_work/transcript

Hoyt, D and Rao, H (2007) *Building a Talent Engine to Sustain Growth (Case No. HR30)*, Stanford Graduate School of Business

Ingham, J (2007) *Strategic Human Capital Management: Creating value through people*, Butterworth Heinemann, Oxford

Kantor, J and Streitfeld, D (2015) Amazon's bruising, thrilling workplace, *New York Times*, 16 August

Labarre, P (2001) [accessed 12 January 2017] Marcus Buckingham Thinks Your Boss Has an Attitude Problem, *Fast Company* [Online] https://www.fastcompany.com/43419/marcus-buckingham-thinks-your-boss-has-attitude-problem

Porter, ME (1995) What is strategy?, *Harvard Business Review*, November, pp 61–78

Thompson, B (2013) [accessed 12 January 2017] Why Microsoft's reorganization is a bad idea, *Statechery* [Online] https://stratechery.com/2013/why-microsofts-reorganization-is-a-bad-idea/

Ulrich, D (2015) From war for talent to victory through organization, *Strategic HR Review*, **14** (1/2), pp 8–12

Ulrich, D, Allen, J, Brockbank, W, Younger, J and Nyman, M (2009) *HR Transformation: Building human resources from the outside in*, McGraw-Hill Education, Chicago

Ulrich, D and Lake, D (1990) *Organizational Capability: Competing from the inside out*, John Wiley & Sons, New York

Vandevelde, M (2016) 'Victorian workhouse conditions' at Sports Direct warehouse, *Financial Times*, 22 July

Vuori, TN and Huy QN (2016) Distributed attention and shared emotions in the innovation process: how Nokia lost the smartphone battle, *Administrative Science Quarterly*, **61** (1), pp 9–51

Wrzesniewski, A, Berg, JM and Dutton, JE (2010) Turn the job you have into the job you want, *Harvard Business Review*, **88** (6), pp 114–17

Linking activities 03 with human and organizational outcomes

Introduction

This chapter provides some initial ideas about how capabilities and other outcomes linked to human capital and organization capital can be created. Chapter 4 will describe how similar links work for social capital as well as explaining why this is the most important of these three capitals. Chapter 5 continues that analysis. The focus of the rest of the book will then be on just the social capital-oriented approaches. However, it will help to understand these social activities if we first review those linked to human and organization capital.

Activities for creating human capital

As explained in Chapter 1, human capital is the value provided by people working in an organization. It is based first on the ability, and second, on the attitude or motivation of people to do their jobs. The diversity of people working in an organization can be a further important aspect of human capital. Some of the rather different activities required to develop these three types of value are reviewed below.

Creating new abilities

Ability can be defined in a number of different ways, including as skills, competencies or strengths. It can also be inferred by someone's behaviours or contributions. Many organizations also try to understand their people's potential to increase their contribution in the future. This is more difficult to assess than current contribution but it often provides a stronger basis for creating value. That is firstly because it is more people-centric – it looks at what people could do differently and the value this would provide, rather than simply whether they can do what the business already requires. And second, the simple fact that assessing potential is difficult offers a competitive opportunity to firms that can do this when their competitors cannot.

Any of these types of ability can be developed by a variety of HR activities. HR professor Dave Ulrich talks about the six Bs (Ulrich *et al*, 2009). However, for most organizations the main choice will be between 'buy' or 'build'. Buying ability, by recruiting people, tends to be the preference for many leading firms. For example, Google's former head of people operations, Laszlo Bock, writes about front loading the company's investment in people into attracting, assessing and cultivating new hires on the basis that big investments in training indicates a failure to hire the right people to begin with (Bock, 2016). Recruitment also tends to be a more successful approach when a firm is not currently performing or when there is a lot of change.

However, building ability, by developing people, tends to be a preferred option by firms applying a growth mindset. This is about focusing on opportunities for improvement and contrasts with a fixed mindset, which emphasizes existing qualities and traits (Dweck, 2012). Research from Wharton business school also suggests that external hires need to be paid about 20 per cent more than internal workers who are promoted into similar jobs. However, the external hires perform less well and leave faster than those who have been promoted. Though if the hires stay in their new firms they still get promoted faster (Bidwell, 2011). This is one more thing I put down to the halo/horns effect – we tend to assess the relatively unknown performance of someone who looks good on paper more positively than the better known and therefore more nuanced performance of an existing employee.

Development may also be seen to fit more naturally in a creating value approach than recruitment, as again, it looks at what people could be capable of doing rather than simply comparing their current skills against business requirements. However, recruitment can be developed into a creating value approach too. For example, whilst I was at EY we introduced an approach we called 'head farming'. We had wanted to insource our headhunting activities and at the same time changed the approach so that our new internal recruiters could be more proactive, mapping out the market and identifying people we might like to employ in the future rather than sitting back and waiting for a requisition.

Behind all of this was our intent to be an employer of choice, and we saw traditional recruitment as a barrier to its achievement. Approaches like post-and-pray advertising can be very good at generating good hires but they are completely unfit for purpose in providing the very best people who could be found. The issue is that the best people are unlikely to be looking for a job, particularly at the time there is a vacancy. So recruiters need to go to these people with their employer value proposition (EVP) and be willing to enter into conversations when the time is right for one of the people being targeted, not because it is a good time for the recruiting firm, eg it has a current vacancy.

At the time, which was well before the development and widespread adoption of social media, this was an unusual approach. Nowadays it is something many organizations do – we just call it talent pipelining. And it is social media that has made the approach more feasible. We can use social tools, primarily LinkedIn, to source people. Then there are other social tools that can be used to manage the relationship with the sourced individuals in an external talent pool. One example of a business using this approach is soft drinks company Coca-Cola, which in the United States uses an external talent pool for most of its professional and managerial hiring. The external pool is stocked from sourcing, employee referrals and potential boomerang hires (returning alumni). When there is a vacancy the firm does not need to start the whole reactive process of recruiting, it just goes to the external pool to see who is ready to join. I have worked with another organization that is also attempting to influence the development plans of the people in the external pool so that when they do join they have even more of the skills that the acquiring organization wants (and also so that the existing employer pays to develop them).

The creation of external recruitment pools has additional value in developing relationship capital (the value of relationships outside of a business). They can also be combined with other external groups such as those created for open innovation, as the people who might have great ideas for a business will often be the same people that the business might like to employ at some point.

Although I think these cases are examples of people-centric creating value (described in Chapter 2) there is still more we can do. For example, once we have set up an external talent pool we can use it for something I call 'career partnership'. This recognizes that people no longer want to work for a firm for life and that many people now work in short term, task oriented contracts. However, it also suggests that there are still opportunities to create long-term, mutually beneficial relationships – partnerships between people and employing organizations. The approach enables these by being open about the potential for someone to develop within an organization or outside. When a relevant external opportunity for someone arises, a firm acting as a career partner would raise it with them and encourage them to apply. If they get that other opportunity the partnering firm simply keeps in contact with them via its external talent pool. This would also have a temporary benefit for the company's relationship capital, much as McKinsey and other professional firms try to have by helping departing staff get jobs with their clients. However, the hope would be that at some point in the future the person would rejoin the partner again. But once again that would probably only be for a relatively short period. The approach is designed to gain the maximum lifetime value from an individual and to offer them the best possible proactive career support in return. You can find out more about the idea in my earlier book on human capital management (Ingham, 2007) or on Gary Hamel's management innovation site, the MIX (http:// www.managementexchange.com) (Ingham, 2010).

Career partnership has not really caught on but examples of its use do exist, for example, 3M and Johnson & Johnson in Germany are currently doing something similar for their HR business partners. Close variants also operate in various areas such as the UK civil service graduate fast-track scheme. In any case, I still think it is a great example of a creating-value approach. I like to compare it to the concept of tours of duty, promoted by Reid Hoffman, the founder of LinkedIn, in his book *The Alliance* (Hoffman, Casnocha and Yeh, 2014). Hoffman suggests that firms should offer short-term tours of duty that enable people and organizations to contract together to undertake pieces of work based upon particular skills and without any expectation of a long-term relationship or career progression. To me, this is an adding-value perspective. It looks at the way businesses are working and seeks to fit people management into this current paradigm. Career partnership is a creating-value response to the same issue. It also responds to people not wanting a job for life but seeks to find a new basis for a long-term and mutually beneficial career relationship within this new context.

However, it is worth recognizing that Hoffman's tours of duty do link closely to the changing nature of employment for many people. In fact, as well as buy and build, a third 'b' – 'borrow' – is also starting to become popular, particularly with the rise of the contingent workforce. This includes contractors, consultants and an increasing number of self-employed and portfolio workers participating in the gig economy. New talent platforms such as UpWork, Tongal and Gigwork are making choosing people for particular tasks based upon particular skill sets very feasible (Boudreau,

Jesuthasan and Creelman, 2015). In fact McKinsey predicts that 540 million individuals around the world could benefit from these systems (Manyika *et al*, 2015). In addition, businesses are finding it is increasingly useful to tap the skills and ideas of people who do not work for their organizations at all, including sometimes their customers and competitors. All of these different forms of contribution inform an organization's human capital.

The opposing opportunities provided by tours of duty and career partnerships also illustrate that creating-value activities are not always applied to everyone working in an organization, but often just those with the greatest net impact on a business – the people who are often referred to as talent. A firm's talent acquisition and talent development activities may therefore be very different from the volume recruitment and development approaches applied to the rest of the business.

Note that it is not just recruitment that has changed – learning and development, communication and, most recently, performance management have all seen huge transformations taking place as well. And often these changes have been designed to connect these processes to the types of human capital that individual businesses have been trying to build.

The other key change is that companies are becoming smarter in what is often called integrated talent management. In a chapter I contributed to the Association for Talent Development (ATD) guide on this topic (Ingham, 2011), I suggest that integration is about horizontal as well as vertical alignment. Vertical alignment refers to the main point I have been discussing in this book – ensuring that HR activities are firmly linked to business needs. Horizontal alignment is about ensuring all the different activities within a firm's HR architecture link to, and support, each other – that what we aim to achieve in recruitment is the same as what we intend to achieve in learning, and so on. Integrated talent management ensures that we are not just able to choose between alternative activities but that we are able to combine them. For example, rather than recruit an experienced hire or develop a novice employee we may be best to combine the recruitment of a semi-experienced individual, supported by some further development. I think this ability to combine activities has led to some more creative creating-value approaches too.

Improving motivation

Motivation is the second main aspect of human capital. People do not provide any benefit to an employer if they have all the skills they need but behave in a way that does not see these applied. Firms are therefore interested in helping their people want to and be able to perform – for example, by optimizing people's health and wellness, their well-being and, increasingly, their mindfulness. Other concepts such as satisfaction, confidence and empowerment are used by some firms too. However, the core concept in this area is engagement, which refers to people's motivation to perform in a way that is aligned with an organization's aims so as to produce benefits for that business.

Much of today's efforts around engagement are still based on insight from the last century, and particularly on the research findings of psychologists Abraham Maslow (1943) and Frederick Herzberg (1959). Maslow proposed a hierarchy of needs that highlights the importance of love and belonging, although social cognitive neuroscientist Matt Lieberman argues, for reasons that will be described in Chapter 4, that these really need moving down to the base of the hierarchy (Lieberman, 2013). This is also the reason for Gallup's question in their Q12 engagement survey about whether people have a best friend at work (Gallup, 1999).

Herzberg proposed that extrinsic (externally applied) motivation and intrinsic (internally generated) motivation are two separate things with separate consequences. Extrinsic motivation is a hygiene factor. Lack of extrinsic motivation, eg insufficient pay, will cause dissatisfaction. Sufficient pay removes this dissatisfaction but will not motivate us. For this to happen, intrinsic motivation is needed, ie we actually need to motivate ourselves. This makes sense when remembering that individuals own their own human capital. This means that people need to be managed carefully to ensure they will want to apply their human capital for the good of the organization they work for. In fact you could argue that management is the wrong word anyway, and that all organizations can ever do is to create the right environment for employees to flourish, increasing the odds of their people becoming motivated.

More recent research by Edward Deci has led to the development of self-determination theory. This suggests that intrinsic motivation requires three key things – autonomy, competence and relatedness (Deci, 1995). You may have come across this research in Daniel Pink's popular book *Drive*, where he repackages Deci's factors as autonomy, mastery and purpose (Pink, 2009). I will describe relatedness further in Chapter 4, and the critical role of purpose will be reviewed in Chapter 5. We will then return to autonomy in Chapter 9.

Engagement is a really important idea but it suffers for two main reasons. One is that it is a financial-oriented rather than a people-oriented term. The other is that people pick up on the business-benefit aspect of the definition and ask themselves what the benefit is for them of being engaged. For both of these reasons, engagement, rather perversely, tends not to be a very engaging idea.

I therefore tend to talk about well-being. It sounds more human and is more about the benefit for the individual, rather than for the business. It is therefore more likely to actually be engaging and to provide the supplementary benefit of better business results.

We tried to respond to the personal and two-way aspects of engagement at EY. The firm created a set of people value principles that described the value the firm would provide to its people in exchange for the value they provided to the firm. These principles were then cascaded into our HR practices. For example, performance management was transformed into a broader management of the employment deal in which we would set clear objectives but also ask an employee how they wanted to be engaged. At the end of the year we would review an employee's performance, but would also ask them to review how well we were succeeding in engaging that individual. This was a particularly brave thing to do. Although it makes sense to ask someone about their personal engagement drivers, because identifying these otherwise is very hard, it also raises the stakes quite considerably.

In Denise Rousseau's analysis of the psychological contract she suggests that someone's emotional reaction to not receiving something they would have liked, but were never quite sure of receiving, is one of disappointment. But when they do not get something they believe they were promised this causes outrage (Rousseau, 1995). Employers should only ever get into conversations around personal drivers of engagement when they are seriously interested in tailoring their approaches in response. The best way of engaging people individually is to ask them about their engagement drivers and then deliver on them. The worst thing is to ask people and then not do anything to address what they say. Ignoring the fact that different people are engaged by different things seems a safer approach for most firms. However, if you want to create rather than just to add value you may need to get into people's personal agendas.

A rather easier means of creating value through higher engagement might be an approach that is receiving quite a bit of attention currently. This is to invest in the employee experience. This builds on an existing effort within IT to improve the user experience with computer and other digital systems. I see this as a creating-value strategy since it is about usability rather than functionality. Functionality is generally going to be about adding value – helping someone to do a job, support a process and meet certain business needs. Usability focuses on helping the person using a system, what this individual needs and what will engage rather than disengage them from its use. An increasing number of organizations are focused on candidate experience in recruitment because they understand the potential damage that can be done by disaffected candidates taking to Glassdoor, Twitter or other social media sites. However, the same principles apply to other HR processes too.

An example of a company applying this broader approach is home-stay network Airbnb where their head of people, Mark Levy, has been given the title of Global Head of Employee Experience. In this company HR processes are improved by exploring the emotions involved in using the processes currently, and what the company wants the process to feel like in the future (Meister, 2015). Other companies use design thinking to build on the current experience. These approaches are positive developments but it is important to remember that employee outcomes are still more important than their experience.

CASE STUDY Recruiting and engaging weird people at Zappos

Zappos's approach to managing its people is already fairly well known, at least in the United States (in fact as a result of this I added the company name to my buzzword bingo template provided in Chapter 2). As a consequence, if this was simply a good case study of creating value through people I probably would not have included it in this book. There are three reasons for doing so.

The first reason is that Zappos is a wonderful example of the changing nature of competitive success I referred to in Chapter 1. Zappos is a US-based online shoe retailer. In fact it was the first company to sell shoes online. At the time, this provided a strategic advantage through competitive positioning. People were already buying clothes over the internet but choosing shoes is a very physical, sensory process and the idea that people might want to buy shoes online was seen as a bit bizarre. Nevertheless, Zappos created this market, showed it could be successful, and now just about all shoe manufacturers and retailers sell shoes online.

Zappos also wanted to differentiate itself by providing very high levels of customer service. It originally needed this differentiation to ensure people would feel safe buying their shoes online. These days it provides immensely high levels of customer loyalty. Zappos also wanted to provide very personal customer service. A lot of customer service is very automated. Think about Amazon, where you will just about always receive your goods by the date that has been committed to but you will never speak to a human being there. Zappos has designed its business processes completely differently, making it more likely that you will get to speak to its people, called Zapponians, because this is when they can find out about you, entertain you and find out about more opportunities to delight you in future. It seems that this core competency in personalized customer service was one of the reasons Amazon acquired Zappos in 2009.

But Zappos's chief executive explains that the above differentiations are not the things that make the company special. Instead of these it differentiates on the people it employs and the way these people are treated (Hseih, 2010). Basically, Zappos employs rather weird people – a little weirdness is one of the company's values. It then makes these people happy so that they can make their customers happy too. This is Zappos's organizational capability, which is the true basis for its competitive advantage. This example therefore demonstrates the point I made in Chapter 1 that competitive positioning is no longer a sustainable source of competitive advantage.

The second reason for including the case study is that Zappos demonstrates a particularly tight relationship between its outcomes and activities. For example, because it does not want to make people unhappy it does not advertise its job vacancies, which would mean having to communicate bad news to people who have not got a job they wanted. Instead, it asks people to join an external recruitment pool called Zappos Insiders and has its recruiters be proactive about who they talk to within this talent pool. These conversations may progress until a hiring manager tells someone they have actually been talking about a job and asks whether the person wants to take it. No unhappiness.

Zappos also maintains its weirdness through its employer branding and its application process – asking people to submit a video explaining, and also asking them during interview, about how weird they are. The company also offers new joiners a financial bounty to leave the organization if they discover that they do not really want to work there. This is a really clever and people-centric approach. So I admire Zappos for being a very funky company, though I realize I am nowhere near weird enough for them. But I admire even more the close links they have made between their desired outcomes and their recruiting and employment approaches.

The third reason for discussing Zappos is that later in the book I will also need to discuss an organization model called Holacracy®, which is now being used by Zappos too. So you will hear about them again in Chapter 6.

Increasing diversity

The other aspect of human capital that goes beyond an individual's 'skill and will' is the diversity of the total workforce. However, this is still about the individual as it is based upon the combination of the different perspectives and ways of thinking of the different individuals who work for an organization. It is particularly important from a human capital perspective, since if everyone thinks in the same way and does things the same, the total value they provide may not increase that much. In addition, increasing diversity seems to make all individuals in a group think more deeply, increasing their individual as well as the group performance (Rock and Grant, 2016).

One well-discussed aspect of diversity is generational difference. This occurs because of the differing experiences that people in different generations have experienced whilst they are growing up, particularly during their teenage years. This area of diversity might be expected to feature heavily in this book as many people believe that generation-Y millennials are particularly collaborative and social media savvy. For example, management thinker Tammy Erickson suggests that those of you in this generation have particular advantages in today's businesses, based on your comfort with technology and the collaborative way in which you communicate with your peers (Erickson, 2008).

I believe there are differences that are generational rather than purely age related, however, I think these tend to be relatively small. I suspect that the most significant difference that generation Y has brought about is helping people of all generations feel more able to ask for the employment deal they want. Generational difference is also only one of a broad range of factors that lead to different perspectives and behaviours. This includes gender, age, nationality, ethnic group, level/type of any disability, socioeconomic status, religion, sexual orientation, personality and many other factors. A good way of responding to these differences is through a technique like Deloitte's mass career customization, which provides the ability to tailor aspects of the employment deal to different groups according to different factors that may be seen as important (Benko and Weisberg, 2007).

However, I also subscribe to cultural theorist Fons Trompenaars's analysis of national behavioural differences in which it is suggested that most nationality-oriented differences will span across a range in a normal distribution. Importantly though, the difference between the averages of any two nationalities will generally be less than the spread within the bell curve for either of these groups – that is, there is generally more variation within one group than there is between groups (Hampden Turner and Trompenaars, 1997). I think that is probably true for generations and any of the other types of differences as well. People are generally more different from each other than is indicated simply by comparing groups of people against each other.

The only way to respond to all these areas of difference (beyond monitoring basic equal opportunities categories) is to abandon the attempt to classify people into groups and simply treat each person as an individual. That again calls for a people-centric approach in which HR and management practices are tailored and personalized to each person and the way they learn and motivate themselves. This is something that technology is making more possible – I will return to this in Chapter 13.

Another important factor in increasing diversity is unconscious bias. This is, first, because bias can easily stop diversity increasing, and second, because a more diverse organization makes it more important to relate to people as individuals rather than simply assuming everyone thinks the same way. The key need is to recognize that we all rely on mental shortcuts and heuristics a lot of the time. These can sometimes help us to make fast and effective decisions but they can lead to biased and illogical decisions too.

Some of the generic problems we all suffer from include the halo/horns effect that I have already referred to. One of the important consequences of this is that we tend to focus on the financial value chain rather than the organization one. This can mean that people and organizational management often receive less investment than they should. Another important heuristic to understand is the overconfidence effect, which means we often believe we can be successful in doing something even when all the evidence suggests that most people or organizations do not manage to achieve it. A good example is making a success of a merger or acquisition – the overconfidence effect might lead us to skimp on internal development actions that would be useful for us.

These and many other heuristics mean we can make repeated suboptimal decisions, particularly around intangibles like people. Some of the most important common biases around people that result from these heuristics include:

- Gender bias: women as well as men tend to favour men in recruitment, compensation, promotion and other areas (Christakis, 2012).

- Physical characteristics bias: we tend to favour beautiful, tall people (Williams, 2012).

- Success versus failure bias: we believe that people who have had positive experiences may be better to hire in order to ensure our work goes well, even though the people with negative experiences may have gained deeper learning.

- Invalid leadership characteristics bias: we tend to believe, consciously or unconsciously, in characteristics like charisma, which have no research-based correlation with success.

- The 'extrovert ideal': many lists of desired competencies and behaviours, communication and development processes and workplace environments are built around the common characteristics of extroverts, making it more difficult for introverts to be successful (Cain, 2013).

These biases can often be best seen in lists of talent, leaders and high potentials, which often include groups of people who do not have any real link to higher performance:

- People who are similar to us – as we are likely to think they perform better.
- People who shout the loudest/flatter us the most.
- Narcissists, psychopaths and sociopaths – often confused with high performers, particularly by those businesses that value charisma (Furnham, 2015).
- Just a random selection of the employee population: this can be the case in organizations that use purely subjective assessments of their talent or do not consider the potential role of luck in people's progression and performance.

These problems raise questions about how well we can ever really assess someone's performance, and even more so their potential – especially as the halo/horns effect may mean we interpret potential through what we can see of someone's performance and end up assessing the same thing twice. To me it reinforces the need to apply a growth mindset and try to develop everyone working in a company according to their own individual potential.

HR to HCM

The HR processes used in the three levels of the value triangle tend to look relatively similar, at least at first glance. Personnel, HRM and HCM all include recruitment, for example. The differences are often nuances in the detailed steps within a process, caused by applying a different focus. Personnel only focused on improving people management activities. HRM links activities to outcomes in order to add value to broader business needs. HCM seeks to create value by managing people in a way that accumulates human capital. The small changes brought about by these shifts in focus can then lead to important changes in activities and to significant differences in people's performance.

As well as these HR or HCM practices it is important to recognize that human capital outcomes can be created by other, broader organizational practices. This can be best explained after describing how these practices also create organization capital (and later in the book I will refer to examples of organizational practices within HCM, including Zappos's workplace design and whether its Holacratic organization can be seen to be part of an HCM-based approach).

Activities for creating organization capital

This type of capital refers to the value of the way people are organized to get work done. It is about how we make an organization greater than the sum of its parts. Some businesses get more out of their people/human capital than others because of the way these people are organized. This is the core reason for having organizations – the belief is that having two or more people work together can ensure they achieve more than working independently. The problem is that increased complexity, petty politics and interpersonal conflict often make working in a large organization, in particular, feel as if it subtracts from, rather than adds to, what someone can achieve on their own. This is not the main reason for the growth in independent working but it is a strong contributing factor for many people working in this way.

Organization capital includes outcomes such as providing clear accountabilities and responsibilities, enabling better alignment with organizational objectives and supporting people to do their jobs. These capabilities tend to be based largely on an organization's design and, in particular, its structure and processes, including for the collection and dissemination of knowledge. Organization capital therefore has the advantage of being fully owned by the company and as a result is somewhat easier to manage and change than human capital.

However, organization capital will usually need to relate to more than the organization's design, or architecture. This can be illustrated with McKinsey's 7S model introduced in Chapter 1 – the most popular form of organization model used by business leaders. This model, as well as others often preferred by organization designers, such as David Nadler's congruence model (Nadler and Tushman, 1997) and Jay Galbraith's star model (Galbraith, 1977), all emphasize the interconnected, holistic nature of different organizational elements and the need to align all these elements in any transformation. Just changing one element, particularly those in the 7S's hard triangle, including processes and structure, are unlikely to produce much in the way of change. Creating organization capital therefore requires all 7S activities. Figure 3.1 shows how six of the seven S's from the McKinsey model are linked to each form of capital (strategy has been removed since this underpins the whole system).

Figure 3.1   Links between the six S activities and three capitals

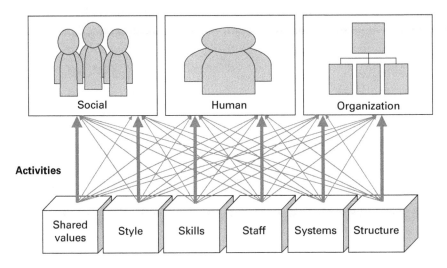

Figure 3.1 suggests that developing each of human, organization and social capital will usually be best supported by using the organizational elements shown vertically beneath them, but may require use of elements shown with a diagonal link as well. So, for example, going back to HCM for a moment, engagement may be best increased by changing the staff and their skills (eg recruiting people who think from a glass half-full versus half-empty perspective, or training managers to spend more time with their people). However, it may also need changes to the organization's structure or systems (eg more autonomous roles or a new performance management process) or to social relationships, ie shared values and style (eg ensuring everyone understands the need to focus on people first or that they act in a more people-centric way).

Applying this idea back to organization capital, the creation of knowledge might be best supported by changes to the organization (eg the knowledge management process including use of an intranet, and perhaps a group of specialist knowledge managers, or the inclusion of knowledge management accountabilities in everyone's job descriptions). But it may also need changes to the other S activities too (eg people with experience in managing knowledge elsewhere, broader development of knowledge management skills, the addition of something about knowledge to the organization's values, and regular discussion groups to review its use and accumulation).

Two of my favourite examples of businesses competing on organization capital are IBM and HCL Technologies (HCLT). Both compete on the way people are organized. I am not trying to suggest they have any better people/ human capital than their competitors – the difference is the way they extract more value from potentially similar quality people to provide a higher contribution. The prime driver of IBM's organization capital is one of its HR processes; the driver for HCLT's capital is its structure. However, both examples are also supported by developments in most of the other S's too.

CASE STUDY   Workforce management at IBM

In the early 2010s technology firm IBM developed a new business mission to be a globally integrated enterprise. This meant that it would spread all of its resources more effectively across the world, operating on a truly global basis. For people management it meant being able to match the best person to perform some work for a client, regardless of which country and office they currently worked in. HR therefore proposed to the CEO that it would develop a workforce management process that would help match the demand and supply of people working in the company (Boudreau, 2010).

To do this HR partnered with IBM's experts in supply chain management who consult for the company's clients, and developed a sophisticated process that would help IBM to manage its people on a global basis. The complicated nature of the process means that it would probably be completely the wrong thing for any other company to use. However, for IBM it is a powerful source of competitive advantage. In fact it is very difficult to see how IBM could have acted as a globally integrated enterprise without it. I therefore suggest that it is an example of creating value, providing IBM with an organizational capability in matching the supply and demand of its people.

CASE STUDY   Upside-down organization at HCLT

HCLT is an India-based IT services firm that has gone through interesting changes in recent years. The stimulus for this transformation was its former CEO, Vineet Nayar, reading Kim and Mauborgne's book *Blue Ocean Strategy* (2004), which as I explained in Chapter 1 echoes Porter's ideas about competing through differentiation in products and services. Nayar found the book's arguments compelling but did not think it would be possible to create a unique competitive positioning in IT services because this is a commodity-based industry. So instead he decided to create differentiation in how the company works, ie in its organization. The particular capability chosen was that HCLT would enable its people to innovate for their clients better than the people working for the company's competitors could do. This outcome was provided by creating an upside-down organization where the top of the hierarchy is the employees on the front line, delivering services for their clients (Nayar, 2010).

A number of firms refer to having an upside-down hierarchy but this has really only been implemented in a very few. In HCLT it is, or at least was, very real. Managers really do spend a large proportion of their time enabling employees rather than in command-and-control mode telling them what to do. This change was enabled though an open 360-degree feedback system in which if someone provided feedback on a manager they got to see the manager's average feedback scores. This transparency generated huge changes in managers' behaviours.

HR at HCLT is also an enabling function rather than a controlling one. This was brought about through a service-ticket approach in which employees can raise tickets about HR processes that constrain rather than enable them, and are also responsible for closing tickets when they decide their problems have been resolved. HR is measured on reducing the time taken to close service tickets and also driving towards zero open tickets.

I think this is a nice example of creating value – for two particular reasons. First, it shows that although organization capital may be created through organizational changes it also needs other S activities to support it, in this case changes in managers' attitudes and capabilities. Second, it shows that big changes can be brought about by small but smart interventions (Nayar called them blue ocean droplets), not just by big transformation programmes.

However, the really important point to note for both HCL's upside-down structure and IBM's workforce management process is that although both of these examples provide tremendous sources of competitive advantage, they are based on organization capital not human capital. Both firms' people are still fairly similar to their competitors. It is the way people are organized that is different, enabling the same type of people to deliver more value.

A new definition for organization design

Although the creation of organization capital is not just about the design of the organization, it is something that traditionally has been led by the organization design function, by HR practitioners with an organization design specialism, or by HR business partners with capability in this area.

But what is organization design? We know it cannot be defined purely based upon the hard aspects of organization design such as the organization's processes and structure. That is because of the need for the design to be holistic. It also cannot be defined based upon all the elements of an organization as that is also what HRM/HCM does and there has to be a difference between the two.

The key to defining organization design appropriately comes from applying the same approach taken to HR and focusing on outcomes rather than activities. From this perspective it is fairly clear that the outcome that organization designers focus on most of the time is organization capital. Organization design is therefore the use of all organizational elements, ie all 7 S's, to accumulate organization capital. Therefore, the whole of the last section of this chapter has really been about organization design.

Managing complicated systems

One of the things that differentiates organization design from HR or HCM is that it tends to be more complicated. This is because the nature of organization capital also tends to be more complicated than human capital. As a reminder, human capital is the value of people – McKinsey's staff and skills. Organization capital is the value of the whole organization – the whole 7S model, not just the structure and systems (though not the value inside staff, skills, style and shared values, which are covered by human and social capital). We also know that both human and organization capital are created by all the 7S activities. This means that organization capital is much more similar to the system of elements that create it than is human capital. Organization design cannot be made optimal if any one of the 7S's are out of alignment. It is not just that this makes the activity of creating the capital more difficult, it is that the actual outcome is affected too. It is this difference that means it is more complicated.

The difference means that organization design has to pay attention to the overall system. It has to be holistic and ensure the effectiveness of the links between organizational elements as well as the elements themselves. In addition, systems are not static in the way they are often represented but change continuously. Organization designers therefore need to pay attention to the dynamics of organizational systems and in particular the role of positive and negative feedback loops. Without doing this, organizations are likely to be constantly surprised by unintended consequences. It is this ability to engage in systems thinking that Peter Senge (1990) called the fifth discipline of the learning organization (see Chapter 11).

Summary and additional comments

1 Organizations can make better choices about the people and organization management activities they undertake by considering the outcomes they are trying to create. Activities will normally change according to the type(s) of capital (human, organization or social) as well as the particular capabilities required.

2 The best and most direct ways to create a particular outcome is to use the activities most closely associated with the type of capital it relates to. However, some other activities relating to the other two capitals will probably be required too.

3 As well as links to particular activities, each type of capital and the approach that develops it require a different way of thinking. People management can be successful using straightforward cause-and-effect thinking (although HCM in particular may require a shift in this perspective). Even value-for-money-based organization design requires the use of systems thinking.

4 This chapter has focused on human and organization capital but some of the ideas and approaches will be relevant to social capital too. Understanding the approaches that can be used within HCM and organization design also helps to understand the similarities and differences that may be required in organization development. In addition, and as will be explained within Chapter 4, social organizations often need well-developed human and social capital too. For all these reasons the points described within Chapter 3 will prove valuable for those concerned with social organizations as you continue to read through this book.

References

Benko, C and Weisberg, A (2007) *Mass Career Customisation: Aligning the workplace with today's nontraditional workforce*, Harvard Business School Press, Boston

Bidwell, M (2011) Paying more to get less, *Administrative Science Quarterly*, **56** (3), pp 369–407

Bock, L (2016) *Work Rules!*, John Murray, London

Boudreau, J (2010) [accessed 12 January 2017] IBM's Global Talent Management Strategy: The Vision of the Globally Integrated Enterprise, *SHRM* [Online] http://www.nationalacademyhr.org/sites/default/files/BasicPage/IBM_Global_Talent_Management.pdf

Boudreau, JW, Jesuthasan, R and Creelman, D (2015) *Lead the Work: Navigating a world beyond employment*, John Wiley & Sons, New York

Cain, S (2013) *Quiet: The power of introverts in a world that can't stop talking*, Penguin, London

Christakis, E (2012) [accessed 12 January 2017] Why are Women Biased Against Other Women?, *Time* [Online] http://ideas.time.com/2012/10/04/womens-inhumanity-to-women/

Deci, EL (1995) *Why We Do What We Do: The dynamics of personal autonomy*, GP Putnam's Sons, New York

Dweck, C (2012) *Mindset: How you can fulfil your potential*, Ballantine Books, New York

Erickson, T (2008) *Plugged In: The generation Y guide to thriving at work*, Harvard Business Review Press, Boston

Furnham, A (2015) *Backstabbers and Bullies: How to cope with the dark side of people at work*, Bloomsbury Publishing, London

Galbraith, JR (1977) *Organization Design*, Addison Wesley, Massachusetts

Gallup (1999) [accessed 12 January 2017] Item 10: I Have a Best Friend at Work, *Gallup*, 26 May [Online] http://www.gallup.com/businessjournal/511/item-10-best-friend-work.aspx

Hampden-Turner, C and Trompenaars, F (1997) *Riding the Waves of Culture: Understanding diversity in global business*, Hodder & Stoughton, London

Herzberg, F, Mauser, B and Snyderman, BB (1959) *The Motivation to Work*, John Wiley & Sons, New York

Hoffman, R, Casnocha, B and Yeh, C (2014) *The Alliance*, Harvard Business Review Press, Boston

Hseih, T (2010) *Delivering Happiness: A path to profits, passion and purpose*, Little, Brown & Co, New York

Ingham, J (2007) *Strategic Human Capital Management: Creating value through people*, Butterworth Heinemann, Oxford

Ingham, J (2010) [accessed 12 January 2017] Hack: Career Partnership, *Management Innovation eXchange* [Online] http://www.managementexchange.com/hack/career-partnership

Ingham, J (2011) Aligning learning and development with compensation and rewards, in *The Executive Guide to Integrated Talent Management*, ed P Galagan and K Oakes, ATD Press, Vancouver

Lieberman, MD (2013) *Social: Why our brains are wired to connect*, Oxford University Press, Oxford

Manyika, T, Lund, S, Robinson, K, Valentino, J and Dobbs, R (2015) *Connecting Talent with Opportunity in the Digital Age*, McKinsey Global Institute

Maslow, A (1943) A theory of human motivation, *Psychological Review*, 50 (4), pp 370–96

Meister, J (2015) [accessed 12 January 2017] Airbnb Chief Human Resource Officer Becomes Chief Employee Experience Officer, *Forbes* [Online]

http://www.forbes.com/sites/jeannemeister/2015/07/21/airbnbs-chief-human-resource-officer-becomes-chief-employee-experience-officer

Nadler, DA and Tushman, ML (1997) *Competing by Design: The power of organizational architecture*, Oxford University Press, Oxford

Nayar, V (2010) *Employees First, Customers Second: Turning conventional management upside down*, Harvard Business School Press, Boston

Pink, DH (2009) *Drive: The surprising truth about what motivates us*, Riverhead Books, New York

Rock, D and Grant, H (2016) [accessed 12 January 2017] Why Diverse Teams Are Smarter, *Harvard Business Review*, 4 November [Online] https://hbr.org/2016/11/why-diverse-teams-are-smarter

Rousseau, D (1995) *Psychological Contracts in Organizations: Understanding written and unwritten agreements*, Sage Publications, Thousand Oaks

Senge, P (1990) *The Fifth Discipline: The art and practice of the learning organization*, Doubleday Business, New York

Ulrich, D, Allen, J, Brockbank, W, Younger, J and Nyman, M (2009) *HR Transformation: Building human resources from the outside in*, McGraw-Hill Education, Chicago

Williams, R (2012) [accessed 12 January 2017] 'I'm Successful Because I'm Beautiful' – How We Discriminate, *Psychology Today*, 18 August [Online] https://www.psychologytoday.com/blog/wired-success/201208/im-successful-because-im-beautiful-how-we-discriminate

Competing and cooperating through social relationships

Introduction

Chapters 4 and 5 build on the review of human and organization capital provided in Chapter 3 by moving the agenda on to social capital. However, these chapters will not delve into the links between activities and social capital very deeply as the activities will be reviewed during the rest of the book. That gives me the opportunity to focus, first of all, on why social capital is so important to a business today. This is based on an understanding of the social brain, social networks and the wider social world.

The social brain

The tendency in Western society and most of our organizations is to think about and treat people as individualistic, rational, competitive and money-motivated *homo economicus*. A lot of this goes back to Thatcherism/Reaganomics and, in particular, Margaret Thatcher's suggestion that there is no such thing as society. There is, however, an alternative, and I would suggest much more accurate perspective. This considers people as also being deeply social, emotional, connected and collaborative. So yes, we are competitive, but we are so much more than this as well. Explaining our opposing tendencies for both cooperation and competition requires an understanding of the ways our brains work, and how these have evolved in humans, and before that in primates and other mammals too.

The role of relatedness in mammals

One of the main characteristics of mammals is our reward and threat systems, which lie behind the fight-or-flight response. There is also a tend-and-befriend response, more common in females. We scan for physical, material rewards and threats but also rewards and threats in our social relations. Social rewards provide pleasure through the effects of neurochemicals such as serotonin and oxytocin in the ventral striatum in the brain, which can stimulate cooperative and affiliative behaviour. Social threats cause social pain, which we experience in just the same way that we do physical pain, in the dorsal anterior cingulate cortex of the brain. This is supported by the release of cortisol and other stress-related neurochemicals, which can lead to aggression between individuals.

This makes mammals deeply focused on our social connections and interactions with other members of our species. For example, dolphins can recognize each other when separated for up to 20 years. We also know that some mammals have a basic understanding of the self. For example, when elephants have marks placed on their bodies and first see these in a mirror they explore the areas with their trunks (De Waal, 2016). This helps in forming relationships with others. Social relatedness in mammals provides a level of synchronization somewhat similar to yawn contagion in humans.

Our social natures help us to live in large groups, which provide safety but also risks. This leads to both cooperation with individuals we know and trust, ie those in our ingroup, and competition with those in outgroups, as well as some aggression and dominance-seeking within an ingroup. Primatologist Frans De Waal argues these behaviours demonstrate basic levels of empathy and reciprocity, including a sense of fairness and justice. In his TED talk, De Waal describes how he trained capuchin monkeys to trade stones with an experimenter for slices of cucumber. As long as each monkey was getting the same deal the monkey would devour the cucumber. However, when two monkeys were placed in neighbouring cages and one monkey received a grape rather than a cucumber, the one receiving the less-treasured cucumber would throw this on the floor, or even back at the experimenter, and would also stop trading stones for any more fruit. Some monkeys receiving the grape even started refusing this until the other monkey got one too. It shows that other mammals can experience a moral sense of fairness and suggests this developed in our common ancestors tens of millions of years ago (De Waal, 2012).

Social psychologist Adam Galinsky suggests the main factors influencing the balance between competition and cooperation are resource scarcity, sociability and dynamic instability. His research demonstrates how all three factors influence the behaviour of Grévy's zebras. When zebras inhabit arid and parched environments the scarcity of water leads their mating relationships to be temporary and unstable. After it rains – when they suddenly have more access to water and there is less need to compete for it – their social relationships shift dramatically, becoming more stable and collective (Galinsky and Schweitzer, 2015).

The role of empathic resonance in primates

As well as relatedness, primates also experience empathic resonance, which provides a shared experience of the motor actions of others and provides the ability to imitate them. This is triggered by mirror neurons in the premotor cortex of primates' brains. Mirror neurons have been shown to exist in macaque monkeys, discharging both when a monkey performs an action and also when it observes a similar action made by another monkey or by an experimenter (Goleman, 2007).

Our mirror system provides a deeper sense of empathy, helping us to internalize and imitate the behaviours of other members of our, or another, species. This also helps us to keep track of friends and foes, to form individual trust relationships and to update these in the light of changes in behaviour. De Waal describes research involving two chimpanzees who were given tokens of different colours. One kind means that the chimp choosing it will get fed, the other feeds them both. The experiment found the second token was used more, though this does depend on the relationship with, and behaviour of, the other animal. This, then, is a demonstration of altruistic, prosocial behaviour, ie a voluntary action that is designed to help another individual (De Waal, 2012). Chimpanzees have since been found to cooperate five times more frequently than they compete (Suchak *et al*, 2016).

The tendencies of primates towards competition or cooperation are driven in part by experience with and positioning against other individuals. Primates have a keen sense of status and become stressed and more aggressive when status differences are unclear. The need to understand how we fit against each other is the reason we have evolved to live in hierarchies.

Advanced resonance in humans

The mirror system in the lateral frontal and parietal areas of human brains provides more complex empathy than in other species, enabling us to take the perspective of, and imitate, other people, putting ourselves in their shoes. The tendency for social imitation between people also becomes more pronounced in social groups. Social psychologist Stanley Milgram, best known for his electric-shock studies, describes an experiment where he planted crowds of actors to stare up at a house window across a street. With only one actor just 4 per cent of pedestrians stopped and stared. But with a crowd of 15 actors 40 per cent stopped and 86 per cent glanced up (Christakis and Fowler, 2009). However, humans have also evolved brain systems providing even more advanced social cognitive skills and an even stronger predisposition to think about the social world.

The roles of mentalizing and harmonizing in humans

These additional human brain systems can be best understood by reviewing the way they have evolved.

Human evolution

Our highly developed social capabilities have been enabled by our large brains and heads. This, together with limitations on the size of the female pelvis, means that human infants need to be born relatively immature. This leads to the majority of the brain's development being completed after birth and our brain development being strongly informed by our childhood environment. This is why mother-and-child attachment is so important to human development and is also a cause of cultural and generational differences. Our relatively short gestation period may even be a response to the need for our brains to develop through social interaction.

Our additional long development period through to adulthood also means that people find it useful to work together to raise their young. Our ancestors therefore evolved into cooperative breeders, or 'alloparents' (Blaffer Hrdy, 2011). That meant we could live in larger tribes, which required abilities to interact socially, facilitated by social grooming. In other primates this involves picking fleas and dirt out of the fur of other members in a group. Although there is a hygiene element to this, it has an even more important role – through the release of serotonin that this triggers – in developing, maintaining and recognizing relationships. However, living in larger social groups humans would have needed to spend up to half their time grooming the other members of their tribe.

Instead of this, humans evolved language so we could maintain our relationships with other tribe members through the use of gossip and chit-chat. One suggestion is that as humans developed and started to coordinate action plans together, we would have communicated through gestures. Mirror neutrons in the Broca area of the brain, which is associated with speech production, would have helped people to imitate these gestures. As these became more commonly used they would have acquired agreed meanings, leading to proto-signs, a protolanguage and ultimately to a true language (Arbib, 2012).

We also learned to tell stories. These appeal to our social brains and our deep interest in one another, providing opportunities to create or re-create people's experiences and to re-experience their emotions. Literature professor Brian Boyd suggests that fiction fosters cooperation by 'engaging and attuning our social and moral emotions and values in the ways our minds are most naturally disposed – in terms of social actions' (Boyd, 2010). Research by psychology professor Emanuele Castano has, in fact, found that reading fiction does improve performance in a social intelligence test (Kidd and Castano, 2013).

I should note that alternative theories have been suggested for human evolution too. However, anthropologist Robin Dunbar has demonstrated a link between the relative size of the brain's neocortex and the size of social groups across primate species. This does suggest that humans' large brains are an evolutionary response to our unusually complex social systems and the need to maintain cohesive social groups. Human social groups often involve about 150 people and this is known as 'Dunbar's number'.

There is, in fact, a layered series of numbers, each about three times the previous one, relating to different levels of social proximity among humans. The number for very close, intimate relationships (which our ancestors would have seen as their core group) is five. The number for close friends (a kinship group) is 15, general friendship (band) is 50, and casual friends/acquaintances is 150. The number for looser acquaintances is 500 and the number of faces you can put names to (your tribe) is 1,500 (Dunbar and Schultz, 2007). You will see these numbers cropping up as you read through this book.

It was the need to maintain relationships within these large and complex social groups that supported the development of two other social systems in our brains: the mentalizing system and the harmonizing system. These systems supplement the mirror system and provide more advanced capabilities to think about ourselves and other people. They are found in the medial, or midline, regions of the brain and are separate to the general intelligence regions, which tend to be on the outer lateral surfaces.

The mentalizing system

The mentalizing system is in the dorsomedial prefrontal cortex and temporoparietal junction. This system provides us with 'a theory of mind' enabling us to predict and infer the thoughts and intents behind people's behaviours. Combined together, the mirror and mentalizing systems provide humans with uniquely well-developed capabilities in mindreading.

They also support empathy, as it is by sharing and understanding other people's states that we naturally come to care about these as well (Zaki and Ochsner, 2016). This extends beyond the affective empathy we share with other mammals, which helps us to experience the emotions others are experiencing. Humans' additional cognitive empathy allows us to take the perspective of others so we can try to work out what it is like to be them and so that we can respond to them appropriately.

The mentalizing system is also called the default network because it becomes active most of the time when we are not thinking cognitively about something else. It is the way this default network switches on during our free time that makes us so deeply interested in the social world around us.

The default network is also inhibited by activity in the rest of the brain – when we are reasoning non-socially our mentalizing system turns off. The emphasis on logical thinking, which is common in many businesses, may therefore make it less likely that we will access the capabilities of this critical system, which makes humans so special. Firms may need to place more focus on emotions and social connection if they want people to benefit from the mindreading capabilities provided by the social brain.

The harmonizing system

The need to focus on the social nature of humans is reinforced by our brain's uniquely strong sense of self, based in the medial prefrontal cortex. Social cognitive neuroscientist Matt Lieberman suggests that the way we tend to think of ourselves as independent individuals, in the West at least, is largely erroneous. What we think of as the self is really just a means of internalizing the social groups we are part of, allowing us to supplement our individual personalities with socially derived norms. This means that although we think we have unique ideas these are actually inseparable from the beliefs and values of the societies we inhabit. Basically, our brains fool us that we are independent in order to make it easier for us to exist within and to harmonize with our social groups (Lieberman, 2013).

Harmonizing leads us to subserviate our own pleasure to the norms of our social groups. This helps us to be sensitive to the other people we are connected with and therefore helps us to achieve more together than we can as individuals. It also encourages us to be prosocial.

Social obsessions

The result of our social brains and the way we are wired for competition, but even more so for cooperation, is that we display an even deeper sense of relatedness, fairness and status than other primates. The Neuroleadership Institute combines these factors, along with certainty and autonomy, in their SCARF model, which indicates the things our social brains obsess about most of the time. It is these factors that lead to our experiences of social pleasure or pain and which, therefore, influence much of our behaviour (Rock, 2009).

Status

Status signals our relative importance within a group. As mentioned earlier, status affects our levels of serotonin and, through this, pride, happiness, confidence and prosocial behaviour. Serotonin is released throughout the social brain in response to submissive behaviours in others, but also in response to recognition and other signs that we have achieved something that others value. Leaders and other high-status individuals tend to gain high levels of serotonin, making it more likely that they will be loyal to and protect those with lower status. In contrast, people who do not feel valued, connected or important to a group will experience lower levels of serotonin. Lack of clarity around status may also reduce serotonin and cause an increase in cortisol, stress and aggressiveness in an attempt to increase status.

Because serotonin is so rewarding it can lead people to spend a lot of time thinking about their own status and how to improve it. We will also put time, energy and resources into doing this. For example, one study showed that salespeople would trade off nearly $30,000 to be recognized in a top salesperson programme where the main incentive was a gold star on their business cards (Larkin, 2009). This example demonstrates that improving status does not need to mean changing hierarchical position or relationships.

Social rewards can be provided in many different ways, which will be described within this book. These actions all provide opportunities to ameliorate low hierarchical status. They will also generally be easier to implement and sometimes more effective than removing hierarchical status differences, which can never be totally removed anyway. Status is relative and people will almost always have relationships with people more senior and well paid than themselves. In particular, there is a psychological tendency called 'hedonic adaptation' in which we recalibrate our comparisons as relative status levels change. This keeps us from getting depressed if our status diminishes but also means we continually push ourselves to increase and then further increase our status. In addition, economists suggest that we perceive our income and purchasing power relative to other people rather than in absolute terms.

Relatedness

Relatedness is about our connections with other people and is triggered by the neuropeptide oxytocin. This is the chemical that lets mammals know they are safe because they in a group. It is also behind maternal behaviour and sexual pair-bonding. The neuroscientist and economist nicknamed Dr Love calls it 'the moral molecule' and suggests it acts as a social glue that keeps society together (Zak, 2013).

Oxytocin is released in the ventral striatum region of the brain, which is associated with the motivation to seek out a reward. It then stimulates receptors in the adjacent septal areas, which trigger the urge to be helpful, leading to our prosocial behaviours. The effect of this is to make it rewarding to be included, liked and cared for by other people. This might be demonstrated by social signs and behaviours such as verbal grooming. The reverse is also true – social isolation has a profoundly negative impact on our health and performance (Cacioppo and Patrick, 2009). However, we also feel good when we altruistically help others with no expectation of a return. As an example, many top business leaders and other wealthy individuals are engaged in giving away large proportions of their fortunes (https://givingpledge.org). We might ask why they felt it necessary to amass such wealth in the first place (status!) but the trend is still a highly positive one. At a more mundane level, even just being treated decently increases people's oxytocin levels, prompting them to behave more decently to others too. This is the case even when we receive praise or compliments from strangers who have no influence on our physical welfare.

Observing altruistic behaviour in someone else also triggers oxytocin and encourages us to be kind to others too. This means that acts of generosity can provide a three-way boost: to a giver, the receiver and any witness to the behaviour too. However, these bonding and cooperative behaviours are only extended within an ingroup and, in humans, to strangers (people we do not know and who are therefore not in an ingroup or outgroup). This may have helped with tribal cooperation and alloparenting. Instead of this, oxytocin acts to increase hostility and aggression towards members of outgroups.

Fairness

The fairness motive, or inequality aversion, is often demonstrated through behavioural economics experiments such as the ultimatum game (Ariely, 2009). In this, one person is given a sum of money and has to decide how to split it with another person. When the second person accepts the split, they each get their money. If they reject it, neither person receives any money. Economic theory suggests that the second person should accept any split, since any amount is better than nothing. In practice, however, most very unequal splits are treated as insults and are rejected.

Experiments using other games also identify tendencies to promote fairness, as well as broader cooperation. For example, in what is known as the dictator game, a person is again given a sum of money and has to decide how to split it. The other person must then accept the money and they each get to keep their part. Again, theory would suggest that the first person should keep all of their money, but in most cases they give some to the second person. The trust game, or investment game, builds on the dictator game. In this, the money received by the second person is increased and they are then allowed to give some money back to the first person who made the split. In most cases the second person will reciprocate the trust shown by the first. Social reciprocity is in fact a common characteristic of social relationships. If someone does us a favour we will generally feel a need to pay this back and will be more likely to do favours for other people too.

The 'prisoner's dilemma' is the best well known of these games. This provides two people with a choice of cooperating with each other or not, ie to defect. The situation is set up so that regardless of what the other player does it makes sense to defect. However, one-third of the time people still choose to cooperate, and when we know the other person has cooperated we cooperate two-thirds of the time (Ahn et al, 2003). Evidence that we will cooperate, trust, reciprocate and punish others, even when there is a cost to us, emphasizes the importance of fairness and underlines that that we do not act merely as narrowly self-interested and competitive individuals.

Both oxytocin and serotonin have been found to increase concern for fair treatment with ingroup members. However, serotonin seems to reduce the desire for reciprocity, hence lower levels of serotonin are seen to correlate with higher rejection of unfair offers in the ultimatum game (Siegel and Crockett, 2013). Effects of serotonin and oxytocin will also be moderated by dopamine, testosterone, cortisol, adrenaline and other neurochemicals.

Behaviour in social groups

Our preferences and behaviours as individuals and in groups are heavily influenced by the neurochemicals that have been described above, the way these impact on social reward and threat responses, and the way they facilitate mentalizing and other neural processes.

Not all of these are useful in an organizational setting. This applies particularly strongly to homophily, which is our often unconscious preference to be with people who are like ourselves. This tends to make communication and relationship building easier, if less effective. Homophily can relate to people's values, status, backgrounds and physical differences. We also have a similar preference for people in our ingroup, with whom we have a shared sense of social identity. Many times, these two groups will largely duplicate each other. The impact of both preferences can include bias, unfair treatment and a reduction in diversity and inclusion of people in groups and across organizations.

Another important preference is for social conformity, in which we tend to align with social norms and the behaviour of other people. Perhaps the most obvious example of this is the herding instinct, ie when we follow people in front of us across a park or a restaurant fills up quickly once a few people sit near the window. It is also seen in the way we seek social proof from other people's behaviours when we are unsure of what to do.

The best well known research on the effect was conducted by Milgram's mentor Solomon Asch. This was a perceptual task experiment in which one participant together with seven actors were asked to match the length of a line with three others, two of which were clearly longer or shorter than the correct choice. During a series of trials, the actors would all announce that a particular line was the best match before the participant was asked for their response.

In the trials where the actors picked a line incorrectly the participant conformed with this choice 37 per cent of the time; 75 per cent of participants gave at least one incorrect answer during these 12 trials. Most of these experienced what Asch termed a 'distortion of judgement' in that they assumed they had misinterpreted something and that the actors must be right. Others had exhibited a 'distortion of action', knowing what the correct answer was but not wanting to answer differently from the majority; 5 per cent conformed in all trials and Ash suggested these had experienced a 'distortion of perception' as they seemed to believe the actors' answers were correct. Similar groupthink effects can be seen in organizational teams and other groups.

We should also note that people do not always apply their abilities to mentalize, even though they could. For example, we tend not to do so when our brains are already under high cognitive loads. People need to be given time, space and opportunities to connect with people to ensure we are optimizing the abilities of our social brains. Not bothering to use our mentalizing abilities to the full can lead us to assume that other people share our beliefs more than they actually do and are more like us than they are. This is the false consensus effect. We also tend to assume that others are more self-interested than they are. This is termed faux selfishness.

Faux selfishness and the brain's clandestine approach to harmonizing are two major reasons why we have built society and organizations in the self-interested way we have. Lieberman describes the way that we forget about the importance of the social brain as our 'social kryptonite'. However, society's increasing interest in neuroscience does give us a greater opportunity to change this. We can decide to balance the focus on our self-serving side with an appreciation of ourselves as connected members of groups. And within this, to recognize that we have the potential to cooperate at least as much as we do to compete.

Evolution has provided strong tendencies towards both competition and cooperation but we are at our best when we cooperate. It is when we do this that we all win. Yet this behaviour is not often encouraged in Western societies or organizations.

The three types of social network

Given that we operate partly through our role in social groups it is important we understand how groups work. The following section therefore moves on from looking at people and their brains to the way that people come together to be social and to do work. We therefore want to understand the groups and networks that people operate within.

One way of doing this is to look at the science of networks. At a very simple level there are three main network topologies, shown in Figure 4.1.

Figure 4.1 Centralized, decentralized and distributed networks

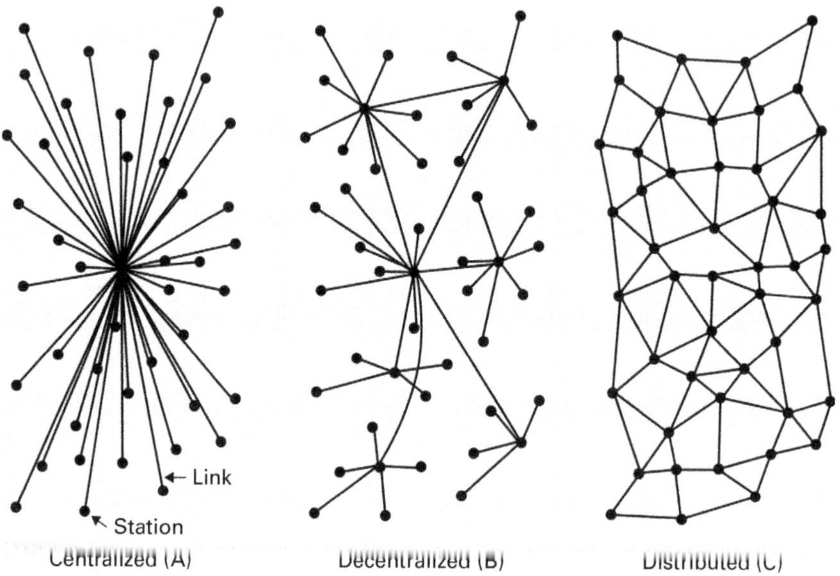

Centralized (A)   Decentralized (B)   Distributed (C)

SOURCE Baran (1964)

The three models in Figure 4.1 consist of nodes or vertices, which can be the people or groups within an organization; and links, edges or arcs, which are the connections between them. Links can be directed/asymmetrical or undirected/symmetrical/mutual, ie they can point in one or both ways. They can also be seen as single or multiple types (eg about learning and innovation) and can be identified at single or multiple value levels (eg rated 1–10 by importance). Degrees are the number of links into a person or between two people. Social networks, featuring the relationships between people, tend to be much more complex than these three models, which were originally drawn to represent different types of computer networks (which is why the diagram labels the nodes as stations). The relative simplicity of these computer networks is the reason I am using them here to explain the basic working of human networks.

It might be interesting to note that the distributed network in Figure 4.1 was the basis for packet switching, which enabled the creation of the internet. However, nothing in this chapter has anything to do with online social networks such as enterprise social networks or 'the social network', ie Facebook. These are simply technology-based platforms for developing the real social networks I am writing about in this chapter (see box).

A network of networks

The Social Organization deals with four different constructs, each called networks. Ensure you understand the differences:

- A social network, also called a social graph, is a system of connections, or representations of these connections, between people within some sort of group or boundary, including within an organization.

- An organizational network is a system of links between groups within an organization. (In both of these top two definitions a group is an organizational or other unit, or potentially the whole organization, whereas a network refers to the relationships within the unit.)

- A network structure is the formal or informal social or organizational networks used as or seen to be part of an organization's structure. All organizational structures are actually social or organizational networks, not just network structures. The specific characteristics of network structures are explained in Chapter 8. (The term network structure can also be used to refer to the structure of a social network, ie its topology. However, I never use the term that way in this book.)

- Online social networks are social media platforms used mainly for forming and developing social networks (the ones in the first bullet point). Within organizations these systems are generally called enterprise social networks. Their role in the social organization will be explained in Chapter 13.

The network labelled (A) on the left-hand side of Figure 4.1 is based around a centralized, single 'hub and spoke'. Social networks often form like this as a result of weaving together a small number of previously scattered relationships. This form of network is simple and efficient but the person or people at the centre may also become bottlenecks and obstacles to communication, performance and innovation. These networks are also not very robust: eg if something happens to the person or people in the centre the whole network fails.

A single hub-and-spoke network can also be represented as one parent with multiple child relationships. This is shown by unfolding the network and moving the central node to the top, with what were the spokes hanging beneath it. This is called a tree diagram and is the basic format of a traditional organization chart.

A centralized network will become stronger and more effective when there are direct, cross-cutting links between people/groups who are not in the hub of the network – eg between a person or group in the top left and one in the top right of network (A) rather than all of these links going to the centre. Increasing the extent of linkages within a network is called 'broking'. This involves reaching across structural holes, which are empty paths between two people who were previously unconnected (Burt, 1995). This creates higher levels of bonding, or closure, within the network. Closure speeds up communication and decision making, which facilitates the emergence of norms and higher levels of trust, and offers more opportunity for change.

As the number of cross-links increase, two particular roles may develop. These are, first, connectors – people who have many links within the network. And second, energizers, who have less links but whose enthusiasm helps new ideas to take hold. All of the links in this network are most likely what are termed 'strong ties'. These are relationships between people who know each other and cooperate together. Strong ties are useful for execution as they bring people together to get work done and support each other.

However, there is generally little diversity in this sort of network as everyone tends to have the same experiences and perspectives. Everyone already knows what everyone else knows.

The most adaptive and resilient network form is (C), a distributed network, which is why the internet uses it. People or groups in these networks have multiple parent–child, or peer-to-peer relationships. However, human networks never look quite like this distributed network. Instead of this, as networks grow, they tend to become clumpy. They form decentralized hubs, clusters or subgroups consisting of many dense connections surrounded by more loosely coupled areas of sparser linkages. Professor of network science Albert-László Barabasi explains that this clumpiness develops because people tend to attach to others who are already well connected. Just as the rich get richer, the well connected get even better networked. This is called a scale-free network, and it follows a power law or 80/20 pareto distribution rather than a normal distribution curve (Barabasi and Frangos, 2002). That is, there is a long tail of very dense hubs and another of empty network spaces.

These multi-hub networks can be either more or less decentralized. Network (B) is still fairly centralized as hubs still connect into one main centre and there is just one lateral connection between hubs shown at the top of the diagram. This is the type of network you might see in a programme management office (PMO) structure. Programmes and projects manage themselves but still report to the PMO.

A more decentralized version of a decentralized network would typically have more of the hubs connected laterally to each other. In addition, these links would often form between people outside the centre hubs, eg between a person in the top left and someone in the top right of network (B) rather than, or in addition to, the two more central people shown below them. This means that the network starts to look like more of a cross between (B) and (C). From now on, I refer to this as a distributed network, whilst recognizing that social networks are inherently clumpy and therefore partly decentralized as opposed to truly distributed.

Additional key roles in this type of network are the people with links across the network, between one hub and another, bridging between different parts of the network. These cross-boundary brokers are known as boundary spanners.

All these lateral connections are most likely to be what are termed weak ties (Granovetter, 2001) – links between people who do not know each other well. These people spread knowledge of what is going on in the different subgroups and provide a basis for sharing ideas across the network, which is important in sparking innovation. However, too high a proportion of intergroup broking or bridging compared to bonding relationships can lead to reduced trust and cohesion (Burt, 2007). It is lateral ties that provide the small-world effect (Watts, 2003) that recognizes the common scenario where strangers can often identify a common acquaintance. This is based upon being able to reach other people through a small number of steps, or a short path length, popularly known as six degrees of separation (Milgram, 1967). This means that networks tend to 'fold back' on themselves, ie our friends' friends tend to be friends (Baker, 2012).

These network chains do more than pass information though. The earlier sections of this chapter on mindreading and harmonizing explained that we are influenced by our connections. We are also influenced quite strongly by our connections' connections and their connections too. For example, research has found that if a person's friends are happy then that person is 15 per cent more likely to be happy too. If the friends' friends are happy they are 10 per cent likelier. And if the friends of those friends' friends are happy the person is 6 per cent more likely to be happy (Christakis and Fowler, 2009). The chain of influence drops off after three degrees, although these days social media means we can also be influenced, eg through online social rewards such as Facebook likes, by people who can have high degrees of separation. Focusing on social networks and online social networks therefore makes ensuring high levels of individual engagement more important too.

Valdis Krebs describes how networks may also evolve into a further form that is a core/periphery network (Krebs and Holley, 2002). This will be reviewed in Chapter 13.

Comparing performance in groups and as individuals

Not everything needs to be done through a group/network. People can often perform most simply, efficiently and sometimes effectively by working on their own. It is in activities connected to problem solving where groups come into their own. In particular, small groups of up to five people have been shown to outperform even the best individuals in complex problem-solving tasks (Laughlin *et al*, 2006). Groups will also often be needed for implementation activities, to cope with the amount of work that is often involved as well as to provide different skills and abilities.

It is in the link between problem solving and execution, ie idea generation, that individuals excel. Brainstorming in groups does not work and lowers the quantity and quality of ideas that are generated (Chamorro-Premuzic,

2015). We are best off being on our own, ideally outside the office (depending on the extent of modern workplace design – see Chapter 10). For example, I took a deliberate decision not to collaborate with another author to write this book. I have found that keeping it focused is difficult enough for one person and even if the end product might have been better it would have been much more complex and difficult to achieve this through a collaborative effort. Organizations can still involve multiple people in idea generation but it helps to keep them separate. This approach is often seen in innovation processes, eg through the use of crowdsourcing. It can also be supported by the use of social tools or approaches such as nominal group technique.

It is the parts of an innovation process before and after the idea generation phase when we need to do work together. Most innovations are not completely new, they are things that already exist in different areas, brought together in new ways. A good example is suitcases on wheels – we knew about suitcases and we knew about wheels well before anyone thought about putting the two together. In a similar way, innovating new ideas often comes from connecting people with weak ties, providing different perspectives and experiences.

To gain benefits from groups it is important that these avoid the tendency for social loafing. This is a free-rider effect that often occurs in individualistic societies when group members decide, often unconsciously, that they are going to let others do the hard work and put less effort in themselves. When everyone does that the group is in trouble! Loafing tends to increase as the size of a group increases. It can be reduced by having clear team and individual goals and measures, and also by having a compelling purpose and high levels of trust and engagement.

CASE STUDY Boundary spanning at Southwest Airlines

Management professor Jody Hoffer Gittell suggests that the main differentiator in Southwest Airlines' success has been high levels of social relatedness, or what she calls relational coordination. This includes Southwest's focus, commitment and passion for shared goals, shared knowledge and mutual respect. These are also supported by frequent, timely, problem-solving communications. In particular, operations agents act as boundary spanners, gathering information on plane arrivals and departures from various different functions, then processing this and communicating adjustments back to the various different groups. Their responsibilities include reconciling conflicting perspectives among these groups in reference to passenger needs, flight safety and other requirements, which also extends their roles into relationship building. Although this is a more costly approach than automating the integration of information, the operations agents provide an additional source of social cohesion and hence a significant role in Southwest's differentiation (Gittell, 2005).

The social world

Our developing understanding of social brains and social networks suggest we need to think about managing businesses differently. However, there is another reason for this too, which is that the whole world around us is being transformed and is becoming more social and complex.

First, the world of work has changed. The term 'knowledge worker' was introduced by management visionary Peter Drucker (1959) to describe a new segment of the workforce concerned primarily with the manipulation of information. Forty years after this, the Cluetrain Manifesto (Locke, Searls and Weinberger, 1999) suggested that 'business is a conversation because the defining work of business is conversation – literally'. This meant that knowledge workers had become people whose job consisted of having interesting conversations. Wind forward another 20 years and the world has changed again. Today's knowledge workers have progressed beyond just having conversations and would be best described as 'relationship workers'. That trend is now starting to accelerate as technology takes over many traditional knowledge workers' jobs.

Supporting this, research from the Corporate Executive Board (CEB, now part of Gartner) suggests that the proportion of work that is collaborative rather than purely individual in nature recently increased from 20 to 50 per cent in just over 10 years (CEB Corporate Leadership Council, 2012). Most of what we did 10 or so years ago would have involved working on our own, on a computer, telephone or production line. Today, a lot of most people's time is spent talking and e-mailing other people, with a large proportion of their time spent in meetings.

CEB suggests people need to be able to achieve through both individual task performance and also network performance, which is about improving others' work and using others to improve their own work too. These combine to provide an overall enterprise contribution. The issue is that most businesses prioritize individual task performance over network performance. As a result, two-thirds of employees feel competitive towards their peers (Kropp, 2014).

It is not that we need to avoid competition. Working in a competitive environment does stimulate people and boosts our performance. However, cooperative relationship working is not going to get performed well if we only focus on competition. Cooperative working also requires skills and interests that are traditionally associated with women, eg listening and empathizing. Increasing complexity also requires more traditionally feminine management approaches, including facilitating and empowering rather than commanding and controlling. Partly in response to these needs and partly in response to societal changes the workforce in many businesses is becoming more female too, if not yet at the most senior levels. So I do sometimes worry about the effect of bias and inequality on my daughters but I think these days I would be more concerned about the longer-term future if, instead, I had sons.

I think the most important issue to emerge from this is that many women find the competitive environment inside most businesses, which was created mainly by men, even more off-putting than many men do. One of the key reasons that so many businesses struggle to keep women, particularly at senior levels, is the increasing display of dysfunctional, competitive behaviour towards the top of many organizations.

My worry is that, with the exception of social media, our focus on social relatedness has seen an ongoing decline since Thatcher's dismissal of society. Particularly within business, our focus on the business rather than the organization value chain has resulted in a transactional and dehumanized approach to management. People have picked up on this and the increasingly fast turnover of their colleagues and have stopped investing in each other in the way we used to do. However, there have been signs of a return to a more cooperative approach since the global financial crisis of 2007. As an example, at the time of writing the UK government had just started talking about creating a 'shared society', and the opposition was suggesting a maximum pay differential of 20 times to apply across the economy.

The importance of social capital

As explained in Chapter 1, social capital is the value of the connections, relationships and conversations taking place between people working in an organization. Various alternative definitions have been proposed but this one comes from the late Sumantra Ghoshal, professor in strategic management, in one of the seminal studies looking at social capital and organizational advantage (Nahapiet and Ghoshal, 1998). This explained that social capital has structural, relational and cognitive dimensions:

- The structural dimension concerns the impersonal configuration of linkages between people or units – that is, who you reach and how you reach them. This deals largely with the topology of network ties reviewed earlier in this chapter.

- The relational dimension describes the kind of personal relationships people have developed with each other through a history of interactions, including their respect and friendship. This includes aspects such as trust, norms, obligations and identification, which result from our social brains.

- The cognitive dimension refers to those resources providing a system of meaning among parties. It includes shared codes and language and shared narratives, often represented as myths, stories and metaphors.

I summarize these three dimensions as connections, relationships and conversations.

Social capital is also based largely on the way people work together within teams, networks and communities. Like organization capital it deals with the extent to which an organization is more than the sum of its parts. This time, though, we are looking at the more informal and intangible links between people, rather than the formal and more tangible environment that a firm wraps around them. Social capital is also an emergent property arising from the organizational system. It is even less tangible than human capital and demonstrates even more attributes of complex systems (see Chapter 5).

Social capital is quite often linked to the production of human capital (Coleman, 1988) or the knowledge aspects of organization capital, sometimes also called knowledge capital (Nahapiet and Ghoshal, 1998). Social capital does support human and knowledge capital and both of these are important. But I also think that the more direct link between social capital and business success through the organization and business value chains is much more important than this.

Because our social brains, social networks and the social world are so important, for most companies, social capital will be more important than human or organization capital. Similarly, business innovator Nilofer Merchant (2012) suggests that whilst the Information Age honoured the value of data, the Social Era needs to recognize the value of a connected human. Professor in lifelong learning John Field makes the same point very clearly in his book on social capital, simply stating that relationships matter (Field, 2008). These points suggest that social capital may offer the prime source of competitive advantage in today's businesses. However, in practice, social capital is often much less well developed than human or organization capital.

This is because the social nature of people and organizations has often not been understood or invested in. Most businesses today still focus on measuring, managing, developing and rewarding the performance of individuals, whereas most organizations really need to start trying to do these things for their teams, and other groups. Even more importantly than this, some of the things we do to create human capital can actually reduce social capital. For example, very exclusive talent management programmes may make perfect sense from a human capital perspective. Paying FTSE CEOs nearly 130 times as much as their average employee (The High Pay Centre, 2016) may help attract an excellent chief executive too. However, as soon as we focus on social capital we understand that our actions are simply disrupting the social fabric of our organizations and are very likely to be making these less not more effective. It is no surprise, then, that many organizations are characterized by turf wars, petty politics and dysfunctionally competitive relationships.

Note, though, that it is important not to forget about human capital in the shift to focus more or additionally on social capital. People say that you need to be able to love yourself before you can love someone else. Bill Ingham, vice president of HR at Visa Inc, suggests that focusing on our own emotional and spiritual needs before we focus on others should not be considered selfish, but simply a starting point. He compares it to the instruction to put on your own mask first in a plane's safety instructions (Ingham, 2015). Building on these points, I suggest that businesses need to be human before they can really be social, ie they need to have a decent level of human capital in place before they will be able to leverage their social capital. People working in an organization need to feel cared for by the organization before they will care for other people. Organizations need to invest in human capital to provide a foundation for their investment in social capital. This is another reason for including Chapter 3 – on human and organization capital – within this book.

The importance of social capital, compared to its low level of development, points to a large gap in organizational effectiveness, and a major opportunity for taking actions leading to improvement. One good case study demonstrating this approach is the previous use of senior executive boards and councils at Cisco, which is described below. Further explanations of the approach will then be provided in Chapter 5 and the rest of the book.

CASE STUDY   Creating a dynamic networked organization at Cisco

Computer networking equipment manufacturer Cisco competes based on the collaboration between its people. In order to develop this collaboration, for a period of a few years it had its top-level executives spend much of their time in horizontal teams called 'boards' and 'councils'.

These were initially set up when Cisco moved to a functional organization. The company did not want to lose its previous horizontal focus and set up its first councils to maintain this. However, the company became very siloed and competitive, with people concentrating on their own verticals. Because of this, people were not necessarily making the right decisions for the company. Some years later, as the company attempted to become more innovative and grow more quickly, it scaled up the number of – and focus on – these groups. The redefined purpose of the groups was now to spread the company's leadership and decision making, creating what CEO John Chambers called 'a distributed idea engine where leadership emerges organically, unfettered by a central command' (Worthen, 2009b).

The reorganization created a meld (explained in Chapter 8) of the existing functional structure with a new network of the horizontally focused groups. This type of change is never easy, and when I met up with one of Cisco's HR directors, Jodi Krause, who led a team facilitating the groups, she described it as moving a battleship onto its side without spilling the ship.

The groups themselves were designed to meet specific market demands and organizational initiatives. Councils were established for $10 billion (plus) business opportunities and boards for $1 billion opportunities. Boards were accountable to councils and councils to the operating committee. Both groups were charged with thinking through business problems and making strategic decisions on their own in an agile manner. Coordination across the groups took place by sharing the groups' 'VSE' frameworks – these provided a *vision* for becoming number one or two in a market segment, plus a *strategy* and a plan for *execution*, supported by measures.

The groups replaced the company's previous hierarchical decision-making structure but the people working in them still reported to, and did most of their work within, traditional functions. Krause explained that it was important that people still felt they had a home. They were led by two to three co-leads and operated as cross-functional, collaborative teams. Each group involved 5–15 senior executives, meaning that people acted on four or five committees and spent over 30 per cent of their time on them. This was part of a deliberate attempt to spread the executives thinly: 'Eventually they realize they can't keep their head above water and if they want to swim they have to give some responsibilities to their teams' (Worthen, 2009a).

Each person on a board or council was given the authority to speak on behalf of the entire company rather than as a representative of their function. Decisions could be made in real time as everyone affected was sitting in one room. Groups were designed to be led collaboratively, but then once the group had reached a consensus they needed to be driven to execute effectively. Chambers noted that 'it is important not to collaborate all the way through the execution phase or the entire engine could grind to a halt' (Fryer and Stewart, 2008).

At one point there were 12 councils involving 120 people, 48 boards involving another 560 people and an additional 100 lower-level working groups involving another 1,230 people. More than 70 per cent of the company's strategic decisions were being made collaboratively.

The organization change was supported by a new leadership model, competencies and a development curriculum (Waltner, 2009). As a self reported command-and-control person, Chambers had to change his own style as well. Rather that telling people what to do he needed to learn to 'lead from the middle' (Bryant, 2009). Rewards were also updated to emphasize the performance of the collective, with a significant portion of senior managers' compensation being based upon peer ratings of how well they collaborated. Cisco also uses its own digital networking technologies extensively. Staff spend more time communicating over the company's TelePresence video-conferencing system than they do face to face at work.

In some ways the boards and councils were very successful. The company reported much faster innovation, eg completing a business plan in 15 minutes rather than six months. The approach also enabled Cisco to manage a large number of opportunities. The pool of identified talent was extended and the number of potential successors vastly increased. A survey of board and council members demonstrated high levels of support for the groups. However, the groups still struggled to become popular. Chambers admitted that for the first two years no one liked working on them but that it made people learn very quickly how to collaborate (Fryer and Stewart, 2008). The approach was heavily criticized within the organization and externally (Blodget, 2009) for being too complex and bureaucratic. It was also blamed for the company's falling market share and a large proportion of senior leaders leaving.

There was even more criticism when the boards and councils were withdrawn a few years later, with many people saying, basically, I told you so! However, for me, the criticism missed the point of the initiative. Cisco wanted to compete on collaboration/social capital, not just on the boards and councils/organization capital (as for HCLT's upside-down hierarchy, discussed in Chapter 3). Once the organization had become more collaborative they no longer needed the boards and councils. Their withdrawal was a sign of the approach's success, not its failure. For example, one of the reported benefits of the change was that what used to be 'me' is now 'we' (McGirt, 2008). That is an outcome very few companies could claim.

Cisco are in many ways my best example of the social organization and I still think their boards and councils contributed significantly and positively to the company's performance.

Summary and additional comments

1 This book focuses on cooperation and collaboration. There is not necessarily anything wrong with competitive relationships – in the right place at the right time competition can spur us to great things – however, I do not focus on competition because I think we already know how to do this.

2 The rational, individualistic and centralized ways in which we manage businesses today fits poorly with our knowledge of the social brain. From this viewpoint, we experience our organizations first and foremost as a social system. The lack of fit between the way we are and the way we are managed can create various psychosocial effects, including high levels of cortisol associated with elevated levels of stress; serotonin and oxytocin levels are also minimized, reducing levels of trust and prosocial behaviour. This all has a significant, negative impact on business performance.

3 An understanding of network science also enables us to be more clinical in our use of groups. This includes deciding when groups should be used, which sorts of groups (see Chapter 9) and how these groups/networks should be set up and facilitated (see Chapter 12).

4 Developing social organizations provides an opportunity for correcting the above issues. The social organization refers to a company of people who devote attention to their relationships as well as the achievement of their business objectives. Focusing on their relationships both supports and enables the achievement of these business objectives, leading to their better and/or faster achievement, or the potential for the creation of new business goals.

References

Ahn, TK, Janssen, MA, Reiners, DS and Stake, JE (2003) Heterogeneous preferences and collective action, *Public Choice*, **117** (3– 4), pp 295–314

Arbib, MA (2012) *How the Brain Got Language: The mirror system hypothesis*, Oxford University Press, Oxford

Ariely, D (2009) [accessed 9 March 2017] Are We More Rational Than Our Fellow Animals?, *The Blog*, 20 August [Online] http://danariely.com/2009/08/20/are-we-more-rational-than-our-fellow-animals/

Baker, WE (2012) *Achieving Success Through Social Capital: Tapping the hidden resources in your personal and business networks*, Jossey Bass, San Francisco

Barabasi, AL and Frangos, J (2002) *Linked: The new science of networks*, Perseus Books Group, Massachusetts

Baran, P (1964) [accessed 12 January 2017] On Distributed Communications: I. Introduction to Distributed Communications Networks, RAND Corporation, RM-3420-PR, as of 27 December 2016 [Online] http://www.rand.org/pubs/research_memoranda/RM3420.html

Blaffer Hrdy, S (2011) *Mothers and Others: The evolutionary origins of mutual understanding*, Harvard University Press, Massachusetts

Blodget, H (2009) [accessed 9 March 2017] Has Cisco's John Chambers Lost his Mind?, *Business Insider*, 6 August [Online] http://www.businessinsider.com/henry-blodget-has-ciscos-john-chambers-lost-his-mind-2009-8

Boyd, B (2010) *On the Origin of Stories: Evolution, cognition, and fiction*, Harvard University Press, Massachusetts

Bryant, A (2009) [accessed 9 March 2017] In a Near-Death Event, a Corporate Rite of Passage, *New York Times*, 1 August [Online] http://www.nytimes.com/2009/08/02/business/02corner.html

Burt, RS (1995) *Structural Holes: Social structure of competition*, Harvard University Press, Massachusetts

Burt, RS (2007) *Brokerage and Closure: An introduction to social capital*, Oxford University Press, Oxford

Cacioppo, JT and Patrick, W (2009) *Loneliness: Human nature and the need for social connection*, WW Norton & Company, New York

CEB Corporate Leadership Council (2012) [accessed 12 January 2017] Driving Breakthrough Performance in the New Work Environment, CEB [Online] https://www.cebglobal.com/content/dam/cebglobal/us/EN/top-insights/executive-guidance/pdfs/eg2013ann-breakthrough-performance-in-the-new-work-environment.pdf

Chamorro-Premuzic, T (2015) Why group brainstorming is a waste of time, *Harvard Business Review*, 25 March

Christakis, NA and Fowler, JH (2009) *Connected: The surprising power of our social networks and how they shape our lives*, Little, Brown and Company, New York

Coleman, JS (1988) Social capital in the creation of human capital, *American Journal of Sociology*, **94**, Supplement: organizations and institutions: sociological and economic approaches to the analysis of social structure, pp S95–S120

De Waal, F (2012) [accessed 12 January 2017] Moral Behavior in Animals, *TED* [Online] http://www.ted.com/talks/frans_de_waal_do_animals_have_morals/transcript?language=en

De Waal, F (2016) *Are We Smart Enough To Know How Smart Animals Are?* Granta Books, London

Drucker, PF (1959) *The Landmarks of Tomorrow*, Transaction Publishers, New Jersey

Dunbar, R and Schultz, S (2007) Evolution in the social brain, *Science*, **317** (5843), pp 1344–7

Field, J (2008) *Social Capital*, Routledge, London

Fryer, B and Stewart, TA (2008) Cisco sees the future, *Harvard Business Review*, November

Galinsky A and Schweitzer, M (2015) *Friend and Foe: When to cooperate, when to compete, and how to succeed at both*, Crown Business, New York

Gittell, JH (2005) *The Southwest Airlines Way*, McGraw Hill Education, New York

Goleman, D (2007) *Social Intelligence: The new science of human relationships*, Random House, New York

Granovetter, MS (2001) The strength of weak ties, *American Journal of Sociology*, **78** (6), May, pp 1360–80

Ingham, WG (2015) Finding our resilient center, in *The Rise of HR: Wisdom from 73 Thought Leaders*, ed D Ulrich, WA Schliemann and L Sartain, HR Certification Institute, Vancouver

Kidd, CD and Castano, E (2013) Reading literary fiction improves theory of mind, *Science*, **342** (6156), pp 377–80

Krebs, V and Holley, J (2002) [accessed 12 January 2017] Building Smart Communities through Network Weaving, *OrgNet* [Online] http://www.orgnet.com/BuildingNetworks.pdf

Kropp, B (2014) [accessed 9 March 2017] Fostering Competition and Cooperation Among Employees: A Performance Paradox, *CEB* [Online] https://www.cebglobal.com/blogs/fostering-competition-and-cooperation-among-employees-a-performance-paradox/

Larkin, II (2009) Paying $30,000 for a gold star: an empirical investigation into the value of peer recognition to software salespeople, Harvard Business School working paper

Laughlin, P, Hatch, E, Silver, J and Boh, L (2006) Groups perform better than the best individuals on letters-to-numbers problems: effects of group size, *Journal of Personality and Social Psychology*, **90** (4), pp 644–51

Lieberman, MD (2013) *Social: Why our brains are wired to connect*, Oxford University Press, Oxford

Locke, C, Searls, D and Weinberger, D (1999) *The Cluetrain Manifesto*, Financial Times, London

McGirt E (2008) [accessed 9 March 2017] How Cisco's CEO John Chambers is Turning the Tech Giant Socialist, *Fast Company*, 12 January [Online] https://www.fastcompany.com/1093654/how-ciscos-ceo-john-chambers-turning-tech-giant-socialist

Merchant, N (2012) *11 Rules for Creating Value in the Social Era*, CreateSpace Independent Publishing Platform, Seattle

Milgram, S (1967) The small world problem, *Psychology Today*, May

Nahapiet, J and Ghoshal, S (1998) Social capital, intellectual capital and the organisational advantage, *Academy of Management Review*, 23 (2), pp 242–66

Rock, D (2009) [accessed 12 January 2017] Managing with the Brain in Mind, *Strategy + Business*, 56, Autumn [Online] http://www.strategy-business.com/article/09306?gko=5df7f

Siegel, JZ and Crockett, MJ (2013) [accessed 12 January 2017] How Serotonin Shapes Moral Judgment and Behavior, *Annals of the New York Academy of Sciences*, 1299 (1), pp 42–51 [Online] https://www.ncbi.nlm.nih.gov/pmc/articles/PMC3817523/

Suchak, M, Eppley, TM, Campbell, MW, Feldman, RA, Quarles, LF and De Waal, FBM (2016) How chimpanzees cooperate in a competitive world, *Proceedings of the National Academy of Sciences*, 113 (36), pp 10215–20

The High Pay Centre (2016) [accessed 12 January 2017] 10% Pay Rise? That'll Do Nicely [Online] http://highpaycentre.org/pubs/10-pay-rise-thatll-do-nicely

Waltner, C (2009) [accessed 9 March 2017] Cisco Creates a New Generation of Collaborative Leaders, *The Network*, 7 December [Online] https://newsroom.cisco.com/feature-content?type=webcontent&articleId=5263198

Watts, DJ (2003) *Small Worlds: The dynamics of networks between order and randomness*, Princeton University Press, New Jersey

Worthen, B (2009a) [accessed 9 March 2017] Cisco CEO John Chambers's Big Management Experiment, *Wall Street Journal*, 5 August [Online] http://blogs.wsj.com/digits/2009/08/05/cisco-ceo-john-chamberss-big-management-experiment/

Worthen, B (2009b) Seeking growth, Cisco reroutes decisions, *Wall Street Journal*, 6/8. Available at: https://www.wsj.com/articles/SB124950454834408861

Zak, PJ (2013) *The Moral Molecule: The new science of what makes us good or evil*, Corgi Books, London

Zaki, J and Ochsner, K (2016) Empathy, in *The Handbook of Emotion*, 4th edn, ed L Feldman-Barrett, M Lewis and JM Haviland-Jones, Guilford Press, New York

Developing social capital in your business 05

Introduction

This chapter provides a process for identifying the social outcomes and activities that may best meet a particular company's needs, and it concludes Part 1 of the book. Parts 2 and 3 then provide more details on the various activities that creating a social organization may need to use. This chapter will cover:

- developing the objectives for social change;
- potential social organization principles;
- choosing the right social activities;
- a new definition for organization development;
- understanding and navigating relationship complexity.

At the end of this chapter, a summary of Part 1 of the book will also outline opportunities for leading the social organization.

Developing the objectives for social change

Organization purpose

The central idea behind Chapters 3 and 4 has been that once we know the outcomes a particular organization requires we can then identify the activities that will generate these outcomes. However, some organizations prefer to focus on something even more important than this, which can include an organization's mission. A shorter-term business plan can be used, but it can take time to create or change an organization's capabilities, so it is useful to have a longer-term perspective on what is important to a business too. An organization's purpose provides a particularly useful hook. This describes a big idea that clarifies what the organization is about and helps people focus on what is most important. It also provides a basis for developing an employee value proposition and employer brand. A purpose statement will often be linked to a company's origin and history as well as the current values of its people.

Importantly, a purpose should deal with more than making money, profit or shareholder returns. These fail to provide a clear focus for people's actions and behaviours and, in addition, often do not engage people either. As Nilofer Merchant notes, 'the social object that most unites people is a shared value or purpose. Money motivates neither the best people nor the best in people. Purpose does' (Merchant, 2012).

It is also increasingly useful for an organization's purpose to deal with more than simply beating a competitor or improving market share. These types of statements increasingly fail to engage people too. Social psychology consultant Gurnek Bains notes, 'the purpose needs to be one that ignites passion. Most people yearn for something bigger. They want to connect to the emergent social themes of the day' (Bains, 2007).

People also want to know that they will be treated well, and put above the needs of shareholders (fairness, status). I therefore, advise companies to develop an internal purpose: a clear big idea about the organization that is internally rather than externally generated. This is about how the organization is going to *be* rather than what it is going to *do*. As an example, Cisco's goal is to be the number one IT company. I think a lot of its employees will find that fairly uninspiring. Why not be the company of people who collaborate the best? I call this having an organizational mojo, as it seems to get close to an organization's real central essence that gives it its life and character and distinguishes it from elsewhere. An organization's capabilities will be closely connected to its purpose. The difference with mojo is that this will be informed by the capabilities rather than the other way around.

I think a somewhat similar idea lies behind the conscious capitalism movement's categorization of great purposes. These are: providing service to others; adding to human knowledge; creating excellence and beauty; and improving the world (Mackey and Sisodia, 2013). It is these types of purpose statements that provide the basis for establishing a sense of meaning for people. Companies cannot give meaning to people, but if they have a clear purpose they can embed this in their employer branding activities, recruit people around it and communicate what they are doing to achieve it. This will make it more likely that people will find their own meaning, potentially aligned with the purpose of the organization. Dave Ulrich suggests that leaders can help facilitate this too. This is by helping meld people's personal strengths with organizational capabilities – for example, through socialization during the onboarding process (Ulrich and Ulrich, 2010).

Meaning often comes from providing value to others. Organizational psychologist Adam Grant has found that reminding people how their work is helping others, especially when this is supported by personal contact with one or more of the people being helped, can boost performance up to a month later (Grant, 2014). Companies should therefore tell, or preferably, show, their people human stories of how their purpose is being achieved. Ideally, this will help people to find the sweet spot where their personal purpose, role purpose and organization purpose are all aligned (Pontefract, 2016).

Organizational capabilities

Once there is a clear organization purpose it is often easier to develop a small number of supporting capabilities. These also need to align with the business strategy, organizational context, workforce make-up and expectations etc. It is also important that they differentiate a company from other similar organizations/competitors and therefore offer the potential for gaining competitive advantage.

As suggested in Chapter 2, many different organizational capabilities are in fact mainly social in nature. However, some of the most common social capabilities – ie capabilities consisting mainly of social capital – are agility, collaboration, cooperation, digital, innovation, speed and learning. Articulating which of these, or other social outcomes, are going to be most important makes it much easier to develop a strategy to provide them. Although all social strategies will include similar approaches, the way these approaches are used will produce significantly different results.

For example, a capability in cooperation will often require people in different parts of an organization to bridge with each other and exploit their weak ties. The strategy that may be needed to achieve this may look very different from one intended to develop collaboration. This may require the development of strong ties and a high level of closure.

Organization values

I was never a fan of the results-only work environment (ROWE) (Ingham, 2008) and it was interesting to see that even BestBuy, where the approach was developed, has stopped using it (Bhasin, 2013). There has to be a focus on how things are achieved, not just on what the results need to be.

Without the *how*, a business may as well just operate as a platform rather than be an organization.

The most common way of articulating the *how* is through a list of values. As I hope you are picking up, I have some fairly definite views on most areas of people management. For example, I love career partnership but definitely do not love competencies or the concept of culture. However, there are some areas I am less decided on. One of these is the role of values. On one hand, I know there are quite a few case studies of very successful values-based change. For example, Bill George led a successful values-based culture change programme as CEO of Medtronic. He suggests that business should start with its purpose and values and use them to engage employees (George, 2004).

On the other hand, I have never worked in an organization where I found values helpful. My current, though slightly half-hearted position, is that it may make sense to use values in recruitment, in order to build an organization that has a tighter and more coherent focus around what it sees as important. But I would still advise against taking this too far and becoming too uniform in beliefs. And I would not use values in development as I do not believe people will change their values to fit those of their employer. Probably the most useful place to use them is in recognition – this is described in Chapter 11.

If you do use values, I would recommend ensuring that they are truly human ones, rather than the things that companies often wish their people would value. For example, some of the organization values I think are becoming more common currently include adaptability, bottom up, integrity, learning, pull (Hagel, Seely Brown and Davison, 2012), self-organization, simplicity, teaming and trust. The Responsive Org movement focuses on autonomy, experimentation and transparency (http://www.responsive.org/manifesto/). WorldBlu promotes freedom and democracy (http://www.worldblu.com/democratic-design/). As a slight aside, an alternative to democracy that is topical today is sociocracy (Endenburg, 1998). This is about a form of social governance based on social relationships and common aims. Many of sociocracy's ideas inform the Holacracy® model that I discuss in Chapter 7.

These are all compelling values, but are not necessarily the sorts of things people would suggest they value individually. For example, see the crowd-sourced list of personal values developed on World Values Day (http://www.worldvaluesday.com/). In addition the above values, as they stand, are not really detailed enough to inform action.

Organization principles

My preference for the *how* is to use organization principles. These explain what a good design will look like and help ensure that designers have got something to focus on as design proceeds, so they will not lose sight of the forest for the trees part-way through a restructure. A good example of organization principles is provided by the Toyota Way (Liker, 2004). Most of these principles are also very social in nature. I particularly like:

- Base your management decision on a long-term philosophy, even at the expense of short-term financial goals.

- Develop exceptional people and teams who follow your company's philosophy.

- Make decisions slowly by consensus; thoroughly considering all the options, implement decisions rapidly (*nemawashi* – 'preparing a tree's roots for the soil').

- Become a learning organization through relentless reflection (*hansei*) and continuous improvement (*kaizen*).

Such principles seem to have some effect since, despite recent difficulties, Toyota is broadly acknowledged to harness the intellect of its people very well. Also, former CEO Fujui Cho once noted, 'We take averagely talented people and make them work as spectacular teams' (Evans and Wolf, 2005).

Dave Ulrich also provides a set of principles for use by HR (Ulrich *et al*, 2009):

- Differentiate clearly between transactional (foundational or essential) and strategic HR work.

- Make the HR organization follow the logic and structure of the business organization.

- Make the HR organization follow the flow of any professional service-oriented organization.

More recently Ulrich has added a fourth principle supporting the increasing importance of social relationships. This is that HR should focus on relationships more than roles (Ulrich, 2015).

Developing organization principles tends to be an iterative activity. Often it is difficult to know what to put in a set of principles, but once a draft set have been developed these can be used to guide reorganizations. As well as ensuring organization change meets the needs of the principles, organizations tend to gain a better understanding of the principles that they really want to have as they go through each reorganization. They can therefore go back to their principles and update them. Over time, the principles become more detailed and unique to a particular organization. Principles work best when they guide organizational actions, eg when there is a choice between two actions and it is clear which one to take because of the clarity provided by the principles.

Cascading objectives across the organization

The organization's capabilities and principles can be cascaded down an organization through the organization's and people's performance objectives, and organizational behaviours or competencies. I have already explained in Chapter 2 that I do not like competencies that much, but this ability to cascade the organization principles into what people do is another benefit they provide.

CASE STUDY   Netflix's culture deck

Organization principles are not that common. Even many large, sophisticated businesses do not have these. However, a large number of organizations have published slide decks about their organizations on LinkedIn's Slideshare system. Many of the statements in these decks look very much like organization principles. The companies that have developed these decks are following a lead taken by Netflix (Hastings, 2009), whose own document has received over 15 million views. Facebook Chief Operating Officer (COO) Sheryl Sandberg considers it one of the most important documents to emerge out of Silicon Valley (Wong, 2014).

One of the reasons that Netflix's deck has been so popular is that it describes a fairly unique way of undertaking HR. The approach was designed to treat employees as players in a pro sports team rather than as members of a family. The company's HR Director believed that when things get too familial, people's judgement can be clouded when they have to let people go, 'because we don't fire our family'. According to Netflix, treating people like sports pros means that people can get cut without getting personal (Giang, 2016).

To develop the new approach, the HR Director pushed back on best practice, suggesting this just refers to a way in which things have always been done. She was more interested in whether something made sense, and whether it was logical. To inform the new approach the HR Director wrote down the things the company valued, what mattered to them, and what they expected in their people. Then, rather than looking at what other companies were doing they took a risk and did something different (McCord, 2014).

Potential social organization principles

Businesses should develop their own organization principles, and not copy anyone else's. However, it may be helpful to suggest high-level principles that some social organizations may want to build on to help shape how they organize and operate:

1 Treating diversity and inclusion as a higher priority than many businesses do now. Both social and other cognitive biases push against creating more diverse workforces. These also act against making it easy for people with different perspectives, or in minority groups, to feel fully included. We therefore need to take more action on both of these fronts. Homogeneous organizations are easier to manage and operate in; however, a reduced number of weak ties often make them considerably less effective. Diverse groups also do more careful information processing. Management professor Katherine Phillips suggests this is down to newcomers creating social awkwardness, which shifts alliances and enlivens group interaction (Phillips, Liljenquist and Neale, 2009). However, people also need to be able to work with others who are different from them without this tipping over into competitive behaviours.

2 Enabling people to connect in multiple networks and ensuring these are of the right type and size. Most of today's businesses are still highly centralized and we need to be more ambitious, brave and creative in experimenting with, and using, distributed or at least decentralized network organizations. Doing this supports the law of requisite variety, which basically explains that the more diverse a network the greater is its ability to respond to change (Heylighen and Joslyn, 2001). Also, when the population of a city doubles, economic productivity goes up by an average of 130 per cent (Bettencourt and West, 2010). This growth is due to greater face-to-face communication (Pan *et al*, 2013). Our organizations should be able to benefit from increased network density too. At the same time, we have evolved to live in tribal groups of up to about 150 people. The book *Tribal Leadership* suggests this behaviour is so natural that – in the same way birds flock and fish school – the main thing people do is 'tribe' (Logan, King and Fischer-Wright, 2008). Retaining a local tribe or village feel within a big city-type environment will be an increasing challenge for many businesses.

3 Paying more attention to the quality of people's relationships. Also emphasizing cooperation rather than competition, helping to reduce the production of winners and losers, and ingroups and outgroups.

Depending upon the context, this may involve ensuring that competition takes place between teams, not between individuals. Achieving this will depend, in part, on ensuring HR and management practices support fairness. It is also about avoiding threat response-inducing status differences, ideally by ensuring everyone feels that they have high status within their groups and the whole organization. MIT's study of high-intelligence work groups demonstrated the need for relatedness, fairness and status. This found that collective intelligence has nothing to do with the individual IQ or engagement of team members or even group cohesion. It was, however, correlated with team members' social sensitivity and negatively correlated with variance in their speaking turns, ie the extent to which a few people dominated the conversation (Woolley *et al*, 2010). Relationships also offer a range of benefits to individual and organizational human capital.

4 Ensuring that the conversations between people are both effective and meaningful. It is by doing this that organizations can ensure the things being discussed are compelling and that the conversations also serve to develop the relationships between people. One way of achieving this is through storytelling. However, this is made challenging by increased separation of people globally and also virtually. Dealing with this challenge requires organizations to get to grips with the potential of social technologies too.

One of the challenges in many organizations, which may evolve over time through iteration of the principles, is how much emphasis on cooperating and collaborating it makes sense to have. Time spent working with others comes at a cost, which is hopefully recouped through improved effectiveness. For example, CEB suggest that 68 per cent of employees find their co-workers' input valuable but 54 per cent find that getting this input is too time-consuming (Kropp, 2014a). There is also often an additional issue in that just 3–5 per cent of people can account for 30 per cent of collaborative activity. These people, who have been particularly generous with their time, will be most at risk from collaboration burnout (Cross, Rebele and Grant, 2016).

Choosing the right social activities

The activities that will be most closely aligned with the required social outcomes can best be identified by following the options identification process presented in Figure 5.1.

Figure 5.1   Options identification process

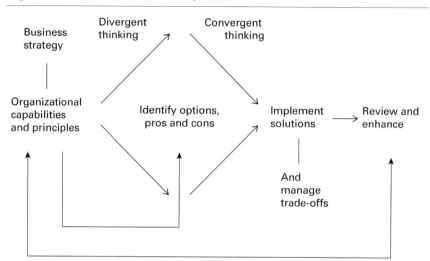

The process starts with clarity over the organizational capabilities and principles, as shown in Figure 5.1. These become the objectives of the process.
This then leads into a period of divergent thinking, identifying various
combinations of activities that could meet the objectives in different ways.

These activities can be usefully split into two categories. The first of these
relate to the design of the whole organization, including each of the various
elements and the links between these. I call this the organizational architecture. Designing the organizational architecture requires the use of tools
and techniques associated with what is traditionally called organization
design (where this is defined by activities rather than by the outcome being
organization capital). Taking this perspective tends to mean that people and
relationships receive a rather superficial treatment.

When my version of organization design is being undertaken (defined as
aiming to create organization capital) it is normally quite sufficient to focus
on the organizational architecture. However, as the social organization aims
to create social capital we need to dive deeper into what is happening within
people and their relationships. This requires more focus on the soft rather
than just the hard aspects of an organization, which using the McKinsey
7S model refers to the staff and their skills, and even more so to the shared
values and style of the organization, ie the elements directly below human
and social capital (shown in Figure 3.1). I call this additional perspective
on an organization an 'organizational society' and it is this that the second
category of activities focuses on.

The various combinations of activities suggested by using the options identification process will generally include activities relating to both the organizational architecture and the organizational society, eg redesigning the organization structure and involving people in thinking through what they need to change in order to operate appropriately within that new structure.

Most often, there is no one perfect way to achieve the objectives that have been identified. Each option will offer certain advantages but certain disadvantages as well. But having identified all the different options it is possible to review the different options, comparing all the pros and cons back to the objectives. This will make it possible to identify which option gets closest to identifying everything an organization wants. This judgement should also include the cost of implementation, as sometimes an option can look better than the current state but is still not worth implementing if it would cause too much disruption. The comparison can be supported semi-analytically, through the use of tools such as harvey balls (mini pie charts). Personally I do not do this, I accept the choice of option will always be subjective and largely intuitive and leave it at that. Note that it is not always a requirement to have a fully coherent organization, in which all the elements of an organization are aligned. Sometimes a small change in one element will be enough. However, very often, organizational options/solutions will involve a bundle of activities as it is the coherence and reinforcement provided by this that will ensure future organizational effectiveness. Bundling may also be required in order to overcome the inertia that often occurs in organizations and that tends to act to keep things as they are.

A good example is provided in Sony's failure to use its leading position as manufacturer of the Walkman to develop something like the iPod and iTunes, and to capture the market that is now dominated by Apple. Sony had everything it needed to do this, including divisions and core competencies in consumer electronics, computing, music and entertainments. However, as Gillian Tett powerfully explains in her book *The Silo Effect*, Sony's divisions failed to collaborate to take advantage of the opportunity (Tett, 2015). Sony's CEOs fought against the organizational silos but were defeated by them. However, Sony's efforts were actually quite limited. Divisional profit and loss accounts (P&Ls) were abolished but not the divisions themselves. A number of cross-group links were set up, including rotations, new higher-level teams and town halls. The workplace was also changed, putting engineers in the centre of the room and co-locating the PlayStation division with the other groups, but letting them create a glass wall around their operations. The CEO also reinforced the importance of collaboration. However, these actions simply were not enough to compete against Apple's coherently collaborative organization. There was certainly much more Sony could have done. Even if it could not change its structure, what about investing in people or team development, some organization development interventions, a social network analysis, or, if the case was being repeated today, implementing an enterprise social network?

Having gone through the process and identified the best solution, an organization designer or design team can then move into implementation. However, it is useful to remember that as well as implementing the solution, another activity will be required. This is to mitigate the trade-offs that come with having selected a non-perfect solution. That is, no matter how good the match with the objectives, the solution will come with disadvantages or drawbacks. If these are not managed, they will stop the solution achieving everything it might have.

Often what happens is that the cons mount up over time. A common example occurs with tensions between centralization and decentralization. A company might centralize to gain benefits from coordination, accepting that this will not give business units so much freedom to innovate. But a few years later, that inability to innovate will have become so large a problem that the company will be forced to reorganize. So it moves to decentralization, improving innovation and accepting less control. This can lead to ongoing oscillation, moving from one approach to its opposite and back again every few years. But actually all that was needed was to manage the trade-offs involved. So the business could implement centralization and find a way to keep business units innovative too. Or it could go for decentralization and ensure the centre can still influence the business units.

However, this oscillation can be part of a positive organizational strategy too. Informal networks and relationships tend to stay in place for some time after a restructure and this can provide a short-term advantage by providing the benefits of the old and new organization simultaneously (Nickerson and Zenger, 2002). In addition, Ronald Burt has found that oscillating between broking within a group (closure) and boundary spanning between groups (bridging) also provides an advantage (Burt and Merluzzi, 2016).

A number of benefits are provided by following the options identification process. First, it makes sure organizations suspend judgement and consider a number of options before landing on a solution. This generates more creativity and can lead to a better solution, eg one that creates rather than simply adds value. Second, it ensures the solutions that are developed are best fit, not best practice. Third, it can be useful politically. For example, if you are working with someone who is wedded to a particular solution, which you think would be the wrong choice, it avoids having conflict over this. You simply say that it is great that the other person has provided one option, but before you start to implement this it will be useful to quickly identify some alternatives and compare them in a logical way. By the time you have done this, that person has often become a lot less emotionally invested in their own proposal and it becomes easier to pick the best option and move on.

Even though you have identified the best option you may not want to implement it in full. Sometimes, it is best just to keep this at the back of your mind and to move towards it more incrementally when you can. This applies, in particular, to something as potentially disruptive as layers and spans – see Chapter 9. If the solution is implemented it will be important to pay attention to ongoing enhancement too. However brilliant a design, once it is implemented things happen. Therefore, even a perfect solution always needs to be supported and enhanced for the context it is working in once it has been implemented.

Increasingly, organizations are moving to an approach where they make ongoing, incremental change, which can make reorganizations feel easier. Whichever approach is taken, it is important to manage the change process carefully, avoiding too much challenge to people's certainty and autonomy.

A new definition for organization development

Whereas developing human and organization capital requires HR/HCM and organization design activities, creating a social architecture – and especially an organizational society – tends to require organization development (OD). Some readers may not be sure what this is and others, even including those in an OD role or function, may have different views. This book therefore gives me the chance to offer my own definition.

Organization design is often seen as a one-off creation activity and OD is seen as involving ongoing enhancement. However, that does not really work because these are then the same thing, just applied in different ways at different times. Sometimes OD is seen as a humanistic way of changing organizations, but good organization design will be humanistic too. Sometimes, OD is seen to relate to the soft aspects of an organization, in contrast to the hard structure and process that are the focus of organization design. However, that does not work either. Organization models, including those used by organization developers – eg the Burke Litwin model – make the same point, combining soft elements such as culture with hard ones like structure. Even the McKinsey 7S model I introduced in Chapter 1 emphasizes how shared values and styles need to be managed holistically with other organizational enablers. (However, for organization development use in today's social world I would expand this model to an 8S one, including an extra 'S' for social relationships.)

Sometimes organization development is defined simply as a set of interventions, but then it is not really anything at all. Having crossed so many potential definitions off the list, OD practitioners often suggest that the thing which makes OD special is the philosophy or values that underpin their work. For example, Edgar Schein (1987) stressed that he never saw OD as being based on a set of techniques, but that it was more about a particular philosophy or attitude to do with working in organizations. Mee-Yan Cheung-Judge talks about OD being 'not exactly communist but shamelessly humanistic in nature' (Ingham, 2011). To me, this is a problem too as OD cannot be defined by its values either – certainly not as long as we want effective organizations to result. The McKinsey 7S model places shared values at its centre because the whole organization needs to be aligned around these values if the organization is going to work. An OD practitioner who comes to an organization with their own individual or professional set of values, rather than the organization's, is going to reduce, not increase, organizational alignment and hence is likely to do more damage than they do good.

The good news is that we do not need to define OD by either its activities/interventions or by its values. We can use the approach I explained earlier in reference to HCM and organization design and define OD by the outcomes it creates. You will probably have already guessed that the outcome I think OD covers is social capital. Therefore, OD is the use of all the levers/possible activities within an organization to create social capital. This means that the social organization is really a new, more integrated, and therefore more effective, approach to doing OD.

The above definition is not exactly right either – OD often creates other types of capital too. For example, it often aims to improve employee engagement (human capital) too. However, the definition is still a good approximation to the truth. Most of OD is about creating more effective relationships and hence it is already well aligned with creating social capital. The definition also helps explain why other fields such as social constructionism and complexity science are so well used within OD. The value of social psychology is fairly obvious. OD is about improving relationships and conversations. And constructionism helps us to see the importance of these conversations in generating shared understanding between people. But complexity relates to relationships as well.

Understanding relationship complexity

I have already suggested that people need to work together to respond to increased complexity. However, the need to acknowledge complexity is also increased when we place more attention on people's relationships. This is because there is a power-law connection between the number of people in a group and the number of relationships between them. The equation for this is:

$$r = p\,(p-1)\,/\,2$$

where:

r = number of relationships

p = number of people

Using this equation, three people in a group create three relationships between them, but four people create six relationships and five people nine relationships etc. A group of 150 people will involve more than 10,000 relationships to keep track of. More detailed equations are also provided by Graicunas (1937).

Relationships also make decision making more difficult. First, because some of these decisions will relate to relationships and groups and, second, because decisions will often be made in groups, meaning that they can be affected by social biases such as groupthink. It is these factors that make OD much more complex than HCM or organization design. Organization design was complicated, OD is complex. The difference between complicated and complex is the difference between a car and an elephant – cars can be taken to pieces, analysed and understood; elephants need to be understood as a whole. The shifting nature of people management, organization design and OD is summarized in Figure 5.2.

Figure 5.2   Moving from cause and effect to complexity

	People	Organization	Relationships
Creating value	Complexity	Complexity	Complexity
Adding value	Systems	Systems	Complexity
Value for money	Cause and effect	Systems	Complexity

Figure 5.2 suggests that people management can be simple, complicated or complex. As we saw in Chapter 4, people are not simple, we are really complex. But people management does not have to worry about this too much because we operate from outside of people's heads. However, at higher levels of value, HR and HCM do take more notice of human psychology than in a basic personnel approach, and are also more interconnected and integrated. This means that they must recognize the complicated and complex nature of organizations. Organization design almost always involves a combination of elements, so this area is already complicated, even at low levels of value. In creating value, organization design becomes complex too, again because of the nature of these strategies. OD is always complex, as explained above.

Navigating complexity

We need to understand organizations as complex adaptive systems rather than as the complicated systems addressed in Chapter 3. The links between cause and effect, complicated and complex systems are well explained in Dave Snowden's Cynefin model (Snowden and Boone, 2007). This suggests that in simple/obvious, cause-and-effect-based systems, everything is known. Taking action in this environment involves identifying a particular situation from a number of alternatives or best practices and then implementing the appropriate action. In complicated systems, things are knowable, as long as there is some time to investigate. Acting is more difficult but can still be done. In the complex domain, relationships are discoverable, but generally only with hindsight. Sociologist Duncan Watts suggests this is true for social networks too, noting that: 'Cause and effect are related in complicated and often misleading ways. We are often only in a position to understand the impact of an action in a network in retrospect' (Watts, 2004).

This means that complex systems, like living systems, can be influenced but not managed. A good way of achieving this is to promote a few simple rules, enabling people to self-organize. I think this is part of the benefit that organization principles provide. Another feature of these environments is that small changes can have large, emergent impacts. Therefore, rather than launching major programmes, it is often more useful to make small changes and wait, nurturing the system to help the solution become the best it can be. The next requirement is noticing what happens and taking more action as a result.

Complexity also requires synthesis and understanding of the whole rather than analysis and understanding of the elements. This is why organization design can afford to rely on models of systems with arrows and boxes – like the various organization models, including McKinsey's 7S – and why OD usually cannot. (In this book I am going to introduce a new organization model in Part 2, focusing on organizational architecture. However, when we move on to the organizational society in Part 3 I will avoid using this.) It also means it is useful, where possible, to bring everyone from the whole organization together to discuss and agree on change.

Complexity also leads to paradoxes rather than dilemmas. Dilemmas involve choices between two options. Paradox involves finding synergies and the potential of doing two seemingly opposite things at the same time. So, rather than deciding on centralization or decentralization, paradox suggests we may be able to do both. CEB suggest there are four main paradoxes in the social organization. These are individual and team performance, direction and autonomy, speed and collaboration, and individual reward plus network performance (Kropp, 2014b).

Harold Jarche explains that different social behaviours relate to each of the different Cynefin domains (Jarche, 2015). Basic coordination amongst people, for example, ensuring we do not duplicate or omit areas of work, relates to a simple, cause-and-effect environment. The next level of more advanced communication is collaboration. This is about people actually working purposefully together with each other in order to solve a problem and produce something together. The relationships between these people, which need to be managed, are now those of a complicated system. The third level is cooperation. This is a voluntary and emergent sharing of interests between people who influence each other based on their reputations. This is a complex set of relationships. We will return to the nature of coordination, collaboration and cooperation in Chapter 9.

Maverick organizations

Many of my case studies come from maverick organizations, eg Zappos and Netflix. These are businesses that have fully aligned all of the different aspects of their organizations around particular capabilities and unique principles that make them very different organizations from most that exist today. This often includes assembling an unusual combination or bundle of organizational architecture elements (described in Part 2). Because they are quite different, and because they often get lots of publicity as a result of this, the cases are often quite well known. Therefore, referring to them runs the risk of boring and alienating some readers. I have still decided to include some of them because they are good case studies, plus I generally describe a new perspective on them, or the same perspective in a different way. But the main reason is that they indicate what it is possible to achieve.

I sometimes think about this as a pond. Most companies using the same best practices are gathered together in the centre of the pond. And then there are maverick organizations out on the periphery doing some completely different things. Studying the mavericks shows how different companies could be. It does not mean you need to turn your company into a maverick. You do not need to come all the way out to the edge of the pond. But perhaps you can come out of the middle, just a little bit, and find some of Kim and Mauborgne's 'blue ocean' water there.

The name maverick, used for this group, comes from the original maverick organization, Semco (Semler, 2001). This company no longer does what it did (Kuiken, 2016) but the case is still a wonderful example of social and self-organization. I will just mention 'Up 'n' Down Pay', which allowed people to set their own pay levels. Semco found that individuals almost always do this fairly, based on the market information they are provided. More mavericks are listed in the book *Mavericks at Work* (Taylor and LaBarre, 2006).

A lot of my case studies also come from the technology sector. These are people businesses, also focused on innovation. But their most relevant characteristic may be that they also use technology to support their innovation. I think this has helped them to move away from the middle of the pond. Most of the case studies are also from the United States, and most of them are large companies. However I still believe that most of what I have written will apply to small companies and public/voluntary sector bodies in most parts of the world.

A good example of a change activity based upon an understanding of relationships and their complexity comes from Juniper Networks. As part of an engagement initiative, Juniper got 500 people together to discuss the organization's purpose. These were the people who the company had identified as connectors, energizers, brokers and boundary spanners (see the section on social networks in Chapter 4). They represented about 5 per cent of the total staff. After the event, each of these socially connected influencers got together with 20–25 of their colleagues to talk about the company's mission. These separate conversations were then integrated by sharing them on Juniper's enterprise social network (Feintzeig, 2015). This enabled the whole organization to participate in the conversation about its shared purpose. More information on the way Juniper identified their influencers is provided in Chapter 13.

Summary and additional comments

1 The options identification process presented in this chapter should help social organization designers to identify appropriate social outcomes and the relevant social activities for their businesses.

2 This chapter marks the end of Part 1 of the book and in many ways is also the end of the book. Parts 2 and 3 will now simply add detail and review options for the activities that can be used to create the required social capital.

3 Part 2 focuses on the organizational architecture, which when used within the context of organization development/the social organization, I sometimes call the social architecture. Developing a social architecture needs to include a focus on relationships. In addition, dealing with the

rest of the organization at a creating-value level also requires an appreciation of complexity (see Figure 5.2). However, most of the activities in Part 2 of the book are mainly concerned with managing the complicated nature of organizational systems.

4 Part 3 focuses on the organizational society, ie the people and relationships and how these need to be developed within a social organization. Doing this tends to require organization designers to take more account of the complex nature of relationships and organizations.

5 Given the complex, unknowable nature of the social organization, using the options identification process to create social capital will not be that simple. Therefore it is not possible to provide an easy-to-use template that provides the top 10 things that every social organization must do.

6 However, I would still encourage even novice social organization designers to try using the options identification process. The more it is used the more gets learnt and the easier and more effective using it becomes. It is always important to do things carefully when dealing with people and their jobs. However, as long as the process is followed it is fairly difficult to get too much wrong. That is, you may not pick the optimal solution but as long as you think there is an option that is better than the current state then you should gain benefit and not do any damage in moving the organization towards it.

Summary of Part 1 – Leading the social organization

Designing the social organization, by using the options identification process, and then implementing the chosen activities to build a new social architecture and develop an organizational society, needs to be a socially based process too. The role of the HR discipline, other functions, and managers and leaders, is to facilitate and support this process.

In general, however, business leaders often act as barriers rather than enablers for this change. For example, the Centre for Creative Leadership (CCL) has found that 86 per cent of senior executives think it is extremely important to work effectively across boundaries. However, only 7 per cent of them believe they are very effective at doing this. CCL suggests the 79 per cent difference between these two figures represents a critical gap in leadership capability (Ernst and Chrobot-Mason, 2010).

The issue might be that leaders are often more self-centred and less mindful than the people they manage. Adam Galinsky illustrates this through a set of experiments using what is called the 'E test'. This involves asking someone to draw a capital E on their forehead. Most people take the other person's perspective and draw the E so that it is backward to themselves but so that a viewer can read it. However, people who are more powerful tend to draw the E so that it is readable to themselves. They also show less activity in the prefrontal cortex and cingulate cortex, suggesting that they have not bothered to empathize with the other person's point of view (Galinsky and Schweitzer, 2015).

The above analysis suggests that we may not be able to rely on business leaders being able to create the social organization. In any case, the social organization requires everyone in an organization to share some leadership responsibilities. The danger of seeing just some people as leaders is that everyone else becomes a follower and we need more from people than this. Therefore, the main thing that managers and leaders need to do is to act the same as everyone else, just with more focus on being facilitators of change, eg by sponsoring social approaches and the use of social technology etc.

This shift in perspective is what business management professor Henry Mintzberg calls communityship (Mintzberg, 2009). It is also supported by Peter Block in his book on managing communities – he suggests that sustainable improvements in community occur when people stop waiting for leaders to do something and discover their own power to act (Block, 2008).

In addition, a similarly reduced role for leaders is seen in the introduction of digital technologies and approaches, which also often require more social behaviours. The 2016 Organization in the Digital Age survey shows that whilst the role of senior leaders is particularly important when starting off with digital, organizational change agents develop a similarly important role during later phases of these projects (McConnell, 2016). This suggests that creating a social organization may depend upon collaborative action taken by change agents working across the organization.

It is for all the above and other related reasons that, despite my desire to integrate the different aspects of the social organization, this book will not review separate requirements for social leadership. Or perhaps a better way of describing this is that I see everyone in an organization as a potential leader and therefore there is no value in using the leadership term. Instead of this, the book will describe the behavioural changes that are required to some extent from everyone. These are reviewed in Chapter 12.

There is, however, one important exception to the above, which occurs because HR professionals usually have very high levels of empathy. This is partly because of the type of people who are often drawn to HR, and partly because even unempathetic HR people often develop empathy skills because of the type of work they do in HR. These skills are another reason for suggesting that HR can play a particularly pivotal role in the creation of a social organization.

References

Bains, G (2007) *Meaning Inc: The blueprint for business success in the 21st century*, Profile Books, London

Bettencourt, L and West, G (2010) A unified theory of urban living, *Nature*, **467** (7318), pp 912–13

Bhasin, K (2013) [accessed 12 January 2017] BestBuy CEO: Here's Why I Killed The 'Results Only Work Environment', *Business Insider*, 18 March [Online] http://www.businessinsider.com/best-buy-ceo-rowe-2013-3

Block P (2008) *Community: The structure of belonging*, Berrett-Koehler, San Francisco

Burt, RS and Merluzz, J (2016) Network oscillation, *Academies of Management Discoveries*, **2** (4), pp 368–91

Cross, R, Rebele, R and Grant, A (2016) Collaborative overload, *Harvard Business Review*, January–February

Endenburg, G (1998) *Sociocracy: The organization of decision-making*, Eburon, Delft, The Netherlands

Ernst, C and Chrobot-Mason, D (2010) *Boundary Spanning Leadership: Six practices for solving problems, driving innovation, and transforming organizations*, McGraw Hill Education, New York

Evans, P and Wolf, B (2005) Collaboration rules, *Harvard Business Review*, July–August

Feintzeig, R (2015) [accessed 12 January 2017] I Don't Have a Job. I Have a Higher Calling, *Wall Street Journal*, 24 February [Online] http://www.wsj.com/articles/corporate-mission-statements-talk-of-higher-purpose-1424824784

Galinsky A and Schweitzer M (2015) *Friend and Foe: When to cooperate, when to compete, and how to succeed at both*, Crown Business, New York

George, B (2004) *Authentic Leadership: Rediscovering the secrets to creating lasting value*, John Wiley & Sons, New York

Giang, V (2016) [accessed 12 January 2017] The woman who built Netflix's culture did it with these 5 things in mind, *LinkedIn Talent Blog*, 2/11 [Online] https://business.linkedin.com/talent-solutions/blog/company-culture/2016/the-woman-who-built-netflixs-culture-did-it-with-these-5-things-in-mind

Graicunas, VA (1937) Relationship in organization, papers on the science of administration, Columbia University, pp 183–7

Grant, A (2014) *Give and Take: Why helping others drives our success*, Orion Publishing, London

Hagel, J III, Brown, JS and Davison, L (2012) *The Power of Pull: How small moves, smartly made, can set big things in motion*, Perseus Books Group, Washington DC

Hastings, R (2009) [accessed 12 January 2017] Netflix Culture: Freedom and Responsibility, *Netflix* [Online] http://www.slideshare.net/reed2001/culture-1798664

Heylighen, F and Joslyn, C (2001) [accessed 12 January 2017] The Law of Requisite Variety, *Principia Cybernetica Web*, 31/8 [Online] http://pespmc1.vub.ac.be/REQVAR.html

Ingham, J (2008) [accessed 12 January 2017] Would a ROWE Get the Right Results?, *Strategic HCM*, 21 October [Online] http://strategic-hcm.blogspot.co.uk/2008/10/would-rowe-get-right-results.html

Ingham, J (2011) [accessed 9 March 2017] Thoughts on CIPD's Organization Development Conferences [Online] http://strategic-hcm.blogspot.co.uk/2011/09/thoughts-on-cipds-organisation.html

Jarche, H (2015) [accessed 12 January 2017] Cooperation for the Network Era, *Harold Jarche* [Online] http://jarche.com/2015/08/cooperation-for-the-network-era/

Kropp, B (2014a) [accessed 12 January 2017] Employees Need Coworker Input, but Still Need to Meet Deadlines: A Performance Paradox, *CEB*, 9 July [Online] https://www.cebglobal.com/blogs/employees-need-coworker-input-but-still-need-to-meet-deadlines-a-performance-paradox/

Kropp, B (2014b) [accessed 12 January 2017] Performance Management: HR's Rubik's Cube, *CEB* [Online] https://www.cebglobal.com/blogs/the-paradoxes-of-performance-management-today-hrs-rubiks-cube/

Kuiken, B (2016) [accessed 12 January 2017] Case: Semco, *neworganising.eu* [Online] http://www.neworganising.eu/management-by-samba/

Liker, JK (2004) *The Toyota Way: 14 management principles from the world's greatest manufacturer*, McGraw Hill Education, New York

Logan, D, King, J and Fischer-Wright, H (2008) *Tribal Leadership: Leveraging natural groups to build a thriving organization*, Harper Business, New York

Mackey, J and Sisodia, R (2013) *Conscious Capitalism: Liberating the heroic spirit of business*, Harvard Business Review Press, Boston

McConnell, J (2016) [accessed 12 January 2017] Change Agents – Nearly as Important as Senior Leaders, *NetStrategyJMC* [Online] http://www.netjmc.com/organizational-change/change-agents-nearly-as-important-as-senior-leaders/

McCord, P (2014) How Netflix reinvented HR, *Harvard Business Review*, January–February

Merchant, N (2012) *11 Rules for Creating Value in the #SocialEra*, CreateSpace Independent Publishing Platform, Seattle

Mintzberg, H (2009) Rebuilding companies as communities, *Harvard Business Review*, July–August

Nickerson, JA and Zenger, TR (2002) Being efficiently fickle: a dynamic theory of organizational choice, *Organization Science*, Sep/Oct, **13** (5), p 547

Pan, W, Ghoshal, G, Krumme, C, Cebrian, M and Pentland, A (2013) [accessed 12 January 2017] Urban Characteristics Attributable to Density-Driven Tie Formation, *Nature Communications* [Online] http://www.nature.com/articles/ncomms2961

Phillips, KW, Liljenquist, KA and Neale, MA (2009) Is the pain worth the gain? The advantages and liabilities of agreeing with socially distinct newcomers, *Personality and Social Psychology Bulletin*, **35**, pp 336–50

Pontefract, D (2016) *The Purpose Effect*, Elevate, Idaho

Schein, EK (1987) [accessed 9 March 2017] Back to the Future: Recapturing the OD Vision, Alfred P Sloan School of Management Working Paper, *MIT* [Online] https://archive.org/stream/backtofuturereca00sche/backtofuturereca00sche_djvu.txt

Semler, R (2001) *Maverick!: The success story behind the world's most unusual workplace*, Random House Business, London

Snowden, DJ and Boone, ME (2007) Providing a leader's framework for decision making, *Harvard Business Review*, November

Taylor, WC and LaBarre, P (2006) *Mavericks at Work: Why the most original minds in business win*, HarperCollins, New York

Tett, G (2015) *The Silo Effect*, Abacus, London

Ulrich, D (2015) [accessed 9 March 2017] The Future of HR is about Relationships, *People Management*, 24 March [Online] http://www2.cipd.co.uk/pm/peoplemanagement/b/weblog/archive/2015/03/24/the-future-of-hr-is-about-relationships.aspx

Ulrich, D, Allen, J, Brockbank, W, Younger, J and Nyman, M (2009) *HR Transformation: Building human resources from the outside in*, McGraw-Hill Education, Chicago

Ulrich, D and Ulrich, W (2010) *The Why of Work*, McGraw Hill, New York

Watts, D (2004) *Six Degrees: The science of a connected age*, WW Norton & Co, New York

Wong, V (2014) [accessed 12 January 2017] Behind the Slides: The Netflix Culture Deck's Rise to Fame, *LinkedIn* [Online] https://blog.slideshare.net/2014/06/11/inside-the-netflix-culture-deck

Woolley, AW, Chabris, CF, Pentland, A, Hashmi, N and Malone, TW (2010) Evidence for a collective intelligence factor in the performance of human groups, *Science*, **330** (6004), pp 686–8

PART TWO
Creating a social architecture

Organizing people to do work

06

Introduction

Part 1 of this book established the importance of creating value by developing social capital and other outcomes in the organization value chain. It also introduced an options identification process that can be used to choose activities that will support the required outcomes. The rest of this book will now focus on describing some of the activities and organizational changes that can potentially be selected and used as part of a particular organization's social strategy.

However, we will not forget entirely about creating human and organizational outcomes. This is because:

- Social organizations need to be human and organizationally effective too, so the actions required to develop these other outcomes are still very relevant.

- Some readers may just be interested in developing social relationships to inform these other outcomes.

- Some activities that can be used to create social capital can be best explained or demonstrated by considering their use in developing these other outcomes too (eg through case studies that concern the creation of human or organization capital, just because these are good cases to understand the activities being described).

In terms of the activities we can use to create social outcomes I have already suggested that actions relating directly to the organizational society, and particularly those focusing directly on social relationships, are likely to be the most useful. Actions relating to people, ie staff and skills, will also be very relevant, particularly for those types of social capital that emphasize deep relationships rather than extensive connections.

However, a lot of what makes social relationships work relates to the organizational architecture. This is supported by research from CEB Corporate Leadership Council (2012), which suggests that enterprise contribution varies with both peer knowledge and relationships. Knowledge of peers' work characteristics had an average impact on enterprise contribution of 4 per cent, double the impact of personal relationships. The two most impactful enablers were: 1) knowing what co-workers are accountable for (6 per cent); and 2) knowing how their own work relates to co-worker's work (6 per cent). It is also supported by a more recent research finding – that knowing others' expertise, and competence-based trust, are both more important in supporting collaboration than interpersonal familiarity and personal trust (Gardner, 2017). Therefore, investing in the organizational architecture may require as much time and attention as building an organizational society.

In addition, focusing on relationships and social capital is a little different to emphasizing people and human capital. As explained in Chapter 3, HR/HCM should include organizational actions as well as people-focused ones; however, the people actions themselves can be addressed largely separately from the organizational ones. For example, learning and development in a flat organization is largely the same as in a tall one. In organization development and when focusing on social capital that principle no longer applies. Relationships are always deeply influenced by the context of the organization they exist within. This means that it makes sense to address the organization first.

Part 2 of the book therefore focuses on what I call the organizational architecture, which is the organization that exists around the people, or the way in which people are organized to do work. As explained in Chapter 3, this is not just about structure and systems but the effect of the whole organization, minus the detail within the people- and relationships-oriented elements (staff, skills, shared values and style in the 7S model). These later elements are then picked up in Part 3 of the book, which outlines activities for building, or perhaps growing, what I call the organizational society, which is about the detail within those people- and relationships-oriented elements.

However, although Part 2 deals with what might traditionally be called organization design, including job and team design, I have now redefined organization design to be a discipline focusing on using all elements of an organization to create organization capital. Here, our aim is to use these elements and techniques that tend to be associated with organization design to create social capital. I have therefore avoided using the term organization design as the title of this chapter and have instead chosen a more generic title, organizing people to do work, which supports the shift in focus. We will also need to broaden out our consideration from teams to also include networks and communities. And we will also address a number of other enablers for organizational effectiveness, including the physical workplace.

In all of the chapters in this part of the book, I will first explain the topics I am addressing, which in this case come from organization design, before shifting our focus from organization to social capital to show how the same areas can be used to build a social organization. To help me do this, I need to introduce you to the organization prioritization model.

The organization prioritization model

Designing an organization requires the use of an organization model such as the McKinsey 7S or one of those I referred to in Chapter 3. However, none of these models are really fit for purpose in today's organizational context, and they all struggle when considering the design of the social organization. In particular, not all of the well-known models recognize the dynamic character of organizations with design of an organizational architecture being an activity that provides the outcomes an organization is trying to create. Many of the models also fail to include sufficient elements to cover the complicated nature of the modern organization. In particular they lack specific reference to social relationships, which I have already suggested in Chapter 4 should really be an additional element in a retitled McKinsey 8S model.

The elements that other models do include are also not always the most important. In particular, they tend to give too much attention to structure. This is an important aspect of organization design but it is not the most important thing. However, because traditional organization charts make structure the most tangible aspect of an organization it is the element that everyone fixates on. It should not be. Structure does what the word suggests, it structures the way people do their work. That is important but not as important as the work, or the people, or the connections between the people.

My own organization prioritization model (OPM), provided as Figure 6.1, gets round these and other difficulties. The top line of this model emphasizes that designing an organizational architecture is about developing outcomes in a way that achieves certain objectives. The objectives are the desired organizational capabilities and the organization principles that explain how the organization is expected to work. The outputs are the three capitals. The other benefits of the model are outlined below.

Figure 6.1 The organization prioritization model (OPM)

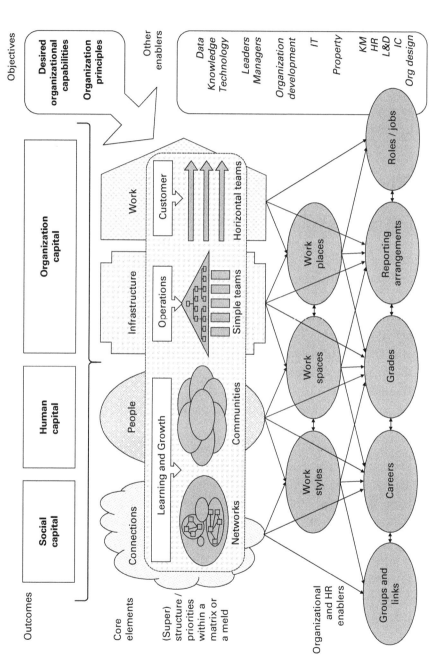

SOURCE © Jon Ingham (2017)

The OPM has been developed for use in organization design and may seem overly 'boxy' for dealing with social relationships. However, even when focusing on social capital, organizational architecture is usually more complicated than complex, and therefore the analytical perspective that underpins this model still applies. However, I accept that any model developed specifically for creating social capital would probably be drawn more artfully, with less use of arrows and boxes, perhaps a bit more like Elizabeth McMillan's fractal web model, which is based on the workings of a heart (McMillan, 2008).

The core elements of an organization

The OPM references more elements than more traditional models because organizations have become more complicated, meaning that a larger group of elements need to be integrated together if the whole organization is going to operate optimally. However, to make using the model as simple as possible it divides these elements into just four core elements, ie the ones we most need to pay most attention to, and a broader set of enablers, which support these core elements and need to be aligned with them but are not so pivotal to organizational effectiveness. These core elements and enablers are the set of activities that can be used in the organization value chain to create the three capitals and other outcomes.

The core elements are the people and the connections between them, the work of the organization, ie its organizational processes and its infrastructure. The OPM's infrastructure element, together with the superstructure, broadly make up what other models such as McKinsey's 7S refer to just as structure. Together with the work element, these are the 'hard', physical, tangible aspects of organizations. (I tend to use the term structure quite loosely to refer to the combination of both infra- and superstructure, or just to superstructure – you should be able to work out which of these options I am referring to.)

You should hopefully recognize some additional links between the OPM's core elements and the 7S model too. In case not, let me explain that the OPM's work element closely corresponds to the 7S's systems. People are the 7S's staff and skills. Connections are probably the closest equivalent to the 7S's shared values. Style falls between the people and relationship elements. As with the 7S, the OPM can be used as an 'organizational excellence' model to demonstrate linkages between the elements (see my description of Spotify's organizational architecture in Chapter 9). And it can also be used for change management. Used in this context, the elements of the model are used to describe the activities needed to make the required changes, rather than the elements themselves. For example, the people element might focus on how the recruitment process has changed, and how many people have been recruited and trained etc, rather than, or as well as, increases in head-count or improvements in skills etc.

Some readers may also notice a similarity to Vlatka Hlupic's six box lead-ership model (Hlupic, 2014). This model is largely based on relationships and individuals (which together with culture make up the model's people-related aspects) and resources and systems (which together with strategy are its process-related aspects). This model was developed based on an extensive amount of other research. The main difference between the core elements in the OPM and the six box model is that the former relates to the whole organization, not just leadership.

The rest of this chapter will use the OPM and, in particular, a review of the core elements to recommend some of the best design choices for social organizations.

Infrastructure

My review of the OPM's core elements will begin with infrastructure, as starting here aligns with the traditional ordering of work steps in organi-zation design. As noted earlier, infrastructure refers to the hard, tangible aspects of an organization that provides the foundation for how, or the container within which, people do the organization's work. It includes:

- Ownership and distribution of profits.
- Budgets and funding mechanisms.
- Locations of the company's operations and offices.
- Support services.
- The head office and arrangements for coordinating with the rest of the business.
- Governance structures, including governance of the organization design.
- Policies on the organization design, cascaded from the organization prin-ciples. These might include guidance on the use of chief operating officers and access to personal assistants.
- Other aspects of power and control such as the entitlements provided at different levels in the organization.

- Knowledge, which refers to the tangible documents and data owned or accessible by a business, eg all the information in its intranet. It also includes all of the company's patents and other intellectual capital. (Tacit knowledge in our brains is included in the people element of the OPM. There is also a form of knowledge embedded in our relationships that means we can pick up conversations where we left off. This is included within the connections element.)

Infrastructure also underpins the organization's superstructure, which deals with how accountabilities are managed. The superstructure will be based on one of several types of social network, including simple and horizontal teams, and communities and networks. The choice of superstructure affects all the other elements in the OPM and significantly influences people's experience of an organization. However, the OPM deliberately delays consideration of the role of superstructure as a response to the way that many business leaders and HR/OD practitioners put too much and too early a focus on it.

For example, my typical experience of meeting a client to talk about organization design is that they will have already scoped out a hierarchical organization chart on a piece of paper. This is the wrong approach on at least four levels. Is the client's problem really about organization or something else, eg the business strategy or the leadership? If the organization is the issue, is superstructure really the thing that needs to be changed? If so, does it really need a hierarchical (probably functional) superstructure, or something else? Finally, now that the client has identified a potential solution are they still going to be prepared to consider other options (for example, by using the options identification process from Chapter 5) or will they become anchored by the option they have developed? Partly to avoid this issue the OPM is designed to make it more likely that superstructure will only be chosen after considering each of the four core elements. Therefore, I will leave explanation about the choice of superstructure until Chapters 7 and 8.

Even without thinking about the superstructure, infrastructure has a direct and critical impact on organization capital and can have an important role for social capital as well. For example, research suggests that clarity about power structures helps relationships to form and develop more easily, whereas lack of clarity leads to dysfunctional competition (Gruenfeld and Tiedens, 2010). Clarity also supports the brain's need for certainty. However, the most important infrastructure-related issue as far as social capital is concerned is the ownership structure of the business.

Ownership structure

Most of the time we categorize organizations into private sector, public sector and the third or voluntary sector. In each of these categories people are directed and managed on behalf of investors, the government or other stakeholder interests respectively. However, there are alternative ways of thinking about and structuring the ownership of an organization, which give more focus to the people working in that organization.

The logic for doing this is that people who put their time into an organization are clearly making a greater contribution and have a larger stake in the success of the organization than its shareholders or other external stakeholders. The need to create value makes it even clearer that we need to see the owners of a business as those who are working in it not merely those who are supporting it financially. Charles Handy puts it well, suggesting that we should see shareholders less as owners and more as financiers, being rewarded for taking a risk with their financial capital. But the owners are the people who loan a company their human capital. He suggests these people need to be treated more like citizens living in a village, having rights and responsibilities to others. In a company the rights need to include access to a share in the profits they have created (Fisher, 2003). Doing this helps align everyone's interest in a business, raises engagement and forms a positive team spirit.

The first option is to make employees the true owners. Employee-owned companies and cooperatives either distribute their shares to their employees or place these in an employee trust. Either option means that each person working for the company has a much more equal share in its future and a more equal vote in how it is run (see the case study on Union Industries below). Other examples include cooperatives that seek to distribute power through equal ownership, such as those in the Mondragon Corporation in Spain, and the B Team movement originating in the United States.

The second approach is to incorporate the employee's voice on the board of directors. The German system of codetermination is a frequently discussed example of this. German union or works council officials take up to half the seats on the supervisory boards of larger companies. This is seen to help communication between workers and management and also encourages a long-term perspective. Employee representatives need to reach a consensus with management and must sell this to the workforce, leading to less adversarial employee relations. It also encourages a fair distribution of wealth.

Some form of employee board representation is also currently being considered in the UK, where current governance systems are increasingly acknowledged to be failing. Alternative ideas include setting up employee advisory panels or appointing particular non-executive directors to take an employee viewpoint. However, non-executives often come from the same circles as executives and can therefore fail to hold them to account. They also often fail to provide good governance of the organizations for the shareholders they currently represent. Placing employee representatives on the board would help to deal with both these problems.

The third main opportunity to ensure employees have a stake in the success of a business is simply to reflect people's contribution through the allocation of equity using an employee share ownership scheme or to simply share success through a profit distribution programme (particularly in those organizations that do not have equity). This approach is being boosted by an increasing number of start-ups, which often incentivize their initial recruits with ownership stakes, although this can also cause conflict between early and later joiners.

Profit sharing helps align people with corporate interests. Share schemes do this and may help people think more like owners too. Neither are as useful as true ownership but both are better than the most common scenario in which most people feel little connection to their company's profits. This can mean that people question why they should work harder when it is mainly investors and fund managers who benefit from their efforts. As described in Chapter 5, corporate encouragements to produce a better return for shareholders do not work for many people now. It is not that people need a share in profits – as discussed in Chapter 4, financial reward – in developed economies at least – often has less relevance too. It is just that a distribution of profits to shareholders firstly reduces the status of an organization's purpose and secondly raises questions around just how much a company really cares about its people.

The situation is even worse where, as often happens, profit sharing is limited to a company's executives. This moves the general employee even further down the pecking order and also further separates the haves from the have nots. Partnership structures such as those found in many professional services firms can suffer similar consequences too. See more on the tensions created by these sorts of divisions in Chapter 11.

CASE STUDY   Employee ownership at Union Industries

Union Industries is a manufacturer of high-speed industrial doors based in my original home town of Leeds in the UK. It became an employee-owned company in 2014. I met up with Paul Schofield (Mr S) who founded the company with his wife back in 1972. Mr S took me on a tour of their premises, which displayed ongoing care and attention and a sense of the firm's history, for example, featuring the original sewing machines used by Mrs S when they started up the business repairing tarpaulin. Mr S noted that both he and his wife enjoyed the theatre and had used their sense of drama and their imagination to develop the premises in their own image – something most corporates do not do. I also noted a prominent display board showing measures of business performance.

The company has developed largely as a result of Mr S's interests in developing long-term relationships with customers and solving their problems as these occur. At different points in time the company has been asked to create new products and has generally said yes. This has led them from their original focus on tarpaulin to selling a multiplicity of innovative products based upon some commonalities in skills. The company's doors are built to last and are therefore relatively expensive but come with lifetime warranty to cover what is expected to be very limited maintenance. Rather than marketing its doors Union relies on its relationships to create pull. To support these long-term relationships and complicated range of products the company needs good people and to retain these people for as long as it can.

Supporting these needs and the founders' own approach, the company operates a little like a family. Mr S explained this as 'if you're with us you're with us, if not you're against us'. As an example of the approach, one of his employees did not have an indoor bathroom so the company put one in for him. This sense of closeness made thinking about retirement bothersome for Mr and Mrs S. Mr S had looked at a trade sale but knew that an acquiring company would probably move to make Union more efficient, which would risk losing the company's ethos and *raison d'être*. When they came across employee ownership this therefore seemed like a natural fit, as it would provide people with an opportunity to take charge of their own destiny.

Initially, this was a difficult sell internally as a lot of people came from mining areas, for example, where they may have never met anyone who owned shares and saw 'the boss' in a very different light to themselves. In addition, the existing directors did not want to become principals of the business so the founders needed to recruit a new managing director (MD). Supporting the new focus on employee involvement the founders got staff involved in this selection process. In total 12 people were involved, which included a welder, storekeeper, bookkeeper, secretary etc, operating in two teams. Each team listened to the presentations of the shortlisted candidates and then agreed together on the new MD, Andrew Lane, as being the best person for the job.

The company was sold to an employee trust at what the founders believe was a fair price, or at least was not ultra-altruistic. Importantly they also left cash in the business, which is now being paid off each month in a way that the business can sustain. The company also runs a share incentive plan so that, as well as owning the company through the trust, people would have their own shares and their own physical share certificates. Everyone was given £250 of shares on the transaction and everyone else who joins since then gets £50 on the first anniversary of their employment. People can buy up to a further £250 of shares each year too.

The company is run by a board of directors but a trust board comprising five trustees – two employees, two independents (one a former HR director) and a chairperson (currently one of the founders) – have a legal duty to oversee the board. The trust works to a list of special permissions such as that to dispose of an asset it has to get the agreement of a majority of employees and the former owners also have to agree. This is largely to protect the building as part of the company's heritage and ways of working. Directors have to resign every three years and reapply for their roles, getting elected at the AGM on a show of hands. There is also an employee council that elects its own people, runs it own meetings and talks about the company. Lane goes in to answer questions at the end of each meeting too.

Lane also organized a choreographed series of events leading up to and beyond the sale in order to keep people engaged in the changes. He also worked to increase people's financial understanding as owners of the business. They got shown the P&L and were trained to understand key financial ratios and simple indicators such as the numbers of doors sold per month. These were the numbers being tracked on the installation board I had noticed on my tour. Lane explains to people that if the board is full then they are making money. Mr S had tended to protect people from bad news but that can lead people towards focusing on the worst possible case. Lane is focused on collective intelligence – the idea that the more people who are involved in making a decision the better that decision will be.

Union also seems like a fun place to work. When I met Lane he was wearing Union Jack socks (the flag is part of Union's logo) to show he is not just a man in an ivory tower. ('I have difficult decisions to explain and am always open to questions. People may not agree but I like them to understand.') Occasionally he will even make a daft decision so that he can later reverse it and people will see that he is human. (I was given an example of a suggestion to shut a machine shop where people liked to work because they loved the fish-and-chip shop round the corner, but actually the employees were right to want to keep it open.) Most senior people spend time wearing overalls, working as an installer to remind them what it is like at the coal face and so that people see them immersed the business.

Lane gave me several examples of people stepping up and taking responsibility because they now know this is what the business requires rather than they are obliged to do so. People are also more collaborative – for example, sales people and installers work together to keep the installation board full.

The company has performed well since the transaction, enabling it to pay good and unexpected bonuses to all employees. Lane tells people that they earned the money, all the board does is to distribute it. Everyone, including directors, now gets the same sum of money rather than the same (or even a graduated) percentage of salary as their bonus. The idea has been to turn away from corporate greed for the greater good. This has obviously helped keep people on board with the new arrangement too.

Work

Work refers to the undertakings of the organization and is performed through the design, implementation and improvement of processes. These are flows of work involving one or more inputs, a logical sequence of related activities that involves some sort of transformation, and one or more outputs or outcomes. These are the central parts of the SIPOC acronym that I referred to in Chapter 1 and which consists of a supplier, an input, the process, an output and a customer. Other aspects of a process definition include governance, management information, automation and in/out sourcing.

Work processes drive the organization and support the rest of the business. Examples include planning, budgeting, reporting and other organizational management processes. Another more specific and unusual example is Zappos's organizational governance process, which is described in Chapter 8.

Processes are in many ways the basic building blocks of organizations. An organization is fundamentally just a group of people organized to do work, ie to undertake one or more processes. We should think about organizations less as structure and more as a set of processes. For this reason I tend to focus on processes before looking at infrastructure.

However, this is not the way organization design is typically done. For example, Jay Galbraith (1977), in his explanation of the star model, suggests that structure needs to come before processes because processes exist to operationalize the structure. But if you think about business strategy this usually proceeds right to left along Kaplan and Norton's strategy map reviewed in Chapter 1. So strategists think about the products they are going to sell to provide margin, then the customers who will buy the products, then the business processes that will support these customers and manufacture the products, and finally move on to the organization. It makes sense to continue focusing on processes by moving from business processes to organizational processes (from outside to inside the organization value chain), particularly as these processes frequently become integrated anyway.

As an example, one of the largest organizational restructuring projects I have ever managed was an internal merger at a travel chain. The idea was to integrate holiday operations with retail bookings by creating better sharing of knowledge between the two groups. This required a new management process. When we redesigned the structure we organized the new roles to implement the business's operational processes selling and operating holidays, but also this new management process passing information backwards between these two divisions.

Therefore, to me, it is more sensible to start with work processes and then develop the required infrastructure around these processes. This is why the OPM places infrastructure between work and the other core elements of the organization. The need for this ordering can also be seen in a best-practice approach or methodology to process design. For example, this is the approach I use when I design processes.

Process design

1 Develop a clear definition of the process and the changes that are required:
  - Agree the objectives of the process, supporting the business objectives/organizational capabilities that the process has to meet.
  - Agree the start and end points of the process.
  - Agree the major changes between the current state and the future state of the process.
  - Specify clear principles, cascading from the overall organization principles, and also clear rules that will ensure the principles are adhered to.

2 Develop high-level to detailed process outlines. This potentially starts with a top-level value chain, which might be referred to as level 1, and drills down into more detailed process maps at levels 2 and perhaps 3, and then, where appropriate, task listings as level 4, and finally work instructions as level 5. This low level of detail may be appropriate when there are high numbers of low-skilled people with high turnover, or when there are certain compliance requirements, or just so that volume metrics can be estimated (doing this tends to be more accurate at more detailed levels). Otherwise it helps to give people certain freedom in how they execute a process.

3 Plan for the execution of the process. This planning is often completed at high and then at more detailed levels, in parallel with step 2 above:

– Identify volume metrics to help size the relevant part of the organization.

– Understand competency requirements to execute the process.

– Organize process by roles/jobs, based upon appropriate clustering of both activities and competencies.

– Complete RACI analysis or similar, identifying the roles/jobs that accountabilities and responsibilities for each process step will be assigned to.

– Develop a structure to help manage the people working in these roles, grouping activities together to minimize handoffs between those involved in delivering the process and also ensuring roles are built on sensible clusters of competencies.

RACI analysis

RACI analysis is a popular tool used in process design, project management and relationship improvement. It suggests that different types or levels of ownership or involvement need to be specified for each step in a process or project. These levels are accountability, responsibility, who needs to be consulted and who needs to be informed, and they form a hierarchy of interests from accountability at the top to being informed at the bottom. I explained the difference between accountability and responsibility in an HR context in Chapter 1. People often think that clarifying responsibility is enough to make things clear but experience suggests this still leaves a lot of unhelpful ambiguity. In particular, it helps to specify both accountability for achieving an output or outcome separately from the responsibility for undertaking an activity.

By the way, readers who have been paying attention may have noticed that since accountability forms the top of the hierarchy the tool should really be called ARCI analysis, but RACI sounds more polite so this is the general acronym that is used. The other thing to note is that there are suggestions that RACI can constrain agility. However, I have often found it helpful, just as long as it is not taken down to too low a level of detail.

4 Plan for the management of the process within the broader organization design:

- Identify interdependencies with other processes and other organizational elements.

- Identify measures and set targets for process activities and outputs/outcomes.

- Use identified measures to document expected benefits from process changes, which can be used to complete the business case for change.

- Document the new process (once the business case has been signed off and go ahead has been given to make the change). This often includes presenting the process flows using 'swim lane' diagrams in which each individual's sets of activities can be easily identified in their own row.

This flow of activity shows very clearly that structure is developed around a process, not the other way around. By the way, it also suggests that roles should be based on competencies, rather than competencies identified for a role, which is what usually happens today.

The approach works for process improvement, which focuses on the current state, or process re-engineering, which starts with a future-oriented blank sheet of paper. Whilst this approach lost popularity after the publication of *Reengineering the Corporation* (Champy and Hammer, 1993) – when many businesses failed to gain the benefits this book suggested they would – it does still have a potentially valuable role. In fact since the time this book was published process complexity has grown substantially, meaning that the opportunities for re-engineering are even more pronounced. This can be seen in Boston Consulting Group's analysis of 100 US and European listed companies, which found that over a 15-year period the amount of complexity assessed by the number of layers, coordination bodies and decision approvals needed had grown by 50–350 per cent. Managers can now spend up to 40 per cent of their time writing management reports and another 30 per cent in coordination meetings (Morieux, 2011). Therefore, re-engineering is potentially even more valuable today than it was in the 1990s.

Processes are less important to organization development and social capital than to organization design and organization capital. However, they still have a significant impact on social organizational effectiveness. Therefore, social organization architects, HR strategists and others should understand how to design them.

Gamification

One interesting change that is impacting process design, based upon the increasing need for people-centricity, which was reviewed in Chapter 2, is gamification. Although this is often confused with serious gaming it really is quite different. To me at least, gamification is simply the design of processes with a joint intent to meet business objectives but also to provide a compelling basis for motivating the people undertaking a process. This is more like the joint objectives people have when they play a game. Step 1 of my approach is therefore amended to refer to both of these objectives. This is then followed by thinking about the way that people can be motivated and whether this can be supported by game mechanics, which are the aspects of games that tend to make them compelling for people. These can often be seen to support autonomy, competence and relatedness – the three factors from self-determination theory that were reviewed in Chapter 3.

The three main mechanics are points, badges and leaderboards, also called PBL. The danger is that a PBL approach can overemphasize status, encouraging unhealthy competition and leading to dysfunctional behaviours. However, there are a broad range of other game mechanics that can be used. For example, gamification can also focus on creating things like meaning and collaboration, using mechanics that drive intrinsic reward. A good, if very simple, example is allowing people who are successful in an activity to do more of this activity. This is an approach often used to reward innovation, for example.

Implementing whatever game mechanics have been chosen may require playing a game, either face to face, as in a board game, or by interacting with an IT system, and potentially other people through this system, on a digital device. For example, boring computerized tasks can sometimes be incorporated into an online game environment that provides points for doing this boring activity, making it seem slightly less dull. Similar systems can be used for work that is already interesting but discretionary, making it more likely that things people know they should do but often do not do them, will actually be done. Taking enough exercise during the working day would be a good example. However, many mechanics can often simply be introduced into normal work processes, without any game-playing activity, helping to support the business and provide a compelling experience too.

John Boudreau provides a good example of PBL-based, non-game-playing gamification at Shanda Games in China, which makes the online version of Dungeons and Dragons. This company realized that its old promotion process and grading structure were boring and decided to gamify them. The system now consists of 100 new levels each consisting of 100 points. Additional points are given out for taking on and implementing particular roles successfully. People now know exactly where they stand and what they would need to do to get promoted. Because this builds autonomy and competence (relatedness could be supported by enabling people to form teams, sharing points between them) the approach now motivates people to take on additional roles and perform well in them – exactly what Shanda wants (Boudreau and Jesuthasan, 2011).

Projects and services

Processes work best for ongoing, continuous workflows such as manufacturing a product or a chemical. A good HR example is social recognition in which people are encouraged to recognize each other on a daily basis. They also work well for discrete time-based but repeatable processes that can be undertaken on a project basis – for example, a quarterly performance review, an annual salary review or an episodic recruitment process.

Processes apply less well when every instance of a discrete project is different from its previous instances. They also struggle in a service environment where work is ongoing but highly variable in nature. Executive coaching and HR business partnering are good examples of these. So would be the support provided by someone who facilitates the agreement process meetings as part of their colleagues' commitments at Morning Star – see Chapter 8.

An explanation for this difficulty is provided by PwC (2011), which describes how the work environments that enterprise workflows operate within range from predictable execution through exception handling to sense making. Predictable execution is an environment where every process instance is the same and processes can follow a completely repeatable series of steps, hence lending themselves to automation via enterprise resource planning and other systems. Unfortunately, very few process environments are like this!

However, processes can also cope when there are a limited number of different inputs or options for activities, which process design refers to as business cases or scenarios. This is what PwC refers to as sense making. An example from recruitment might be where a candidate could be a recent graduate or an experienced hire. A company might decide to have two processes for this, or they might design one process that at some points in the process splits into parallel streams for the two different possibilities.

Unfortunately, a large proportion of environments do not present like this either. In fact, very often these days, things are changing all of the time. This is the exception-handling end of the continuum and processes need to be more highly tailored and can be best enhanced through systems for social collaboration (see Chapter 13). It also helps to keep their design high level and their execution loose and informal. However, the environment eventually becomes so variable that a process has no value at all and every input requires an individualized project or service response.

Verna Allee, a business consultant and writer, builds on similar ideas to suggest that value chains (of the sort explored in Chapter 1 of this book) need to be replaced by a new concept of value networks. The approach basically suggests that in complex situations, processes evolve into networks of value exchanges. Allee shows, for example, how back-and-forth interactions between people and groups can be mapped on a swim-lane diagram normally used for process flows (Allee and Schwabe, 2015).

This is the reason that some businesses in service-based or agile working environments push back against processes and instead focus on approaches such as service design and customer experience management. We will return to this point again when we take a look at process-based organizations in Chapter 7.

Hacks and hackathons

Where processes do still apply the need is often to shorten their cycle time and make them more agile. Process design approaches often need to become more agile as well. Some organizations encourage people to get together on a regular basis to 'hack' their processes. Hacks are simple, iterative and incremental improvements in products and processes. One particular approach to doing this is a hackathon, developed like agile for use in IT but also being extended into other areas of business, including HR. Hackathons can often involve getting together a group of people from different areas of a business to generate more collaborative approaches. They typically start with an initial phase of general divergent brainstorming. This is followed by more specific and directed sharing of ideas and experiences on a few particular opportunities, and the development of new possible solutions. This helps to converge on the areas of greatest opportunity and then to complete a small number of new hacks.

Online hackathons are also possible, such as those organized by Gary Hamel's Management Innovation Exchange (http://www.mixhackathon.org/). These work in a very similar way to a face-to-face hackathon but take place over a longer period, allowing for asynchronous contributions. The two approaches can also be combined, allowing people to get together in different locations that can then be connected together online. This was the approach used for the 'breakathon' organized by Cisco (Meister, 2016). Both the physical and online variants are useful ways to develop processes but are also great activities to develop people's relationships as well.

Hacks are useful but it is important that they do not become kludges! A kludge is an inelegant, superficial solution that fixes a symptom of a problem but not the real problem itself. Many technology customizations are really just kludges, which is why customizable software has developed a bad reputation and why many organizations are moving to cloud-based, configurable not customizable, software as a service (SaaS), which stops them tinkering with their processes.

People

The people element of the OPM deals with creating qualities such as ability, motivation and diversity, ie the same areas reviewed in Chapter 3, but whereas this was about human capital, our need here is to develop social capital. The concern of a social architect will therefore focus on particular, relevant qualities of people such as their skills and motivation to invest in cooperation and collaboration. This is especially as collaboration skills are some of the hardest to develop in people. Increasing diversity is also important, and is potentially even more important for social capital than it is for human capital.

Activities to develop the people element include implementing and improving HR processes and undertaking individually focused development interventions to improve the important social aspects of an organization's people. These actions concern organizational society rather than its architecture, so specific suggestions about these activities are left over to Part 3 of the book and are provided in Chapter 11.

Connections

This last core element reviews how well the people in an organization work together, and in what way, and whether this will provide value for the particular organization. It is the most important element in the OPM as far as social capital is concerned. Although the element is titled 'connections' there are in fact three major parts to it. In addition to people's connections – ie the links they have to other people – these are the relationships that are built upon these connections, and the conversations that take place within these relationships.

Thinking about connections can be usefully informed by reviewing which boundaries between groups might lead to structural holes. CCL suggests that the most common type of challenging boundary (71 per cent) is horizontal, eg across functions and expertise. Just 7 per cent of the most challenging boundaries are vertical, ie between hierarchical levels. Other internal challenges arise from geographic and demographic boundaries (Yip, Ernst and Campbell, 2016). This is one reason that this part of the book focuses more on designing the right groups (Chapters 7 and 8) than it does on managing or reducing hierarchical layers (included in Chapter 9). I also suggest that the biggest problems to do with hierarchy result from hierarchical thinking, not hierarchical structure. In the main, therefore, problems to do with hierarchies need to be dealt with by influencing people's behaviours (see Chapter 12).

The main requirement in terms of people's connections is to make sure people are linked to those they need to inform, be informed by, be able to work with, or otherwise be in contact with to fully participate in the organization. This might include, for example, to support needs for coaching or mentoring. Sometimes the importance of a role may mean people need to be closely connected to social influencers to ensure they are able to receive and send communications to the rest of the organization effectively. The organization may also need to connect people to others who are not necessary or at least not core to people doing their jobs – for example, to include weak as well as strong ties. These are often the hardest connections to develop and maintain.

Social organization designers also need to think about the number of connections they are asking people to have. However, this is addressed as part of the groups and links element in the OPM and you will find more suggestions on this in Chapter 9.

Once the right connections have been identified these can be associated with a particular role or job – for example, by being included in a job description or as a source of feedback in a performance review etc.

The relationships and conversations aspects of the connections element will be largely defined by the organization's superstructure, which will be reviewed in Chapters 7 and 8. Other relevant activities include social HR processes (ie those that are about improving relationships rather than just individual effectiveness), team facilitation, organization development, use of enterprise social networks and social network analysis. These are reviewed in Part 3.

Organizational enablers

Directly under the core elements, the OPM also includes three organizational enablers. The first of these is the workplace, which will be reviewed in Chapter 10. The second is the digital workspace, which will be discussed in Chapter 13. The third organizational enabler is the organization's workstyles. These include the implemented policies and lived values that are demonstrated through the organization's social norms and people's ongoing, informal behaviours. Four important workstyles are reviewed below.

The first of these is the way people are involved in the organization. This can result from the formal cascade of decision rights and the flow of information in the organization, as well as whether managers are authoritarian or consultative. Another aspect of this workstyle is the symbols of privilege that reinforce status differences and lead to people being included or excluded from decisions and activities. These symbols include parking spaces, separate restaurants, corner offices and proximity to the windows. The importance of involvement and also of symbols of privilege are what leads to Isaac Getz's suggestion that creating a liberated company starts with treating everyone with similar rights and privileges. Doing this leads to higher trust, initiative and engagement within the organization (Carney and Getz, 2009).

Flexible working is another important workstyle factor and includes both home working and flexible working time. These approaches normally involve a trade-off between making work easy for people and bringing people together to connect and collaborate, ie between being human and social. The importance of the social side of this balance was demonstrated by Yahoo! cancelling home working, for example, and asking everyone to come into the office. Unfortunately this change was not introduced in a very empathetic way (Lindsay, 2013).

A third important workstyle concerns uniforms and dress codes. Formal clothes signal authority and control and get in the way of more personal connection. (There is a similar distinction between hardback and softback books, which is why this book comes with a soft binding.) Also many companies suggest they encourage dress flexibility but managers and sales people still often wear suits or expensive chinos whilst other staff groups wear jeans. It means nothing on its own but it signals and reinforces a great deal. It is for this reason that one NHS Trust in the UK has experimented with having all their staff wear the same uniform rather then demarcating their status as doctors, nurses, health-care assistants, ward clerks, students or cleaners (I think they have something in place so that you know not to call over a cleaner if you are having a heart attack).

A final interesting and important workstyle relates to the amount and type of physical contact in an organization. From a social brain perspective, proximity and human touch are central to human relatedness, producing high levels of oxytocin. However, in today's workplace, an increasing focus on digital communication and social and legal restrictions over physical contact mean that touch is increasingly limited to a handshake. There is no easy way to change this but I do think it can suboptimize connecting. Certainly, in my own experience, the most trusting organizations I have worked in have all been ones where there has been a level of hugging and kissing. Psychology professor Dacher Keltner suggests that touch provides its own language of compassion and is essential to what it means to be human (Keltner, 2010).

Other enablers

Shown below the organizational enablers in the OPM are the HR enablers – other supporting elements of an organization that are more likely to be seen as HR rather than broader management practices. These HR enablers are reviewed in Chapter 9. However, the OPM includes one further set of enablers on the right-hand side of Figure 6.1. The first three of these other enablers are data, knowledge and technology. These are all having increasingly profound impacts on organizations and it is possible I do not do them justice within the model. However, they are not completely absent. Data is created and used in each of the elements. Knowledge flows across the model too and is particularly relevant within infrastructure (explicit knowledge), people (tacit knowledge) and relationships (social knowledge). Technology is everywhere too, particularly in work processes (automation and operational reporting), infrastructure (management information), people (productivity systems) and connections (enterprise social networks). We will also return to the use of technology and data in Chapter 13.

Other enablers also include the role of leaders and managers, which was addressed in Chapter 5. The final set of enablers are the roles of all the service groups responsible for organization development, property, IT, knowledge management, HR, learning and development, internal communication and organization design. These all need to be designed and set up appropriately, and also be formed in a way that will enable collaboration across the different professional areas.

Summary and additional comments

1 All the elements in the OPM are aspects of an organization that could contribute to organizational capability. These can be developed by actions that could be included as activities in the organization value chain. The core elements of the OPM provide a particularly important area of focus for organizing people to do work and these all need to be considered before turning attention to organizational superstructure.

2 Social organization designers will want to consider how all four core elements support the development of a social organization. Key areas to consider include the role of company ownership; the design of processes, services and projects and how these promote social exchanges, including through gamification and hackathon-type activities; as well as the attitudes and diversity of people and the connections and relationships between these people.

3 The OPM and the core elements in the model also help to identify the type of superstructure that will be most useful for a particular organization. This will be explained in Chapter 8.

References

Allee, V and Schwabe, O (2015) *Value Networks and the True Nature of Collaboration*, Meghan-Kiffer Press, Tampa

Boudreau, J and Jesuthasan, R (2011) *Transformative HR: How great companies use evidence-based change for sustainable advantage*, Wiley & Sons, New York

Carney, BM and Getz, I (2009) *Freedom, INC.: Free your employees and let them lead your business to higher productivity, profits, and growth*, Random House, New York

CEB Corporate Leadership Council (2012) [accessed 12 January 2017] Driving Breakthrough Performance in the New Work Environment, *CEB* [Online]

https://www.cebglobal.com/content/dam/cebglobal/us/EN/top-insights/
executive-guidance/pdfs/eg2013ann-breakthrough-performance-in-the-new-work-
environment.pdf

Champy, J and Hammer, M (1993) *Reengineering the Corporation: A manifesto for
business*, HarperCollins, New York

Fisher, LM (2003) [accessed 12 January 2017] The paradox of Charles Handy,
Strategy+business, **32** (Fall) [Online] http://www.strategy-business.com/
article/03309

Galbraith, JR (1977) *Organization Design*, Addison-Wesley, Boston

Gardner, HK (2017) *Smart Collaboration: How professionals and their firms
succeed by breaking down silos*, Harvard Business Review Press, Boston

Gruenfeld, DH and Tiedens, LZ (2010) Organizational preferences and their
consequences, in *Handbook of Social Psychology*, 2, pp 1252–87, ed ST Fiske,
DT Gilbert and G Lindzey, John Wiley and Sons, New Jersey

Hlupic, V (2014) *The Management Shift: How to harness the power of people
and transform your organization for sustainable success*, Palgrave Macmillan,
Basingstoke

Keltner, D (2010) [accessed 12 January 2017] Hands On Research: The Science
of Touch, *Greater Good* [Online] http://greatergood.berkeley.edu/article/item/
hands_on_research

Lindsay, G (2013) Engineering serendipity, *New York Times*, 5 April

McMillan, E (2008) *Complexity, Management and the Dynamics of Change:
Challenges for practice*, Routledge, London

Meister, J (2016) [accessed 9 March 2017] Cisco HR Breakathon: Reimagining the
Employee Experience, *Forbes*, 3 October [Online] https://www.forbes.com/sites/
jeannemeister/2016/03/10/the-cisco-hr-breakathon/#4667db51f5ee

Morieux, Y (2011) Smart rules: six ways to get people to solve problems without
you, *Harvard Business Review*, September

PwC (2011) [accessed 12 January 2017] Transforming Collaboration With Social
Tools, *Technology Forecast* [Online] https://www.pwc.com/us/en/technology-
forecast/2011/issue3/assets/transforming-collaboration-with-social-tools.pdf

Yip, J, Ernst, C and Campbell, M (2016) *Boundary Spanning Leadership: Mission
critical perspectives from the executive suite*, Centre for Creative Leadership,
North Carolina

Selecting an organization structure – traditional opportunities

07

Introduction

Organization structure – or really, here, superstructure – builds upon the rest of the infrastructure core element. It provides a way for organizations to enable, coordinate and motivate their people so that they can deliver their work. It does this by arranging individuals into groups and by creating organizational networks to allocate objectives, tasks, responsibilities and resources to these groups, subgroups and individuals. Structure is also supported by organizational reporting arrangements that define the flow or cascade of accountability – for example, from a manager to their reports – but this is included in the OPM as a separate enabling element – see Chapter 9. And it is also supported by policies on decision rights and on flows of information but these are included within the workstyles element that was reviewed in Chapter 6. It is important to note that there is nothing in the superstructure element that suggests all decisions need to take place at the top of a hierarchy or that communication can only flow within, not between, groups.

The easiest way to explain the different structures an organization may want to use is to describe the main structural archetypes that have developed over time. Most organizations use one or more of these archetypes, suitably tailored and adapted to meet their own specific needs. Providing this description will be the focus of this chapter and the next. This chapter deals with the more traditional and still most prevalent organization structures that most readers will recognize, often from personal experience. The structure of the chapter is shown in Figure 7.1. Chapter 8 will then deal with the more modern organization structures that are not so common but deserve more attention in the social organization.

Figure 7.1 Traditional organization structures

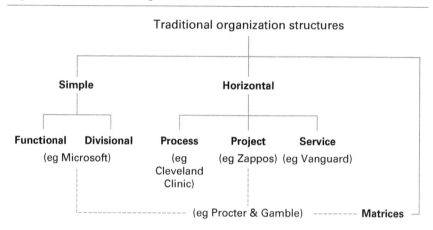

Each of the archetype descriptions is supported by an example (I just use one example to cover functional and divisional structures since these are generally well understood already). These are not necessarily focused on generating social capital, they are mainly just good case studies of the particular archetype. Social organizations would use these archetypes, or modified versions of these, slightly differently from the case study organizations in order to create social capital.

Most of the examples are also quite well known maverick organizations. However, other commentaries on them are not always clear about what these models are demonstrating (partly because they are not using a model that defines structures as clearly as the OPM). Using these same examples provides me with the opportunity to demonstrate the archetypes I am describing and also to show what is really so special about the examples, which should help reinforce understanding of the archetypes.

As you read through these archetypes you should notice links back to the core elements of the OPM described in Chapter 6.

Simple/functional organizations

Simple organizations are centralized networks that divide work into specialisms. This arrangement often results in higher productivity than having generalists undertaking a broader mix of activities. People within the specialisms are normally organized in a tree structure (like the connections shown with a solid line in Figure 7.1) with multiple reports for each manager (one person reporting to a manager is generally a bad idea – see Chapter 10). Social relationships tend to point towards the top of the structure (ie the centre of the network). This tree structure can look very simple but organizations that use only this structure may find that it does not reflect the actual way in which works get done.

Simple organizations were the first formal organizations to emerge in history. An example is the organization of legions in the Roman army. These consisted of about 5,500 men led by a legatus and a camp prefect together with an aquilifer who carried the eagle standard. Legions were divided into 10 cohorts. Nine of these consisted of 480 soldiers divided into six centuries, each headed by a centurion. The first cohort consisted of around 800 specialists such as surveyors, builders, blacksmiths, medical staff, veterinaries, soothsayers and priests. This cohort was divided into five centuries and was led by the highest-ranking centurion in the legion, who was called the Primus pilus. Each century also included a small number of specialists such as the optio, who helped provide training. The organization was supported by well-developed career paths – for example, the legatus was often a development role to be a future provincial governor. The exception to this was the centurion role, which was generally only vacated when the role holder was killed in battle.

In modern times, simple structures were popularized by companies like Ford assigning work to specialized production workers and then bringing work to them via the assembly line. They are also often the first to be implemented as an organization grows, once it realizes that its lack of organization is starting to result in disorganization. This is usually once it employs about 50 people, which is the point that it will typically get its first HR person too.

The vast majority of simple organizations are organized around functions (eg the procurement, manufacturing and distribution departments of a traditional financial value chain) or divisions (see below). For example, a larger HR department organized on functional lines would probably have specialists for areas such as recruitment, learning, performance management and employee relations as well as a service centre. The model is still very similar to that used by the Roman military. Those who criticize functional organizations should perhaps be grateful that at least today's bosses do not carry around 3-foot staffs and use these for beating their reports!

Most simple organizations also arrange their people in hierarchies, which is part of the reporting-arrangements element in the OPM. However, doing this is not a requirement and simple organizations are best characterized by their separate vertical specialisms rather than by their hierarchies of horizontal layers. Other structures can have hierarchies, only simple structures have vertical specialisms.

People within a function or other simple structure can work together as a team. A good example is a manufacturing cell, which places people in close proximity together with the supplies and equipment they need in order to facilitate the flow of production work. However, particularly in larger organizations, the term 'team' is often used to refer to the people working at a particular hierarchical level within a function, ie the people reporting directly to the same manager. We still tend to call them a team even if people do little work together and potentially experience a level of competition with each other. Even when people do work as a team they tend to work in series to each other, each focusing at a particular point within an overall business process. As Peter Drucker suggested, describing the development of functional units at Ford, they 'play on the team; they do not play as a team' (Drucker, 2009). This is why I tend to refer to people organized this way as a grouping rather than assuming them to be a true team.

A simple structure can also be based on geographies, products or really anything else. The key is that everything is organized around one single dimension. The advantages of simple structure, including the main functional version, include efficiency, clarity and professionalism. These structures are also easily scalable. The main disadvantage is that focus on a single area can distract people from things that are even more important, such as the work that needs to be done and the customers who need to be served. However, this does not need to result in silos. When this occurs it is often a result of badly designed or poorly implemented simple organization, rather than being a consequence of a functional or other simple structure itself. Nothing in my general description of organization structure, nor my more specific outline of simple structures, suggests that people cannot work with others outside of their own group.

Divisional organizations

Divisional organizations are not as simple or as centralized as functional organizations but they are built on the same type of thinking, applying the logic of specialization to organizational management too. They were the next archetype to be developed after functional organizations, particularly in General Motors, where the creation of divisions (Buick, Oldsmobile etc) enabled Alfred Sloan to establish more control over this company. Each divisional head could focus on running their division, with the chief executive focusing on the performance of the divisional heads and the financial or broader high-level performance of the divisions.

Divisional structures are also often the next model to be taken on as organizations grow and become more complex. They help deal with this complexity but can also suffer from lack of coordination across the divisions. However, this move from functional to divisional is not a one-way street.

Functional reorganization at Microsoft

An example of an organization moving in the other direction is Microsoft, which returned to a functional structure following its acquisition (and before the subsequent part disposal) of Nokia.

Rather than divisions representing each of the major product groups (Cloud, Windows, Windows phones, Xbox etc), each with its own engineering, HR and other functions, Microsoft has now organized around these functions, each one managed centrally and covering all the product groups. The formal purpose of the change was to leverage synergies across services and devices. However, if this was its sole objective Microsoft could have created a matrix of the previous divisions together with new cross-divisional units focused on services and devices respectively. This point has led to a lot of speculation in the IT press that the real point of the restructure was to avoid the siloed attitudes that tend to be so prevalent in divisional organizations (Thompson, 2013). This does seem to have been a significant issue in Microsoft, with one well known representation of its organization structure featuring three separate groups shooting at each other (Cornet, 2011).

However, if the real purpose of the reorganization was to create a more social organization then Microsoft may have been better off moving to one of the more modern structures described in Chapter 8. Having said this, social organization architects should not ignore functional and divisional organizations. Most organizations are structured like this – and that is not likely to change. The main opportunity may therefore be to manage the trade-offs involved in the use of these structures so that they can be implemented without causing extensive siloization etc.

Horizontal/process-based organizations

Process-based structures organize people along process lines with most of these people working in parallel along the whole end-to-end process. Social relationships are more horizontal, providing greater, or at least a higher quality of network closure, than in a simple organization. This type of structure was the next model to develop, after functional and divisional structures, emerging in the 1960s and 1970s due to increased focus on customers and a push back against the bureaucracy of divisional organizations. They then gained further support during the short-term burst of attention given to process re-engineering during the 1990s. Today the model is much less popular, at least in its pure form, and most published case studies date back to the 1990s too (Ostroff, 1999). Partly because of this I normally explain the model by describing how different HR would look if part of a process-based organization.

First, of course, you would probably not actually have anything called HR as that is a function and part of a functional perspective on an organization. So instead of this we need to start with the people management process. This might be defined as a level-2 process below the organization value chain, or it might be split into two – a people acquisition process and an internal management process. If we take the first of these, the recruiting process, we might split this into graduates, experienced candidates and contingent hires. Graduate recruitment may then be split by university, and then even by course. So you might have someone at the bottom of the organization responsible just for recruitment from, say, the Chemistry course at Bath University. This is a focused area of activity but it is still very broad because one person might need to do all of the advertising, selection, offer and other activities for this one university course. Compare this to a traditional functional recruitment department where there may be specialists for employer branding, sourcing, advertising, assessment testing, interview administration etc, all working at different points in the overall process.

In practice, you would probably never drill down this far – process-based organizations tend to need a mix of people with different skills and so are usually much more team-based and less hierarchical than functional ones. Teams are generally quite small with just a process manager in charge, supported if necessary by a couple of other management roles.

You might also find that the organization in my example just subsumes people management within each major business process. This would mean the recruiter I referred to above would need to have an even broader span of business as well as HR responsibilities. This means that working in a process-based organization can be exciting work. It is also great for customer service as each customer has one clear person or team focused on them, using the end-to-end process to provide them with value. But it also requires substantial cross-skilling. It may also take people away from their previous identity – for example, they can no longer be an employer branding specialist but must cover the entire high-level process. It is because of the challenges involved in changing mindset and capability that we do not see many process organizations. A possible additional reason is that the development of enterprise resource planning systems since the 1990s has made these structures unnecessary – businesses can now get enough control over their processes without needing their people to be aligned with them.

For all these reasons I have thought about removing process-based organizations from this book. I have left them in for the following five reasons:

1 The logic of process-based organization still makes absolute sense. If organizations want to focus on their core competencies/business processes or the work of the organization then there is no better way of achieving this focus than having everyone working on the process that delivers this.

2 Process-based structures also offer social organizations substantial advantages over functional or divisional structures as their horizontal teams become very much the focus of the business. Teaming becomes a critical imperative for these businesses.

3 There may not be many pure process-based organizations around but there are quite a few examples of organizations that have embedded process organization into parts of their businesses. As an example, the business partner role is somewhat process-based as it focuses on executing HR's relationship management process.

4 There are also a few examples of modern process-based businesses – for example, hospital operator Cleveland Clinic (see the case study below) organizes its consultants, nurses and other medical staff into cross-functional teams working together on particular treatment areas.

5 There are also an increasing number of businesses that in many ways look very similar to process-based organizations – these project-based organizations will be reviewed after the Cleveland Clinic case study, below.

CASE STUDY Medical process-based teams at Cleveland Clinic

Cleveland Clinic is a large medical centre run by a non-profit community trust in Ohio. It focuses on delivering patient-centred medicine and is organized in the same way that its patients think, ie around their conditions. So instead of having its 4,000 doctors and over 40,000 other medical staff structured by their 120 specialisms, Cleveland Clinic is organized into pathology-focused groups called 'institutes'. This means that rather than dealing with multiple departments and negotiating different appointments on a variety of campuses, everything a patient needs is available within the one institute.

This group practice model allows the clinic's people to take a collective and cohesive approach to delivering care. Professionals within an institute work together as a tightly knit team, sharing their knowledge and experience for the benefit of their patients. This is important as there are about 4,000 medical journals publishing about 1,500 medical articles each day, meaning it is impossible for any single individual to keep up with all this knowledge. Working as a team provides a much greater opportunity to provide high-quality, fully informed care.

Each institute works around care paths, which define the standard of care required for a specific disease. Designing these processes is helped by having doctors, nurses, administrators and others on the same team. Executing a care path requires a team to follow the developed process from start to finish. However, at each stage in the process, caregivers can exercise judgement based on their knowledge, experience or gut feeling. Teams are led by physicians who are salaried but on one-year contracts with continuation as well as pay increases subject to an annual performance review. This contrasts with the more common model in the United States where doctors are self-employed and are paid by the numbers of procedures they carry out.

Using a team-based approach to undertake care paths reduces the number of process handoffs; avoids wasteful duplication of tests and scans; makes mistakes less likely; and increases convenience for patients. Chief Executive Toby Cosgrove provides an example from the clinic's epilepsy centre, where before the care path the average time between diagnosis and surgery was seven months. However, only 11.5 days of this time was devoted to direct patient care. The care path reduced the time input to just nine days and the full cycle time was reduced to 3.5 months (Cosgrove, 2014).

Project-based organizations

Project-based organizations are designed around projects focusing on the sort of discrete process instances discussed in Chapter 6 and/or other business requirements. They allow people to come together and collaborate to meet a particular objective. This way of organizing is very popular in a number of business sectors such as IT software development and professional services firms. An example for HR could be a group of HR specialists, business partners and service centre advisers pulled on to a project to manage a particular employee relations issue, or to undertaking a specific project – for example, identifying opportunities for introducing digital HR. Many HR consultants (ie business-partner-level staff owned centrally) also operate in this way.

Typically, there is a resource pool of people who are assigned short term to a particular project or multiple projects. Whilst people are on a project they work for and are reviewed by a project manager, but there is generally someone back in the resource pool who can help deal with conflicting demands from different projects and who looks after people's longer-term skill and career development. This model is also being updated by the trend towards people-centricity I reviewed in Chapter 2. For example, I worked in one business that set a six-month period as the maximum time someone would be assigned to a project before being rotated back into the resource pool. Generally, this was perceived negatively by the company's clients but was believed to be necessary if the people in the organization were to be developed and engaged effectively.

The fact that someone working on a project team can look forward to rotating off their project makes the mindset and capability challenge of this type of organization less of an issue than for process-based organizations. Project-based organizations are also being enabled by enterprise social technologies, which support the coordination of teams without a traditional, hierarchical programme management office structure. This is also making these structures more popular and they are what Deloitte is describing in its 'network of teams' concept (Bersin, 2016). Deloitte sees this type of structure as the main organization model for the future of work – see more on this in the section on melds in Chapter 8.

A focus on projects rather than processes provides more flexibility in what teams do than in a process-based organization. Teams do not need to focus exclusively on processes but can also look at challenges, opportunities or other things. Projects also provide more opportunity to organize around people rather than simply around work. However, the main focus is always on the project. So, for example, even agile teams are only people-centric in terms of looking at different ways in which people might be able to implement a system, there is still often no intent to create extra value from what the people may be able to achieve. Teams can also focus on organizational as well as business projects, helping to make social ways of working easier to implement.

CASE STUDY Holacratic circles at Zappos

I mentioned in Chapter 3 that Zappos had recently implemented an organization model called Holacracy® (Robertson, 2015). This sounds like something very new and different but at its heart it is simply a sociocratic approach (referred to in Chapter 5) applied to a project-based organization. Like other project organizations it has a strong focus on roles rather than people. For example, I understand that Zapponians now refer to each other by role titles rather than by their first names. That does not sound like a very positive thing, particularly in an organization that used to be so people-focused. However, sociocracy also brings to the model a strong focus on teams, called 'circles'. These can focus on specific projects, functions or overall business operations.

The model does have several unique features. Chief amongst these is that circles are self-managing, meaning that there are no mangers (see comments on self-management in Chapter 9). Instead of having people reporting to each other the model has circles reporting into other circles through the use of coordinating 'link' roles in both the higher- and lower-level circles. Lead links are appointed by a higher-level circle to represent its needs to its subcircles. Representative links are elected by members of a subcircle to represent it to the higher-level circle. Cross-links can also connect circles in different hierarchical chains. The process for filling roles and jobs is also unusual as people construct their own jobs as portfolios of roles from different areas of the organization, including from multiple circles.

All of this is enabled through some predefined processes designed to make self-organization simple for people. These are based on a novel selection of organization principles defined in Holacracy's 'constitution'. As an example, this includes the use of 'tensions' to point to ways of closing gaps between current realities and future opportunities.

The most important process focuses on governance within a circle and on improving its 'role-ationships', ie the way roles have been designed to work most effectively with each other. The process is undertaken through monthly meetings of the people working in a role in the circle. These meetings agree on changes to roles and subcircles within the circle or to policies governing the circle's domain, and they also elect circle members to fill the special roles of facilitator, secretary and rep link. There is also a knowledge management system called Glass Frog, which maintains agreements reached during these governance discussions. I think this process is the most positive feature of the model. The organization value chain does need more attention in organizations, regardless of the structure that is used.

However, other organizational processes, particularly those around HR, are not defined by the model, though suggestions for taking action in these areas are provided in Holacracy's 'app store'. For example, the '3-tier partnership app' (HolacracyOne, 2013) provides a means of moving towards employee ownership. The approach categorizes people as regular, tenured or core, depending upon a person's commitment to the organization. People in the latter tiers are seen to have a greater stake in the organization and play a bigger role in recruiting and exiting other people from the organization. They also have greater employment security.

I can understand why Zappos was attracted by this organization model as it is a bit weird and they are too. However, as you may well have seen reported (McGregor, 2015), the company has been struggling with the model's implementation. Partly this is because Holacracy® is so different it was always going to be a challenge (just moving from a functional to a project-based organization is quite challenging, never mind all the other changes around roles and self-management that are required by Holacracy®). Partly it is because Zappos compounded the problem by offering the same type of bounty they offer to new recruits (described in Chapter 3) to their previous managers who would no longer have manager roles to work in. A large proportion of these people took this offer and caused the company a huge loss of its human capital.

However, the main reason for Zappos's problems comes from the choice of the Holacracy® model itself. As described above, the model's focus is very much on roles and not on people. I understand that by enabling people to self-organize Holacracy® can create a liberating environment for people to work in, helping them to be more fully themselves. The clarity provided by its constitution also provides a sound base for people to form trust-based personal relationships. However, the model only creates value through organization capital not human or social capital. Organization designers should consider whether this is enough. For Zappos, with its focus on creating value through happy weird people, I do not think it was. Zappos wanted to create a structure that allowed people to be themselves, a bit like the inhabitants of a city. However, cities are networks not projects. A community- or network-based structure, both of which will be described in Chapter 8, may therefore have been a better choice.

Despite these problems, Holacracy® does offer some advantages for HR and organization designers because there is so much focus on the management of the organization rather than ignoring this in favour of a focus on business requirements.

However, the use of Holacracy® still faces the biggest problem, which is that organization designers should never implement a standard model. Instead, designers should focus on the organizational capabilities and principles they want to achieve. They can then use the sequence of divergent and convergent thinking in the options identification process to select the organization model that best matches these objectives. I think if Zappos had done this they would have ended up with a very different and probably a much more appropriate solution, avoiding a lot of their current problems.

Service-based organizations

Most service-based companies rely on customer service staff following a set process. However, companies that want to provide the highest levels of service need to provide very high levels of freedom for their people, potentially dispensing with process altogether and enabling their people to do whatever is necessary to satisfy a customer. Doing this will often require assembling a short-term network of company staff to resolve an issue, enabling the customer's problem to be dealt with right away.

This is what Dave Gray refers to as a connected company (Gray and Vander Wal, 2014). One of his examples is Vanguard Group, an investment management company, which gives its customer service representatives authority and control to handle a customer's call. The rest of the company acts as a support network that the rep can access if they need to. All members of staff do 'Swiss Army duty', meaning that they go on the phones once every month. This is all part of the company's broader strategy to balance 'I' with 'We'.

Network organizations will be reviewed further as one of the new opportunities outlined in Chapter 8. However, they clearly do occur as an evolution of a horizontal organization as well as the way in which they will be described in the next chapter.

Matrices

The next organization form to become popular for a while was the matrix. This archetype responds to requirements to meet multiple demands or stakeholder needs by incorporating multiple dimensions, eg product and geography, functions and processes etc, within the structure.

Today the archetype is frequently criticized and there are popular alternatives such as the front–back organization, where supply-and-demand-oriented dimensions of a matrix are brought alongside each other and connect together through market-oriented rather than organizational mechanisms.

However, even multidimensional matrices can be made to work. IBM, for example, is currently an eight-dimensional matrix based on functions, products, solutions, customers, geographies, channels and a front–back hybrid of customer facing and a product-and-solution back end.

Design principles that can make matrices effective include:

- Having a soft rather than hard matrix, ie choosing which dimension will be the most important (there will always be one dimension that is most important so design it in rather than leave it to chance).

- Ensuring the dimensions have different types of accountability (eg one for revenue and one for costs).

- Only ever using two dimensions for people management (ie people should never have more than two managers).

- Only having one layer between the two-manager employee and the head of the matrix so that challenges in reconciling the needs of the two managers can be dealt with relatively easily.

- Double-hatting responsibilities across the matrix, eg someone could be both a specialist and a business partner.

However, and once again, success tends to depend upon other elements of the organization, particularly the mindsets of people managing the matrix (Ghoshal, 1990) and their relationships with other managers, rather than the structural choice itself. As long as these other things are done, my advice would be that if you do not need a matrix then you should not use one unnecessarily. But if you need one – ie if you need to reflect a number of different priorities though your structure – then do not be put off. And does a matrix organization work well for a social organization? I think the link probably works the other way around – that an organization needs to be at least partly social in order to operate a matrix.

CASE STUDY Organizing a matrix at P&G

Procter & Gamble (P&G) provides a particularly interesting case study of organization design. From 1987 to 1998 this company used a global matrix of product categories and countries, supported later by global functions. However, the matrix had not been implemented very well – there were too many layers of management and not enough management processes or systems and, as a result of this, the matrix had become off-balanced, with power moving to the wrong dimension (global functions versus regional product categories).

CEO Durk Jager and his successor AG Lafley restructured the company to create a 'four-pillar front–back hybrid matrix'. The front–back organization consists of two independent, parallel units connected via internal market mechanisms. These are the global business units (GBUs) looking after brands and products, and the market development organizations (MDOs) supporting consumers and retailers within countries. The matrix part of the organization comes from corporate functions spanning across and within these groups. The model is also supported by global business services (GBSs), which provide a shared service for internal business processes (Galbraith, 2008).

Most of the routine activities conducted by GBSs were outsourced and the remaining project-oriented activities were reorganized into a project-based, or 'flow-to-the-work' organization. Within this approach, new projects are created to respond to urgent and high-impact opportunities, and as people complete other projects they are assigned to these. The flexibility provided by this model was seen as a key enabler in the successful acquisition and integration of Gillette in 2005 (Martin, 2013).

P&G's model works very well and has therefore been kept in place, with fairly small adjustments (eg most recently a reduction in the number of GBUs from four to two), since 1998. It allows the company to focus on two different dimensions (products and customers). It combines global scale with local focus, and it provides strong and efficient organizational processes. P&G suggests the structure plays an important role in providing its capability to grow, removing many of the traditional overlaps and inefficiencies that exist in many large companies (P&G, 2009b).

The model is also supported by various enablers, many of which I will discuss in Chapter 8, and others that will be reviewed later in the book:

- Aligned management processes such as a single business planning process in which plans and budgets can be reviewed by the various groups working across the matrix.

- An emphasis on cross-functional working, combining existing technical expertise in different ways to help innovate new products. For example, Whitestrips were developed by bringing together people from oral care (who knew about whitening teeth) with people from the fabric and home-care area (who were experts in bleach) as well as people in research and development (who developed new film technologies for the product).

- Communities of practice – described in Chapter 8 – with over 20 communities involving over 0,000 people sharing best practice and solving business problems (Cloyd, 2004).

- The use of social technology, for example P&G's intranet has an 'Ask Me' feature that directs people's problems to 10,000 technical people around the globe.
- Open workplaces with even corporate executive (CXO) offices arranged around a central open space. (Based on an analysis of CXO communication patterns the offices next to the CEO were given to the chief marketing officer and the vice-president of HR. This decision was not popular with the heads of the organization pillars, but AG Lafely noted he was perfectly satisfied with the allocation because P&G is only about two things: its brands and its people.)
- Egalitarian working styles – eg only very few executives have secretaries.
- Updated incentive systems, increasing the variable portion of top executives' pay from 20 to 80 per cent and extending stock options from less than 1,000 employees to over 100,000 people.
- Proactive career development moving people around geographically and through both functional and line positions.
- A collaborative CEO. This applied particularly strongly to AG Lafley who led P&G from 2000–09 and again from 2013–15. His collaborative leadership style complemented the complicated matrix structure and contrasted with that of the previous CEO Durk Jager, who is reported to have boasted about breaking kneecaps and making heads roll (Brooker, 1999), which is never going to be helpful but is particularly inappropriate in a matrix.

I think P&G competes mainly through organization capital but I believe its matrix structure and approach will have created high levels of social capital too. It is worth noting that, upon becoming CEO, AG Lafley suggested he wanted P&G to be known as the company that collaborates better than any other in the world (P&G, 2009a). This statement expressing P&G's mojo probably referred mostly to a desire to increase focus on open innovation through an approach named 'connect and develop'. However, I think the above points show that the company understands the importance of internal social relationships too.

Summary and additional comments

1 Not too surprisingly, given that Chapters 6 to 10 are looking at organization architecture, most of the case studies in these chapters support the creation of organization capital. This is particularly the case for those traditional structures that have been reviewed within this chapter, ie simple and horizontal teams plus matrices.

2 However, I also think that all of the cases, especially P&G, demonstrate the creation of a level of social capital too. P&G in particular has clearly developed a very connected and collaborative organization, which competes not just through its matrix structure but also through the relationships formed within and as a partial result of this matrix. P&G's case also illustrates the benefits of a long-term approach and ongoing tweaking of the organization structure, avoiding the organizational pendulum swinging that I described in Chapter 5.

3 I think the fact that social organizations can work very effectively using one of the traditional structures reviewed within this chapter is part of the reason why they remain so prevalent. In my view, they probably always will remain the most popular archetypes. Social organization designers do therefore need to understand these, and in particular, know how to address the trade-offs inherent in these models.

4 For example, we know that unless we think about the organization holistically, including all of the enabling elements in the OPM, functional and divisional structures will tend to limit or at least will not naturally encourage cross-functional or cross-divisional working. Therefore, we should make sure we set up links between simple, and if appropriate, other, groupings to make coordination happen. Similarly we have a choice as to whether important decisions are taken at the top of an organization or by the person closest to, or otherwise best placed to make the decision (see Chapter 9).

5 Despite this point, other more modern options are almost certainly going to become more popular and these are reviewed in Chapter 8.

6 In practice, most organizations will develop their own structures by combining or tailoring some of the archetypes from this chapter and from Chapter 8. For example, one organization may decide to use a functional organization but use a matrix structure part-way down the functional hierarchy.

References

Bersin, J (2016) [accessed 12 January 2017] New Research Shows Why Focus on Teams, Not Just Leaders, is Key to Business Performance, *Forbes*, 3 March [Online] http://www.forbes.com/sites/joshbersin/2016/03/03/why-a-focus-on-teams-not-just-leaders-is-the-secret-to-business-performance

Brooker, K (1999) Can Procter & Gamble change its culture, protect its market share, and find the next Tide? *Fortune*, **139** (8), pp 146–52

Cloyd, G (2004) [accessed 12 January 2017] At P&G, It's '360-Degree Innovation', *Bloomberg*, 11 October [Online] http://www.bloomberg.com/news/articles/2004-10-10/online-extra-at-p-and-g-its-360-degree-innovation

Cornet, M (2011) [accessed 12 January 2017] Organizational charts, *Bonkers World*, 27 [Online] http://www.bonkersworld.net/organizational-charts/

Cosgrove, T (2014) *The Cleveland Clinic Way: Lessons in excellence from one of the world's leading health care organizations*, McGraw-Hill Education, New York

Drucker, P (2009) [accessed 12 January 2017] Drucker on Management: There's More Than One Kind of Team, *Wall Street Journal*, 18 November [Online] http://www.wsj.com/articles/SB100014240527487042043045745443129162 77426

Galbraith, JR (2008) *Designing Matrix Organizations that Actually Work: How IBM, Proctor & Gamble and others design for success*, John Wiley & Sons, New York

Ghoshal, S (1990) Matrix management: not a structure, a frame of mind, *Harvard Business Review*, July

Gray, D and Vander Wal, T (2014) *The Connected Company*, O'Reilly Media, California

HolacracyOne (2013) [accessed 12 January 2017] 3-Tier Partnership v1.0, *HolacracyOne LLC* [Online] http://www.holacracy.org/wp-content/uploads/2015/05/3-tier_partnership_app_-_v1.01.pdf

Martin, R (2013) Rethinking the decision factory, *Harvard Business Review*, October

McGregor, J (2015) [accessed 12 January 2017] At Zappos, 210 Employees Decide to Leave Rather Than Work With 'No Bosses', *Washington Post*, 8 May [Online] https://www.washingtonpost.com/news/on-leadership/wp/2015/05/08/at-zappos-210-employees-decide-to-leave-rather-than-work-with-no-bosses

Ostroff, F (1999) *The Horizontal Organization: What the organization of the future looks like and how it delivers value to customers*, Oxford University Press, Oxford

P&G (2009a) [accessed 12 January 2017] Innovating from the Outside In [Online] http://news.pg.com/blog/innovation/innovating-outside

P&G (2009b) [accessed 12 January 2017] Media Pack, *P&G* [Online]
http://www.pg.com/en_US/downloads/media/Media_Kit.pdf

Robertson, BJ (2015) *Holacracy: The revolutionary management system that abolishes hierarchy*, Portfolio Penguin, London

Thompson, B (2013) [accessed 12 January 2017] Why Microsoft's reorganization is a bad idea, *Stratechery*, 12 July [Online] https://stratechery.com/2013/why-microsofts-reorganization-is-a-bad-idea/

Selecting an organization structure – new opportunities

08

Introduction

This chapter continues the review of potential organization structures I began in Chapter 7 and moves this on from the traditional to more modern archetypes, which are also ones that can best fit a human or social organization. These models, which provide the structure of the initial sections of this chapter, are outlined in Figure 8.1.

Figure 8.1 New organization structures

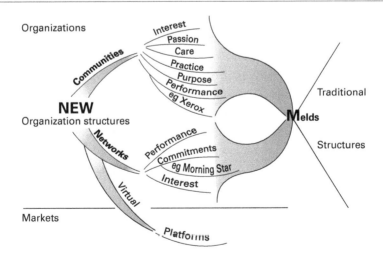

Later sections of this chapter will deal with:

- formal and informal organization;
- prioritizing organization structure;
- defining the organization form.

Communities

A community is a group of people built around a particular topic they care about, commonly called a domain. It is also decentralized, bounded and tightly knit within its boundaries. Organizational relationships focus on bonding, as they also do in a horizontal team; however, communities are denser, with higher levels of closure. This does not mean that everyone needs to know everyone else but there does need to be a high density of connections supported by high trust and caring relationships. This means that most communities are kept fairly small.

This tight focus helps people to work together as a unit but to do this in a more human way than a team, with people bringing their whole selves to their work, deciding for themselves what is important and what they need to do. The real benefit provided by a community is the value it creates for its members, not just the outputs it provides to a business. Its lifespan therefore depends on the continuation of this value and utility for the people in the community.

Communities have been used in organizations since the 1970s but have become increasingly popular over the last few decades. They are most often used as a basis for open conversation, learning and knowledge sharing between members, helping people reach agreement and make decisions, often through consensus. Communities work best when membership – or at least contribution – is voluntary and the group of people is at least partly self-organizing. This helps make participation feel like a social contract rather than a commercial one, so that people feel able to use and apply their skills, unleashing their passion and excitement around a particular domain. Communities also need some external links so they do not become cliques.

Organizational communities are quite like Charles Handy's villages. Just like villagers, community members have rights and responsibilities though these tend to be soft and informal. However, there are differences too. Peter Drucker notes that true communities are 'defined by the bonds that hold their members together, whether they be language, culture, history, or locality'. In comparison, organizations are purposefully designed, specialized and are defined by their tasks (Drucker, 1992). Combining these two points, organizational communities are defined by their bonds, and by their purpose. Villages just *are*.

In fact, building on Etienne Wenger's analysis (Wenger, McDermott and Snyder, 2002) I would suggest all communities (not just communities of practice, which are the subject of Wenger's analysis) are defined by three fundamental elements – a domain of concern, a group of people who care about this domain and a desire to do something together:

1 The domain is a concern, a topic or area of focus that it makes sense for people to spend time on together. This could be an opportunity, a problem or just an area that these people are passionate about. It is the domain that brings the community together and gives it its identity. It also defines the key issues that community members will collectively want to address. An organizational community is different to a village because it is *about* something.

2 The people who use the community do so to come together to share thoughts, ideas, experiences, needs and opportunities. This deepens insight about the domain, the cohesiveness of the community and also the community members' sense of belonging and relatedness. It helps for communities to be clear about the benefit, value proposition, bargain or 'plausible promise' that it is offering community members. Just as with an overall employee value proposition (EVP), this community proposition can be implicit or explicit. And also just like an EVP, individual community members can have very different perspectives about their own value proposition. This can include needing support, wanting to learn, sharing knowledge, building reputation, receiving recognition, helping other members of the community, and helping develop the community or whole organization.

3 A desire or motive to do something together is the sense of mission that provides a basis for people's voluntary participation. It also enables a categorization of community types, as listed below:

   – Communities of interest connect people with content and subject matter experts to help them learn and stay informed by interacting on an ongoing basis. Membership tends to be very fluid so these communities have the least strong level of shared identity. Potential opportunities include interest groups focused on an organization's products, services or processes. For example, quality circles bring together people doing similar work to identify and analyse problems using techniques such as statistical process control, and then to suggest solutions. When I met Vineet Nayar at HCL Technologies he drew a diagram of the company as a star combining its traditional and upside-down simple organizations (reviewed in Chapter 3) plus circles around the points of the star, representing communities. Nayar explained that he encouraged employees to get involved in communities related to their own interests to further their engagement. He also suggested that in the future these communities will become more important than either of the simple structures included in the rest of the star (Ingham, 2010c).

– Closely related to communities of interest are communities of passion, which bring people together over shared interests that are often unconnected to the work of the organization: book clubs, sports, social responsibility etc. However, these communities can also act as advocates for particular needs within an organization.

– Communities of care – also known as affinity groups, special interest groups (SIGs), employee forums or employee resource groups (ERGs) – place the community as the domain of interest or passion. They act as support groups focusing on helping community members – who are often minorities within their organization eg women leaders; people from ethnic groups; lesbian, gay, bisexual and transgender (LGBT) groups; people from specific religions or with disabilities; or development groups for newly recruited or promoted people managers etc. They are used by organizations to help them achieve diversity and inclusion goals and can also play a role in areas such as leadership development, innovation and change management. They can also help community members by providing support such as mentoring programmes or by establishing visibility with senior leaders (Welbourne, Rolf and Schlachter, 2015).

– Communities of practice help people to share and develop their knowledge within a domain, as well as to use and develop the community's body of knowledge, including tools, practices, methods, documents and resources etc. This scope extends beyond a community of interest as it focuses on practitioners who have a desire to improve their practice, going beyond just sharing information.

– Communities of purpose help people to connect over a common desire to develop an aspect of the organization as a whole. People tend to come from different areas of an organization, which helps them to create a shared view of the future and to address issues and work on tasks that are important to them. These communities can be a useful source of new business or organizational innovation. An example is the partnership layers within professional services firms. Another is

Cisco's boards and councils, which were described in Chapter 4 (these demonstrated aspects of both teams and communities). A further example at Xerox is described below.

- Communities of performance. Communities are increasingly being extended into other areas too. This includes short-term collaborations to meet particular business needs. However, because of the need for trust between community members they do need time to become established.

Any or all of these types of community may be appropriate within an organization. However, communities of purpose or performance are the ones that lend themselves most naturally to being incorporated into an organization's structure.

There is a widespread belief that the formation of communities needs to be spontaneous, emergent and bottom-up. However, the trend has clearly been towards a more top-down, managerial approach. See, for example, how Andrew Cox (2005) describes the shift in the thinking of Etienne Wenger between his two main books on communities (Wenger, 1998; Wenger, McDermott and Snyder, 2002) or how John Seely Brown writes about structuring spontaneity (Brown and Duguid, 2001). Whilst some commentators regret 'a displacement of the emancipatory aspirations of the original notion' (Swan, Robertson and Scarbrough, 2002), a more intentional approach to community management does provide much more opportunity for generating value.

However, even communities of performance need to be moulded and tended rather than constructed in the way of a simple or horizontal team. Communities do not exist just because someone announces they have formed a community, they exist when the members or potential members act and behave in a way that suggests a community. Wenger suggests that communities, like gardens, benefit from attention that respects their nature. Cultivating them depends on identifying the right communities, providing them with the appropriate infrastructure and assessing their value using non-traditional methods (Wenger and Snyder, 2000).

In a similar way, leaders generally emerge or are elected from within a community's membership rather than being appointed. For example, many open-source software communities elevate their founder into a position called a benevolent dictator for life. However, leaders can be imposed on a community too. There may also be other roles taken on within a community such as coach or facilitator. These can be shared, or shift as required, and structures are only kept in place for as long as they are useful.

The most common community role is called community manager (though this is very much a facilitating role). Community managers involve people, attract new members, bring people together and help share and curate knowledge through events, forum discussions and other opportunities such as hackathons. However, this does not dispense with the need for all community members to also care for the health of the community itself, in addition to supporting other community members.

Because of all these potential benefits, Etienne Wenger suggests communities have as much potential to reinvent organizations as teams have done previously (Wenger and Snyder, 2000).

CASE STUDY   Communities of performance at Xerox

This case study relates to Xerox Corporation's transition from promoting proprietary information technologies to using industry standards. Supporting this shift, the company set up what they called a strategic community, the Transition Alliance, consisting of about 50 IT professionals working at corporate headquarters and in the business units (Storck and Hill, 2000).

Xerox suggests this purposeful community was an alternative to a matrix organization and contrasts it to a functional or divisional approach. The functional approach would have been to create a function in the group head office working above the divisions. The divisional approach would have been to create separate functions in each of the business units and tie them together through a matrix. However, these approaches would have resulted in either too much or too little centralization. Developing a community as opposed to creating either a function or divisional groups in a new matrix allowed the company to keep people where they were and have them work together, avoiding either of these problems.

The operation of the community also differed from that of a task-oriented (ie simple, process- or project-based) team. Its organization structure was very fluid with roles emerging based on issues and people's ability to contribute. Although membership was managed and defined primarily around someone's role, individuals chose what contribution to make based mostly on their own needs.

Knowledge leaders emerged on an issue-by-issue basis after demonstrating relevant insights and experience, and were then able to share their knowledge with the group as a whole. There was also a small group of people who were acknowledged as 'knowing who knows' because they were able to link people with questions to others who might be able to provide them with answers. Both groups were seen as leaders because of their ability to contribute, not because of their role or seniority in the rest of the business.

The community also had only loose links into the rest of the business, which sponsored the community but avoided integrating its management processes. Communications were ad hoc and there was limited reporting, encouraging people to take risks. Xerox called the group a community because this term captured the sense of responsible, independent action that characterized the group.

The community enabled highly effective learning and knowledge sharing, which was then filtered into the business units, and people willingly applied what they learned. Xerox suggests the community represented a strategic knowledge management capability for the company as it provided a means of more broadly exploiting tacit knowledge than would have been possible in a matrix structure.

However, the community was not what most people think of as one, because it was also about doing work and supporting the formal business requirements of managing IT infrastructure more effectively. The community was successful in providing high-quality, validated solutions to issues; in handling unstructured problems; and in supporting new technological developments. In addition, although the community was relatively autonomous it was also guided by headquarters, which, for example, selected the community facilitators who promoted certain discussions within the community.

The company did not have a clear set of principles for the community when they set it up, and perhaps this would have been too top down and enforced even for a community of performance. The Alliance therefore developed its own ways of working, including a 'zone of safety for candidness'. Xerox also suggests the principles for other such communities include that the community should establish its own governance processes. I agree that this is a good idea.

The case also demonstrates something else that I frequently notice as a byproduct of social activities, which is that although The Alliance was established to meet business goals, community members also took away new and improved relationships that helped them be successful even after having moved out of the community. The community's management processes, encouragement of individual learning, and the general appreciation of community resulting from experience with The Alliance have provided lasting value (social capital) for the company.

Networks

As explained in Chapter 4, all of the structures reviewed in Chapters 7 and 8 are forms of networks. The simple hierarchical tree structures of functional organizations are centralized networks. Reduced centralization leads to horizontal teams and communities, which are both decentralized, multi-hub networks. Even further reduction in centralization leads to the type of network that we are looking at in this section, which is a more (but not totally) distributed network. From this point forward I will follow the common practice of simply calling this type of structure a network, with its semi-distributed nature being implied.

Networks are relatively unbounded, often consisting of highly distributed and largely autonomous individuals or groups cooperating with each other through peer-to-peer relationships. They are loosely coupled, meaning there are a large number of links or pathways between people and that problems relating to one person or one link do not have much impact on the system as a whole. Relationships focus outwards, on bridging with other groups and networks. They are easily scalable, often growing much larger than is possible for a community. This is important as the 'network effect' means that adding a new person to a network makes it more useful for all of its members (think about adding more phones to a telecommunications network or devices to the internet).

Each member of a network is linked to at least one other person but most other members will be unknown to them. Most network communication is therefore indirect or through intermediaries. Whereas the organizational and individual view of a community is the same thing, these perspectives will look very different for a network. Organizations will look at a network as a whole but this will generally mean very little to an individual operating in the network. Instead, they will have a view of their one set of connections, often called an egocentric, or ego, network which may span across several organizational networks. It may therefore be rather misleading to talk about a network as an example of a group, since there is often very little in the way of a group visible to the people in the network. Based on this point, Henry Mintzberg (2015) suggests that if you want to understand the difference between a network and a community, you should ask your Facebook friends to help paint your house!

Connections in a network can be between people who have very limited knowledge of each other – as, for example, is often the case in an online network like LinkedIn. However, in most business contexts, organizations need people to develop some level of relationship between themselves on top of these connections.

Acting like most living systems, networks are very robust, dynamic and flexible. Because of this, they work well in complex environments in which centralized systems struggle. Network structures are also very good at communicating information and surfacing new ideas. The best ideas are often generated from a large group of diverse contributors, rather than just one expert. Though there is nothing to stop a simple or other organization generating ideas in this way, a network makes doing so more natural and, often as a result of pre-formed connections, more effective.

Network structures emerged in the 1970s and were a hot topic of the 1980s and 1990s, supporting globalization and rapid technological charge (Powell, 1990). They have recently received a further boost in popularity, supporting the desire to be more agile. New technologies have also made them much easier to set up and maintain. They are most often seen in knowledge-oriented organizations such as technology start-ups, research firms, consultancies and universities.

Networks are also seen to be behind the limited success of the Occupy movement and the Arab Spring etc, which have been very effective in gaining the engagement and participation of large groups of people. However, these have been much less effective in bringing about change. Malcolm Gladwell infers that whilst networks may start revolutions, they cannot finish them (Gladwell, 2010). Speaking at an SHRM conference he has suggested that organizations therefore need to sell the value of hierarchies (by which I think he means simple tree-structure organizations) to their millennial employees, as Gladwell believes that this group has a strongly negative reaction to them (Hollon, 2012).

Just like communities, networks also have a domain, people and a desire. The domain can cover the whole organization, linking everyone together – for example in a social club network – or it can just relate to a particular aspect of the organization, connecting a smaller group of people, as is seen in diversity networks. However, information is often open to everyone in an organization.

The people involved are those individuals who can see a benefit from being part of the network. The reciprocal benefit offered by the network lies in extending the reach, enhancing the reputation and disseminating the value of each member's contributions. This empowers each person to act in their individual interests while contributing to the good of the whole network at the same time.

Desire can include a range of different options, from sharing information to more business-oriented activities. For example, network analyst Karen Stephenson suggests that organizations include networks for social connection, work, expert knowledge, career guidance, innovation and learning (Kleiner, 2002). In my experience the sweet spot for networks focuses on sharing ideas, exchanging information and curating knowledge. Therefore, the community that a network most closely resembles is a community of interest. The difference is that the focus in networks of interest is outwards across the organization rather than on sharing within a small group of people. A network's size and breadth will usually offer an advantage for information sharing as compared to a community. Networks of interest are also the most popular form of network linked to an organization structure.

Adriana Lukas suggests five laws or requirements for distributed computer networks. These include abundance or at least sufficiency, freedom and ability to bypass, and asymmetrical balance (TEDx Talks, 2011). Distributed social networks require similar enablers, which also include abundance. Other requirements include autonomy (see Chapter 9) and diversity (Chapter 4). However, the most stretching requirement is trust (Chapter 12). The need to meet these combined requirements, supported by a focus on best practice and the effects of organizational inertia, mean that network organizations have not yet become very common.

Networks also suffer similar difficulties to communities in playing a major role in taking actions linked to business objectives. Lack of interconnectivity between people, particularly with increasing network size, makes this particularly difficult. However, some networks do support performance too. For example, employee resource groups can be used to help ensure customer marketing efforts relate to the needs of particular minority groups. Another example is the use of networks of expertise that exist in HR and other areas as alternatives to traditional centres of excellence. These provide the same level of insight and support, but in the networks people have not been brought together so tightly. Also, see the following case-study example of using networks of commitments at Morning Star, and then the analysis of virtual and market-based networks that follows afterwards.

CASE STUDY A network of commitments at Morning Star

Morning Star is a US tomato-processing company employing between 400 and 3,000 people, depending on the season. It has a philosophy of self-management (or, really, self-direction), which will be reviewed further in Chapter 9. It articulates this philosophy and, in particular, the importance of mutual accountability in a published set of organization principles (Morning Star, 2016).

Morning Star's people do not have job titles and instead of this develop their own personal mission statements. All permanent and seasonal employees are encouraged to identify new opportunities in their own area or in the rest of the organization and can issue a purchase order or recruit a new colleague to work with them. However, before they do this they must seek input from their colleagues.

People must also manage interdependencies in their mission statements and coordinate their ongoing activities with their colleagues. This takes place by writing an annual 'colleague letter of understanding', or 'CLOU', which is done without the help of managers or central functions. CLOUs need to be negotiated face to face, often with around 10 other colleagues, and are then signed off by these other people to indicate their agreement. Therefore, although people do not have managers they do report to each other, but more as suppliers and customers. Relationships are supported by people's CLOUs and also by their personality assessment (MBTI) scores being available for others to check, helping to frame and tailor their conversations with each other.

The commitments made between people form a distributed network of relationships across the organization, which involves about 3,000 connections. Authority flows between people over this network, based upon people's expertise and achievements. People's connections and relationships can change quickly and Morning Star believes this means that the network is more flexible and agile than if people were managed from the top of the organization. Gary Hamel suggests the network helps people 'work together like members of a carefully choreographed dance troupe' (Hamel, 2011). The network of commitments is also used to track progress and address performance issues and is recognized by the company as their organization chart (Green, 2010).

Morning Star's self-managing approach is also supported through other aligned organizational management processes. Business units present their plans to the rest of the company in an annual planning meeting. Priorities are then agreed by having people express their preferences using a virtual currency (see Chapter 11). Individual negotiations between colleagues are supported through an advice process and a separate agreement process. Problems are settled through mediation or, if necessary, a panel of peers or even a final decision by the company's founder and president, Chris Rufer.

Each factory is monitored through a few hundred measures called 'stepping stones', which are published and which anyone can question at any time. Every two weeks, the company provides detailed reports of finances and other measures to everyone in the business and this information is also used to review and manage the performance of business units. Performance and reward is managed by elected compensation committees and this peer-based approach keeps differentials low, with the highest-paid person receiving no more than six times the lowest, including seasonal staff. There are no promotions but people can progress from simpler to more complex roles when they find ways to innovate and provide additional value to their colleagues.

Virtual, market and platform-based networks

Virtual organizations extend networking approaches to cover an ecosystem of independent companies rather than just a single firm. Each company in the network surrenders some individual control to share risks and potential rewards. Participating companies are usually chosen based upon their individual core competencies. In fact many of these virtual networks are formed by major organizations refocusing on their own core competencies and outsourcing other activities. An example is Boeing's repositioning as a systems integrator assembling planes from components manufactured by a large number of separate companies, all working together as a virtual network.

In this environment straightforward value chains need to include supply chains outside of an organization, which has led to the growth of supply chain management. The more complex value networks described in Chapter 6 become market networks, with each company potentially playing a variety of roles within the virtual network. Although virtual networks can work on a collaborative basis they are usually based on market mechanisms as these help to balance supply and demand and to identify the best organizations to perform particular activities.

Markets work primarily through market pricing (the cheapest offer gets the work) or competitions (the best entry wins it). They can provide a cheaper alternative to organizations, particularly as these grow in size and complexity. Market transaction costs are generally stable or will fall with volume whereas the costs of managing and organizing people often increase. As originally suggested by Ronald Coase (1937) this means that there is an optimal balance between the size of an organization and its use of external markets and therefore in the proportion of internal to external relationships.

In today's world, increasing levels of transparency and digital technology, now aided by blockchain, are lowering market transaction costs (Spence, 2017). These shifts mean that work traditionally performed by organizations is increasingly being put out to tender through markets. This distribution of effort is the basis of much of the gig economy and also open innovation. For example, digital technologies and the ability to rent rather than hire people are seen to provide the basis for 'exponential organizations' whose ability to scale quickly provides a basis for competitive advantage (Ismail, Malone and van Geest, 2014). This is why business strategy professor Rita McGrath suggests that companies need to be ready to operate as market-places (McGrath, 2016).

A particular opportunity relates to the use of talent platforms such as Upwork, Tongal and Gigwork, which allocate work to a network of independent, gig workers nominally outside the organization rather than to a traditional group of employees working within an organization. Traditional employing organizations bring people together to do work. They do this by employing or contracting with people to undertake a variety of activities supported by organization design and management processes – everything we have been looking at in this book. In contrast to this, platforms break down work to assign pieces of this to different individuals. They do this by arranging to rent or access people to undertake specific tasks when people are needed to do them.

The opportunity to use platforms depends on the conditions identified by Coase but also on work which can be broken down easily into small parts. This means that whilst internal and virtual networks are good responses to complexity, the use of platforms only applies to conditions that are simple, or potentially that are complicated, but definitely not to ones that are complex. Building on Chapter 5's review of complexity, platforms can be seen to work for approaches focusing on managing people and organization but not those emphasizing relationships. They also fit best at lower levels of value. Therefore 'talent platforms' is not a great name for these platforms since most of their focus is on value for money roles, not the people whom most organizations would see as their talent. This latter group of people, focused on adding and creating value, will generally want to find other more direct ways to connect with organizations.

However, the extension of work and relationships beyond a single organization is not the focus of this book and I will leave further discussion on virtual and market-based networks to others. Yet I do still want to take a deeper look at talent platforms as these may also point towards an opportunity for the use of internal networks of performance.

Topcoder is a good example of these platforms. The company runs a crowdsourcing platform that administers competitions in IT programming and graphic design. Requirements are divided into smaller pieces of work to provide multiple challenges, which can be undertaken on an individual basis or within groupings. Where project managers are needed these are also independent workers rather than line managers of the others working on a project. In fact there are no line managers as this function is taken over by the platform and market mechanisms.

Competition entries are reviewed by experienced platform members to identify the winners, who get to develop their solutions. The software produced can then be licensed out to clients.

Organizational networks of performance can look similar to this but can also benefit from an even stronger shared sense of purpose and higher levels of trust, and there may therefore be a benefit in using this type of network internally. Additionally, both external and internal platforms benefit from developing strong relationships rather than just relying purely on the platform-based connections. For example, Topcoder uses star ratings as well as the coders' pictures and bios to help build trust in the individuals. The trust or relationship capital generated through these relationships reinforces the general background level of trust provided by people's reputations generated through the system's algorithms.

Similarly, when using organizational platforms, social capital within a network reinforces the general level of trust across the organization and the trust in the internal platform that supports the network. Social platforms are likely to be based on technologies, especially corporate social media systems (see Chapter 13). However, they do not need to be. For example, the use of large-scale events (see Chapter 12) could also be seen as a type of platform (and a large cross-selection of staff brought together for such an event could best be seen as a network). Dave Gray also emphasizes the need for cultural as well as technological platforms as the backbone behind a podular organization (Gray and Vander Wal, 2014).

This means the opportunity provided by market platforms is not getting rid of managers, as is often reported (O'Reilly, 2015), since internal platforms can do this too. The opportunity is replacing organizational planning by market mechanisms in situations were work is simple and can be broken down in order to be assigned to independent people. This is a major downside of these platforms. The major benefit of networks is that they thrive in environments of high complexity. Market platforms impose a set of simple requirements around the organizational boundary, which reduces the benefits the network can provide.

Melds

In Chapter 7, I suggested that matrices provided an effective means of responding to multiple goals and dimensions of performance. The new types of organization reviewed within this chapter tend to be best brought together not through matrices but what I call a 'meld'. These provide a more human equivalent to the structured approach provided by a matrix. Whereas a matrix is a combination of two separate dimensions a meld is more of an integration between them.

Melds can be used to link together traditional structures. An example is the front–back organization mentioned in Chapter 7, which is a meld of process-based (upstream and downstream) divisions, linked to each other through internal market-based mechanisms, acting over the top of more traditional functional groups.

Melds can also link traditional and new structures. Both communities and networks are very human ways of organizing but they can present problems in getting things done. For this reason both archetypes are often melded with traditional structures. For example, pure network organizations are completely flat but most networks that want to achieve something will want to add some hierarchy/simple structure. A distributed network can therefore be melded with a functional structure to create a network that at one point has a centralized tree-network structure. Alternatively, a flat network can be created within a hierarchical simple structure. A community structure can be melded with a functional structure to create functional resource groups consisting of overlapping communities with people assigning themselves to these, depending upon their personal interests. A slightly different example of this approach was demonstrated by the case study of Xerox's Transition Alliance described earlier in this chapter. This was a community incorporated on top of a divisional organization.

These melds help optimize the benefits of both traditional and modern structures – something John Seely Brown and Paul Duguid refer to as the balance between process and practice (Brown and Duguid, 2000). It is also the basis for what John Husband refers to as wirearchy – a network operating alongside a hierarchy (meaning a simple structure) allowing people to work together collectively through connection and collaboration rather than relying on hierarchical status (Husband, 2016). John Kotter makes a similar point in reference to his dual operating system combining existing hierarchies (simple structures) used to maintain certain business processes in parallel with a complementary emergent network to discover and experiment with new opportunities. Kotter notes these must be two systems, but part of one inseparable organization united by a constant flow of information and activity. These are based, in part, on the fact that network volunteers are the same people who are working within the simple organization (Kotter, 2014).

The most popular example of this type of meld is a combination of networks and project team-based structures. This is the model that Deloitte refers to as a network of teams, which I referred to in Chapter 7 (McDowell *et al*, 2016). One example can be found in the US Joint Special Operations Command's 'team of teams' set up to mirror and outperform Al-Qaeda's network structure. This approach decentralized authority and empowered teams to act more independently and to take appropriate actions in real time. At the same time the organization acted to strengthen coordination across the teams. This was first through a common purpose articulated through a 'meta-narrative' about winning the war on terror. Second, the central operations group was charged with collecting and sharing real-time information, helping teams see the patterns in the data. Third, a new communication process was set up to link and synchronize with liaison officers representing each team for 90 minutes every day. Each synch started with learnings at local team level since the last synch. This re-created the ability of a small team for everyone to see things together and provided the same benefit of scale (McChrystal *et al*, 2015).

The changes were not just about the organization structure but the leadership approach too. McChrystal describes this as moving from a chess-master model to something more like a gardener – not forcing things to happen but letting the things in the ground do what they can do. This required working with senior people in the organization, encouraging them to allow junior people to experiment and get things wrong. Creating trust across the network required everyone to be appropriately skilled as otherwise people would just run towards the wrong solution faster. The transparency of the organization's processes highlighted anyone returning to traditional behaviours. These combined actions mean that thousands of people working around the world are able to synchronize and align at strategic, operational and tactical levels every day (McChrystal suggests fortnightly is probably a sufficiently fast operating rhythm in business). They have created a shared consciousness across the network of teams and empowered execution at a scale in which decisions can be made locally quickly. Local teams are able to act ahead of rather than behind strategic plans. This is uncomfortable but has to be done in order to act sufficiently quickly.

The network of teams meld also has an opposite equivalent – teams consisting of people working with an organization through networks (Barozzi, 2016). Melds can also be created just from modern archetypes by nesting communities within an existing network or combining communities within a broader network. This meld can create a core and periphery network. An example relates to the case study earlier in this chapter on Xerox's Alliance, which included about 50 community members but which was also linked into a broader network of about 250 IT systems professionals working on infrastructure management issues. Alternatively, if there is more than one centre, it can create a multi-hub network.

It is also worth noting that whilst pure structures can only really be based upon communities or networks of purpose or performance (ie 'doing' groups), melds can also incorporate communities of interest, passion, care, and practice; as well as networks of interest and commitments.

As noted by the Community Roundtable (2016), communities also tend to evolve into networks over time as a natural consequence of their growth and success, or in a more deliberate way as their objectives change. For example, developing from a community into a network helps employee resource groups advocate the perspectives and needs of their members, promote learning about their causes and highlight positive changes to the rest of the organization. However, this may reduce the personal attention they can give to members of the network. This experience equates to that of people who are drawn into living in cities but experience environmental disorientation and dream about a quiet village life. However, social technologies also allow integrated communities and networks to coexist more easily than was readily possible before these systems were available – see Chapter 13.

The ability for communities to morph into networks means that whereas there is a hard separation between simple and horizontal teams there is a much softer and more graduated distinction between communities and networks. This is one of the reasons that many groups described as communities clearly act as networks given the numbers of people they contain.

A good example is provided by Shell's use of 'communities' of practice. At one point, Shell had over 300 of these groups. Community managers then helped amalgamate these smaller groups into three very big ones, mostly focused on upstream technologies, as well as some smaller ones, often linked to business functions. Some of these groups have several thousand members each (Milton, 2010). Community managers support the networks by collecting and sharing stories of their activities to generate enthusiasm (Wenger and Snyder, 2000).

Finally, melds and matrices do the same sort of jobs but achieve what they need to do in different ways. If you can say something like 'I am at this point in the organization, reporting to a manager in one dimension and another manager in another dimension and having a role in a third dimension', then you are fairly obviously operating in a matrix. If your positioning is something more like 'I am somewhere around here, in this community and that network as well as some other informal groups', then it is much more likely that you are working in a meld.

Melding network and communities at Connecting HR

My best personal experience of a meld was acting in a voluntary capacity as a community manager for a group I co-founded called Connecting HR along with digital HR strategist Gareth Jones. This was a meld of a network and a number of interlinked, shifting communities, linked to particular events. The network was designed to bring together people within or interested in the HR profession and working in the UK into a community/network of interest/passion/care, rather than just being an opportunity for networking (Ingham, 2010b). The example illustrates some of the inherent difficulties of using communities and networks, and perhaps suggests why they often have limited application within organization structures.

The group's main focus was organizing a series of around 20 tweet-ups and five unconferences – fabulous events, which are explained in Chapter 12. We were lucky to find a disused warehouse in London to use for the unconferences. The environment was dirty, dilapidated and a bit cold – and the difference from a typical office environment helped people to behave in a very different way. We could sit a large group in a single circle but also break into subgroups around the balcony without any noise interference and everyone could still see everyone else during the whole day.

We generally had close to 100 people attending most of these events and levels of engagement around them were consistently high, creating short-term communities in the build-up, during and following on from each one. In particular, by the end of each unconference people would often be tweeting and blogging about how much they loved each other – and for a reserved Englishman like me there was often a slightly worrying amount of kissing and hugging going on. In Chapter 12, I write about love and I only really feel compelled to do this because of my experience at some of these unconferences and seeing how easy it is for people to love each other when organizational or other barriers are not put in place to stop them doing this.

The above short-term communities were held together by a virtual network using a number of tools including Yammer and Ning and with on-going conversation on Twitter, including a few Twitter chats (Ingham, 2010a). The network was largely self-managing with just me and my co-founder acting as voluntary and time-limited community managers. For example, unconferences were organized by members of the group who volunteered to do this (the group was also self-funding over a couple of years after an initial input of beer money).

Connecting HR was highly successful and demonstrated some of the potential of communities and networks. So, over a four- or five-year period this self-managing network involved more than 1,000 people interacting online or attending its events; it also succeeded in generating high levels of passion during this time. It also led to similar groups being set up in the internal communication and learning and development (L&D) professional areas, and within HR in other cities in the UK.

However, experience in the group also highlighted some of the specific requirements and potential pitfalls of these structures. First, communities and networks need a particularly clear purpose – we did not have one. This prob-lem was compounded by the two founders having rather different visions for the group, and when we introduced a core group to help us facilitate the larger one this problem was made bigger as we all had different ideas about what we wanted to do. This led to increasing instances of uncooperative behav-iours. In addition, although the environment was generally very amiable we did not succeed in creating a support group – eg people's requests for help would often go unanswered. And although people were generally helpful and often happy to organize and facilitate the unconferences there was often little broader support forthcoming for developing and maintaining the community itself. This meant the group was difficult to sustain, particularly as the found-ers had limited community manager time available to devote to it.

The biggest issue of all was inability to control. For example, the one thing I asked the volunteers facilitating the unconferences was that the events should make a surplus that was key to maintaining the network. However, the last event used up most of the surplus, making it difficult to continue. This is not a criticism of the volunteers who put time into organizing it, or even really of myself, but is a comment on the limitations of community. Communities are not always good at running projects. We really needed the unconferences to be implemented by something that felt a bit more like a project team, which could have been directed more easily. However, without the ability to compensate people and relying purely on volunteers and their discretionary effort that was not going to be possible.

Formal and informal organization

The traditional structures reviewed in Chapter 7 and the new structures described in this chapter are often distinguished as formal and informal organizations. However, the new structures are too important to be left alone because they are informal. McKinsey notes that because informal networks rely on serendipity and cannot be managed, their effectiveness varies considerably: 'At worst, informal networks can make dysfunctional organizations even more so by adding complexity' (Bryan, Matson and Weiss, 2007). To avoid this problem I suggest they should be seen as formal parts of the organization structure.

Both communities and networks certainly need to be managed with a lighter touch and ideally be generated by the people who are going to partici-pate in the network or community, but this does not mean they cannot be influenced. They can, for example, be nudged to improve their effectiveness. For example, where two communities cover the same ground these can be combined, and where a community is no longer serving a useful purpose it can be wound up. Supporting this analysis, team performance consult-ant Jon Katzenbach suggests organizations can often influence the informal organization more than they think they can. However, they also need to avoid the temptation to manage it (Katzenbach and Khan, 2010).

Similarly, you could have a formal network-based organization where a group of functionally oriented people come together and decide to set up an informal functional grouping, operating either as a community or reporting into a head of the group, ie in a simple structure.

Obviously, it depends what we mean by formal and informal. Xerox called that company's community of performance informal and it was certainly managed differently to a task-oriented structure but it had a very defined role and purpose. If you are happy calling that informal then fine – networks and communities are informal. But in my work and in this book I define things a bit differently. To me, formal is not just what we make happen but what we pay attention to. Informal is all the other stuff that goes on, some of which is a necessary backdrop to making the formal piece happen too. This suggests the key difference is not between traditional and new structures but between the different desires supported by communities and networks: interest, passion, care, practice, purpose and performance.

From this way of seeing things, communities or networks of interest are probably best left being informal. But you would need to be a fairly brave and very hands-off leader to leave communities or networks of performance as informal parts of your organization.

Prioritizing the organization structure

In Chapters 6, 7 and 8 I have reviewed the top part of the organization prioritization model (OPM), including the four core elements of infrastructure, work, people and connections; and the four main structural archetypes of simple groupings, horizontal teams, communities and networks. You may well have noticed some links between the four elements and the four archetypes. This is in fact one of the things that makes the OPM such a useful model.

Nearly all organizations, certainly those over 50 people or so, will use all four core elements from the OPM. However, some of these elements will generally be more important than others. This prioritization should inform the selection of structure (which is why I call the model an organization prioritization model):

- If infrastructure is the most important element, the organization should probably use a functional or divisional superstructure.

- If work is the most important aspect then the organization may want to organize around horizontal teams.

- If people are the most core element they may benefit from being organized into communities.

- If connections are key then a network-based organization may be the most appropriate structure.

You can also back up even further than this and consider the key priorities in the business strategy map (not the financial chain as that only has value-for-money impacts as far as people and organizational management is concerned):

- If customers and branding are the most important part of the strategy map the most important core element is likely to be work, meaning that horizontal teams may be best suited.

- If operations and core competencies are key to the strategy map then the infrastructure element may have priority and simple functional/divisional groupings may be required.

- If learning and growth is key then people and connections may need the most attention and these may need to be organized through the use of communities and networks.

The structure indicated by this prioritization may therefore be the one an organization is best using. It may not – the OPM is only a model and no model is reality. There are plenty of other factors that may lead to a different choice. Also an organization may find that several of its core elements are of roughly equal priority and this may lead towards selecting multiple structures to be combined as dimensions in a matrix or a meld.

Using the OPM in the way described above, the identification of the most useful type of group to be used for an organization's structure becomes much less of a challenge.

Defining the organization form

The prioritization provided by the OPM does not just determine the organization structure but will inform all the other aspects of an organization too. Therefore, rather than thinking about structure it is better to consider changes to the broader organization form. The form includes structure, but also how the rest of the organization wraps holistically around this. This includes the core elements from Chapter 6, the structure from Chapters 7 and 8, and also all the enablers from Chapters 9 and 10 too. Form is what people are often referring to when they talk about structure. They are not actually that interested in the cascade of accountabilities provided by the superstructure but are trying to articulate the type and nature of the organization – the basic model it is built upon. This is the organization form.

For example, an organization that prioritizes its own infrastructure and therefore selects a functional structure will also need to ensure that its people's skills, their relationships and other aspects of the organization – eg the grading system – align alongside these. To me, the reason that functional organizations get so much criticism has little to do with the merits or otherwise of a functional structure but is because organizations do not focus sufficiently on alignment within this organization form. If they did they would not end up with the functional silos that many of them have now.

Summary and additional comments

1 Simple and horizontal teams, communities and networks are the four fundamental archetypes available to use in an organization structure. For example, these are the ones that Etienne Wenger compares together in his article in *Harvard Business Review* (Wenger and Snyder, 2000).

2 All types of structure organize people together and hence can form social capital as well as contributing to organization capital. Structures define some of the most important organizational relationships, which will

provide a large proportion of our broader social relationships at work. They are therefore important to get right. They respond to our needs for relatedness and help show how we fit into our organizations.

3 Communities and networks in particular organize people around other people, whereas simple and horizontal teams organize them around tasks. Both communities and networks are therefore particularly relevant to the formation of social capital. For example, both Xerox's communities and Morning Star's network will help create social capital, although the organization capital provided by Morning Star's system of colleague letters of understanding (CLOUs) is that company's main competitive advantage.

4 I link communities to human capital and networks to social capital for two reasons. First, although communities do form social capital their main contribution is to human capital. People in communities look after and support each other, helping one another to grow. This activity boosts relationships between them but it boosts the individuals even more. Most people in most communities already know each other so they act to improve existing rather than create new social capital. In comparison, whilst networks do contribute to human capital by developing knowledge and insight they add much more to social capital. The benefit they provide is normally more about the network (eg what people could do or find out) rather than being about the individuals within the network (eg what people have already been able to find out).

5 The ideal choice of structure/form in a social organization will often be to use communities and especially networks, but employers can also make best use of simple and horizontal organizations. These may be less innately social but the trade-offs involved in their selection can usually be managed and they do offer other advantages over communities and networks.

6 Managing these trade-offs will often centre on creating and improving connections and relationships. The key need is often to transfer focus from individuals to whole groups – this opportunity will be a major focus of Chapters 9–13.

7 The success of communities and networks relies on deep relationships between the people participating in them. These relationships can be developed and facilitated within a particular group but will often need developing in advance as well. Social organizations may therefore also need to develop good relationships across the whole organization – something that I call the organizational society and which I will return to in Chapters 11 and 12.

8 Communities and networks are usually enabled by technology and I will return to them again in Chapter 13.

9 New organization forms also tend to be complex rather than complicated – something that can be seen best in considering melds in comparison to matrices.

References

Barozzi, G (2016) [accessed 12 January 2017] When 'Work' Is No Longer Work, *Medium*, 14 November [Online] https://medium.com/@gianpaolo.barozzi/when-work-is-no-longer-work-72ea1798ef1b#.sar56pw7c

Brown, JS and Duguid P (2000) [accessed 12 January 2017] Practice Vs. Process: The Tension That Won't Go Away, *Knowledge Directions*, Spring, pp 86–96 [Online] http://people.ischool.berkeley.edu/~duguid/SLOFI/IKM_Practice_vs_Process.pdf

Brown, JS and Duguid, P (2001) Structure and spontaneity: knowledge and organization, in *Managing Industrial Knowledge*, pp 44–67, ed I Nonaka and D Teece, Sage Publications, London

Bryan, LL, Matson, E and Weiss, LM (2007) Harnessing the power of informal employee networks, *The McKinsey Quarterly*, **4** (November), pp 13–19

Coase, RH (1937) The nature of the firm, *Economica*, **4**, pp 386–405

Community Roundtable (2016) [accessed 12 January 2017] What is Community?, *The Community Roundtable* [Online] https://www.communityroundtable.com/community-101/what-is-community/

Cox, A (2005) What are communities of practice? A comparative review of four seminal works, *Journal of Information Science*, **31** (6), pp 527–40

Drucker, P (1992) The new society of organizations, *Harvard Business Review*, September

Gladwell, M (2010) Why the revolution will not be tweeted, *The New Yorker*, 4 October

Gray, D and Vander Wal, T (2014) *The Connected Company*, O'Reilly Media, California

Green, P (2010) [accessed 12 January 2017] The Colleague Letter of Understanding: Replacing Jobs With Commitments, *Management Innovation eXchange*, 15 April [Online] http://www.managementexchange.com/story/colleague-letter-understanding-replacing-jobs-commitments

Hamel, G (2011) First, let's fire all the managers, *Harvard Business Review*, December

Hollon, J (2012) [accessed 12 January 2017] SHRM Atlanta 2: Malcolm Gladwell on Why Millennials are so Very Different, *ERE Media*, 25 June [Online] https://www.eremedia.com/tlnt/shrm-atlanta-2-malcolm-gladwell-on-why-millennials-are-so-very-different/

Husband, J (2016) [accessed 12 January 2017] What is Wirearchy?, *wirearchy.com* [Online] http://wirearchy.com/what-is-wirearchy/

Ingham, J (2010a) [accessed 9 March 2017] #Chrchat, Strategic HCM, blog, 23 November [Online] https://strategic-hcm.blogspot.co.uk/2010/11/chrchat.html

Ingham, J (2010b) [accessed 12 January 2017] Connecting HR: Networking and Community, *Strategic HCM* [Online] http://strategic-hcm.blogspot.co.uk/2010/08/connecting-hr-networking-and-community.html

Ingham, J (2010c) [accessed 12 January 2017] HCL Technologies – Collaborative Organization Structures, *Social Advantage*, 2 July [Online] http://blog.social-advantage.com/2010/07/hcl-technologies-collaborative.html

Ismail, S, Malone, MS and van Geest, Y (2014) *Exponential Organizations: Why new organizations are ten times better, faster, and cheaper than yours (and what to do about it)*, Diversion Books, New York

Katzenbach, JR and Khan, Z (2010) *Leading Outside the Lines: How to mobilize the informal organization, energize your team, and get better results*, John Wiley & Sons, New York

Kleiner, A (2002) [accessed 12 January 2017] Karen Stephenson's Quantum Theory of Trust, *Strategy + Business*, **29** (Winter) [Online] http://www.strategy-business.com/article/20964

Kotter, JP (2014) *Accelerate*, Harvard Business Review Press, Boston

McChrystal, S, Collins, T, Silverman, D and Fussell, C (2015) *Team of Teams: New rules of engagement for a complex world*, Penguin Books USA, New York

McDowell, T, Agarwal, D, Miller, D, Okamoto, T and Page, T (2016) [accessed 12 January 2017] Organizational Design: The Rise of Teams, *Deloitte University Press* [Online] https://dupress.deloitte.com/dup-us-en/focus/human-capital-trends/2016/organizational-models-network-of-teams.html

McGrath, RG (2016) Is your company ready to operate as a market?, Frontiers: exploring the digital future of management, *Sloan Management Review*, Fall

Milton, N (2010) [accessed 12 January 2017] KM Success Story Number 17 – $200m Per Year at Shell, *Knoco Stories*, 21 October [Online] http://www.nickmilton.com/2010/10/km-success-story-number-17-200m-per.html#ixzz4VDEQgRc0

Mintzberg, H (2015) [accessed 12 January 2017] We Need Both Networks and Communities, *Harvard Business Review*, 5 October [Online] https://hbr.org/2015/10/we-need-both-networks-and-communities

Morning Star (2016) [accessed 12 January 2017] Colleague Principles, *Morning Star* [Online] http://morningstarco.com/index.cgi?Page=About Us/Colleague Principles

O'Reilly, T (2015) [accessed 12 January 2017] Networks and the Nature of the Firm, *The WTF Economy*, 14 August [Online] https://medium.com/the-wtf-economy/networks-and-the-nature-of-the-firm-28790b6afdcc#.jm6molpba

Powell, WW (1990) Neither market nor hierarchy: network forms of organizations, *Research in Organizational Behavior*, **12**, pp 295–336

Spence, A (2017) [accessed 19 April 2017] How Will Blockchain Impact HR?, HR Transformer Blog, 3 April [Online] http://www.glassbeadconsulting.com/how-will-blockchain-impact-hr/

Storck, J and Hill, PA (2000) Knowledge diffusion through 'strategic communities', *Sloan Management Review*, Winter

Swan, J, Robertson, R and Scarbrough, H (2002) The construction of 'communities of practice' in the management of innovation, *Management Learning*, **33** (4), pp 477–96, December

TEDx Talks (2011) Balanced asymmetry of networks or how to avoid hierarchies: Adriana Lukas at TEDxKoeln, *YouTube*, 16 December [Online] https://www.youtube.com/watch?v=mNwn49YuFa0

Welbourne, TM, Rolf, S and Schlachter, S (2015) [accessed 12 January 2017] Employee Resource Groups: An Introduction, Review and Research Agenda, CEO Publication G15–13 (660), *Center for Effective Organizations, University of Southern California* [Online] https://ceo.usc.edu/files/2016/10/2015-13-G15-13-660-ERG_Introduction_Review_Research.pdf

Wenger, E (1998) *Communities of Practice: Learning, meaning and identity*, Cambridge University Press, Cambridge

Wenger, EC and Snyder, WM (2000) Communities of practice: the organisational frontier, *Harvard Business Review*, January–February

Wenger, E, McDermott, R and Snyder, WM (2002) *Cultivating Communities of Practice*, Harvard Business Press, Boston

Enabling the organization 09

Introduction

The OPM's core elements, structures and organizational enablers, all addressed in Chapters 6–8, are the main drivers of organizational effectiveness, at least in terms of organizational architecture. But to ensure a fully optimized organization other aspects of an organization design also need to be addressed. This chapter will use the OPM and in particular a review of the HR enablers from within this model to recommend some of the best design choices for social organizations, but also to describe how other, perhaps less optimal, choices can be made more social when looking to mitigate the trade-offs involved in their selection.

After having reviewed the HR enablers the chapter will return to the concept of 'organization form', explaining how the form, including HR enablers, can help understand the properties of maverick and other organizations.

HR enablers

The HR enablers in the OPM address aspects of an organization architecture that are more specific and not as important as the core elements of an organization. However, if these enablers are either poorly designed or are simply misaligned with the core elements or the organizational enablers then they will still interfere with the way the organization runs. Addressing the HR enablers as separate elements within the OPM is designed to ensure that they will be addressed. As a reminder, the HR enablers from the OPM are:

- roles and jobs;
- reporting arrangements;
- grades;
- careers;
- groups and links.

Roles and jobs

The purpose of designing and enabling an organization is to help people perform the work of their business. The aspect of this design, which is central to what most people do on a normal working day, is their role(s) and job. This makes designing roles and jobs a particularly important part of the overall design activity. However, it is also one that, other than for senior management jobs, is often overlooked and would therefore benefit from receiving more attention, including when designing organizations to be more social.

Roles are assemblies of work tasks and activities that a certain person or people will need to perform. A job will then often consist of several roles. (This is slightly confusing as we often think of a role description as being broader than a job description. We might therefore do better to think of a role description as a role portfolio description – a high-level outline of the various roles one or more people might be performing. A job description provides more specific detail on the expectations for one particular job holder.)

The most critical need is to design roles to enable the effective execution of business and organizational processes by bundling together sensible combinations of activities and of required competencies. Doing this will depend on the organization structure – for example, functional organizations will have lots of functional roles whereas project ones will have lots of project-based roles. This can lead to the use of techniques like job simplification to make it as straightforward and efficient as possible for people to do their work. Some organizations do this by using RACI analyses (described in Chapter 6) in place of traditional job descriptions, or at least using the accountabilities and responsibilities from their RACIs, along with other points such as competency and relationship requirements, as the main basis for describing people's jobs.

But human and social organizations will also want to think about the needs of job holders, particularly as the autonomy and coherence of jobs is one of the biggest drivers for employee engagement. This may lead towards job enlargement rather than simplification. One trend I have already referred to is to move away from tight job descriptions and towards broader descriptions of role portfolios. People are also swapping their roles between themselves more frequently.

Another trend is to give people more freedom in picking their own roles as this ensures they have work they are interested in, or which provides a variety of activities, rather than just because these roles sit next to each other in the execution of a business process. This approach to job construction is used at Zappos, as described in Chapter 7, and in Buurtzorg, as described below. A linked trend I referred to in Chapter 2 is job sculpting.

These approaches are helped by having a broad range of roles available to people. This is why one of the things I did at EY was to increase the range of roles making up an audit team so that rather than everyone just being an auditor, people could take on the specific role of being a business process specialist, business analyst, knowledge expert or team coordinator etc. The change meant that people were able to contribute in different ways on different teams and were less constrained by their grade or position in the team or organizational hierarchy (see my comments under reporting arrangements, which follow below). This helped improve team performance but also contributed to providing people with a more interesting career and therefore higher employee retention.

Other organizations seek to provide their people with more flexibility through initiatives such as innovation time (used by Google, 3M, Gore etc), where 10 to 20 per cent of time can be devoted to activities outside of a job's normal focus; or ideas like hackamonth (used by Facebook), where engineers can spend a longer period away from their normal jobs to focus on particular opportunities. Much of this time is typically spent in groups and conversations.

Where job design needs to start with the current organization rather than a future-oriented approach, role and job design will need to be supported by role/job analysis. One useful idea to support this is provided by psycho-analyst Elliott Jaques (2006). He suggests that people work in natural hierarchies that are mainly dependent on the time span for their decision making. Some people focus mainly on their day-to-day work, others on the next few years ahead. A CEO of a major global oil company may need to be thinking about how things will change over the next 50 years. These time horizons sort people into different hierarchical levels, which Jaques calls strata (you may have met this idea in the career-path appreciation system of estimating future potential). Job analysis in an effective or requisite organization helps ensure that a role holder's time horizon will match the time span of the role they are working in.

Many organizations will also want to continue use of job evaluation, ie identifying the appropriate level of pay for a particular job depending upon its accountabilities and other related aspects. Job evaluation helps provide internal consistency around reward and this can help promote positive group and interpersonal behaviours. It can, however, both constrain agility and promote focus on extrinsic rather than intrinsic motivation. Organizations that want to focus on broader roles rather than detailed jobs will generally want to limit job evaluation to jobs at the ends of a pay range and use more flexible approaches to progress people's pay during the range. Also see the section on reward in Chapter 11.

In many project-based and other organizations, people end up taking on so many roles, and changing them so frequently, that their roles and job descriptions becomes less important or meaningful. These organizations need to put more focus on the person rather than the role, and assign people work, review their performance and pay them etc, based upon their personal behaviours and results rather than focusing on the roles they operate within. This approach may also be needed in community or network organizations since in these businesses people are the main focus of attention – not the work, processes, roles or jobs.

Reporting arrangements

The reporting arrangements element concerns how accountabilities are cascaded down or around the organization and also how people's performance against these accountabilities are reviewed. These are the activities that lie behind the lines on an organization chart.

The connections used for reporting are defined by the organization's structure. For example, someone in a functional organization will normally report to a higher-level functional manager. Some people in a matrix organization will report to two managers representing different dimensions of the matrix. The reporting arrangements element concerns the nature of the relationships used over these connections. There are various options available to organization designers in this area. Reporting arrangements can be group to group rather than individual to individual, as is the case in Zappos's Holacracy® – also see the section 'Groups and links' later in this chapter. People can also report in to small groups or pairs of people, rather than just to individuals. And people within a reporting relationships can also be seen to be working together as a pair or dyad. This is the perspective used by Samuel Culbert to inform his suggestion of using performance management previews. In previews, a manager and the person reporting to them assess their own performance working together as a pair in a relationship (Culbert, 2010).

However, there are two other important areas addressed within this element. The first of these concerns the level of influence or direction one person has over another. This ranges from heteronomous (subject to an external influence) to autonomous (self-governing according to their own laws). The second aspect of reporting focuses on the management of organizational layers created by heteronomy in reporting relationships. This ranges from hierarchical (literally meaning ruled by angels but usually interpreted as being arranged by levels of importance) to heterarchical (unranked or having the potential to be ranked in a number of different ways).

Direction and nature of reporting

There are four main types of relationships that can play a role in the cascade of accountability within an organization and which can be applied to groups or, more traditionally, to individuals. These are heteronomous, bottom-up, semi-autonomous and autonomous, as set out below.

Heteronomous

This is the traditional top-down management relationship that exists in most organizations today. Everyone within the organization, other than usually just one person at the very top, is directed and managed by the person operating above them who decides what they need to do, and often how they should do it. The relationship is often described as hierarchical, autocratic or command and control. However, heteronomous relationships do not need to be any of these things. In particular, although most heteronomous relationships are hierarchical, they do not need to be. For example, an organization could have one group of specialist people managers and separate groups of project staff working in horizontal project teams. People managers could then be connected to project staff through a melded network of line management relationships. These relationships would be heteronomous but not necessarily hierarchical.

Even when reporting arrangements are hierarchical, this only means that the manager and their reports are at different levels. It does not necessarily imply that these relationships exist within a tree structure. For example, an organization could allocate people management to just one individual at each organizational layer with everyone else focused on operational tasks. Management relationships would then be heteronomous and hierarchical but would not necessarily form a tree structure. Even when reporting takes place in a tree structure, relationships do not need to be autocratic or totally commanding. It also does not mean that people cannot communicate outside of their own area.

I use the term heteronomous rather than hierarchical because this aspect of reporting is about the nature of influence or direction, not about the number of levels, but also to ensure people do not infer a command-and-control-oriented approach when they read or think about this type of relationship.

Heteronomous relationships are a very natural part of human life and when they are not imposed they tend to evolve very naturally. One example comes from open-source projects, which are highly self-managing but still tend to have a lot of hierarchical roles, including module owners and super-reviewers etc, and where the founders are often granted the status of 'benevolent dictators for life'.

One explanation for this natural formation of heteronomous relationships is provided by Jaques's strata. From this perspective hierarchies are not an aspect of organizational bureaucracy but a critical part of people-centric management.

It is certainly the case that much of the criticism of hierarchy is often more about poor design or implementation of structures or reporting arrangements. The most common issue is that a manager only has one person reporting to them, meaning that they tend to interfere in this person's job. Another problem occurs when there are inappropriately sized distinctions between a manager and their reports. Jaques suggests a requisite organization ensures reporting relationships always align with changes in strata. If a strata is missed a manager will be too distant from the people reporting to them and will not spend time coaching them. If both are from the same strata they will end up attempting to perform the same job, causing conflict as well as inefficiency (Jaques, 2006).

Issues can also be behavioural rather than structural. The main problem here is when the organization structure becomes the basis for communication and other activities rather than being limited to the cascade of accountability etc. This can lead to hierarchical thinking in which people only focus on their respective positions. In this scenario the potential contribution of a person will always be judged by their organizational layer or grade rather than by their ability to contribute on a topic. Even worse than this, of course, is when managers interpret their hierarchical position to mean that they can talk down to and belittle anyone who works below them. Or when people only concern themselves with satisfying their manager.

None of these problems have to be experienced though. Hierarchical thinking results from a lack of respect and humanity it is not a consequence of any particular structure or reporting arrangement. People with good managers generally appreciate and sometimes very highly value the support they can receive from them. It is not having a manager which is important, it is having a good manager if there is one.

However, as we will see below, there are alternative options available for reporting arrangements too.

Bottom-up

Relationships can be heteronomous but bottom up rather than top down, as in true coaching or a mentoring relationship where a more senior coach and their more junior coachee focus purely on the latter person's agenda. This could then be used to understand issues at the bottom of an organization and pass them up to the top. HCLT's upside-down organization model, reviewed in Chapter 3, also fits within this bottom-up approach.

Semi-autonomous

There are a range of options that provide higher levels of autonomy within a reporting relationship. The most common of these is for a manager to specify what people working for them need to do, but to provide them with a free choice over how they achieve this. This is the basis of agile software development in which a product manager specifies what a project team needs to achieve but the team together decides on how they are going to achieve it. The approach also relates to what Gerard Fairtlough (2005) calls 'responsible autonomy' and which is his preferred approach to organizational coordination.

Empowerment is another approach to increasing people's autonomy. However, to be effective, this needs to be real. Encouragements to be empowered but with ongoing requirements for approvals and sign-offs simply increases cynicism in the workforce.

Semi-autonomous workers can also be self-organizing or self-managing. Self-organization refers to groups that can include managers. Self-management refers to individuals and groups who do not have managers. For example, Niels Pflaeging *et al* (2012) suggest that complex environments call for functionally integrated self-managing cells controlled through peer pressure and self-regulation within the cells.

Self-managing groups can still be organized into hierarchies, eg through the self-managing arrangements in Zappos's Holacracy® and the broader concept of sociocracy (Endenburg, 1988), which are achieved by arranging double links between groups, as described in Chapter 7. Zappos's self-managing circles and roles have collective freedom in how they work but what they need to work on is informed by the higher-level circle. HolacracyOne describes this approach as a mix of integrative processes at the governance level and autocratic authority at the operational level (Compagne, 2014).

Autonomous

Autonomous workers are completely self-directing, defining their own goals and self-organizing to meet them. This is a common approach in network-based organizations – and Stowe Boyd argues it will increasingly become the norm: 'The old demands to subordinate all personal interests to those of the collective will be displaced by a personal re-engagement in our own work' (Boyd, 2015a).

In this approach, 'reporting' relationships are lateral or heterarchical. This means that people are either all seen to be at the same level or that their levels can be judged in a number of different ways, so that two people in a relationship can both be seen as the more senior person at different times for different things. Power will shift according to skills, interests and broader abilities to contribute, eg having the time and availability could be a basis for taking a more senior role as well. Boyd suggests that these relationships function like a brain: 'In the brain – and in fast-and-loose companies – different sorts of connections and groupings can form. People can choose the sort of relationships that most makes sense' (Boyd, 2015b).

This is also sometimes called 'situational' or 'actualization' hierarchy and is most common in distributed networks. These act a little like a fishnet. For example, Bob Johansen describes how you could grab a single mesh of a fishnet and lift it up with the rest of the net latticing underneath it. This is a temporary, soft hierarchy that lasts for as long as you hold the net. The number of layers in the hierarchy depend on how high you lift the mesh and the width of the net (Johansen, 2007).

The lateral nature of this type of reporting means that requirements for both *what* and *how* can be agreed between people in an egalitarian way. (Note that relatively heterarchical, egalitarian relationships can exist without autonomous roles – for example, this is what we were working towards in EY's project teams.) Where functions exist these should see themselves as supportive to the self-directed teams, often delivering out of a shared service structure.

Examples of self-directed organizations include Morning Star (reviewed in Chapter 8) and Buurtzorg (described below).

CASE STUDY Self-directed communities at Buurtzorg

Buurtzorg is a Dutch organization of 9,000 community nurses. Built on trustful relationships and the idea of placing humanity above bureaucracy, it operates through self-directed groups of 10 to 12 people, each looking after about 50 patients within a neighbourhood. These groups are responsible for the complete care process within that area. However, nurses focus on individual patients, getting to know them and supporting them at a personal level, and so the process does not predominate as it does at, for example, Cleveland Clinic (reviewed in Chapter 7). Groups also decide how they will deliver this care, including how many patients to support, which partners to work with, where to rent an office, and even whether they need to expand the group or split it in two. This may happen if a group is getting too big and people are finding it more difficult to coordinate their activities. There are no managers, so responsibilities for all these decisions are distributed across the nurses within a group.

Not only are there no group managers but there is no regional management either. There are coaches but these have no responsibility or decision-making authority over the groups. Coaches cover 40–50 groups, which stops them getting too involved and ensures that groups remain independent of them. There are also no staff functions, eg HR, although experts are sometimes hired centrally to work in advisory roles on a contract basis, often to build up the nurses' own capabilities so the experts become surplus to requirements.

However, people are not treated equally and decisions are not made by consensus. Nurses take leadership roles within their teams or the whole organization where they have particular expertise, interest or can make the greatest contribution. Groups are also linked through an organizational network, allowing nurses with particular specialisms to share their expertise outside their own community or to participate in voluntary task forces. However, these additional contributions are made based upon the individual person not just because of the role they are operating in, as it would be in Zappos, for example.

Also, instead of having a formal set of principles, as found in Zappos's constitution, Buurtzorg just has a few ground rules, which include, for example, the need for group members to appraise each other every year. However, groups decide how they are going to do this for themselves in order to ensure local ownership of their appraisal process. People cooperate easily and there is little need for structured meetings. CEO Jos de Blok shares ideas through a blog for developing the company – and these posts may eventually lead to agreement on a new policy.

Buurtzorg call their groups 'teams', but it is evident to me that the company is a community- not a project-based organization, internally as well as externally (ie the nurses work within internal communities as well as supporting their external communities). The company is able to make these internal communities work effectively for business purposes because their nurses are so intrinsically motivated, something that is supported by both the organization's social purpose and its self-directing approach.

Layers and spans

Layers are the hierarchical levels involved in a chain of heteronomous reporting relationships from the top to the bottom of an organization. An organization's number of layers is the maximum length of the reporting chain in any area of the business.

This is another area like structure, which tends to receive excessive attention within organization design. It is, after all, only one part of the reporting arrangements element, which is a small part of the entire organization. The concept also only really makes sense in functional organizations as these tend to be the most hierarchical. Other structures usually have very few layers and often very large spans. Some organizations, particularly those using community or network structures, may be completely heterarchical – meaning they have just one layer.

However, in functional organizations where there can be a lot of layers this is still an important part of organization design. A large number of layers can be useful in providing clear control and progression in this type of organization. However, layers increase costs, particularly because more managers require even more managers to manage the additional managers. Gary Hamel notes that, assuming a management span of 1:10, a small organization with 10 non-managing employees will need just one manager, but a large organization with 100,000 will need 11,111 managers because an additional 1,111 manager managers will be required (Hamel, 2011).

Having lots of layers also slows down and distorts communication (a bit like an organizational version of Chinese Whispers) and this can reduce customer focus too. For example, when I worked with one client on a major organization design initiative, their head of customer service suggested that moving to six or seven layers had helped them get closer to their customers. Doing this can help spot issues more quickly and resolve problems faster and more effectively. Delayering can therefore improve customer satisfaction.

Changing the number of layers also impacts average management spans, as approximately the same number of people will still need to fit into the organization being redesigned. Therefore, the choice tends to be between tall, narrow organizations and short, broad ones. Broad, flat organizations work well when people work autonomously; people, and particularly managers, have high levels of competence in their roles; and teams are mature. Tall and narrow organizations can work better when there are distributed locations and managers have high non-managerial workloads. They are also often recommended when there are complex tasks and unstable environments in order to gain more control over what is happening. However, to me, narrow spans only provide the appearance of control. It is flat organizations that are the best adapted for complex environments, as these help people to experiment and innovate (a bit like McChrystal's network of teams from Chapter 8). I would therefore suggest making organizations as broad and flat as possible in both complex/unstable and simple/stable environments.

However, layers also need to align with the nature of the business. For example, a sales function may obviously need a Head of EMEA leading a Head of Europe leading a Head of UK leading a Head of the North of England etc. Adopting this breakdown may provide a more fundamental requirement than any of the above concerns about tall or flat etc.

When reviewing layers and spans I always suggest that layers are the more fundamental concern, therefore I normally advise on getting layers right and then working out how to manage the corresponding spans, rather than the other way around. Delayering from eight to seven layers makes a big difference, whereas having to manage 12 rather than 10 people is a less significant change. There are also steps the organization can take to make it easier for managers to respond to broader spans, which often includes the use of new technologies. Spans are in any case increasing, though not by that much. For example, Deloitte suggests that US companies now have an average span of control of 9.7, which increases to 11.4 in large companies (McDowell *et al*, 2016). Spans are also higher at lower organizational levels, which must result at least in part from the fact that those people designing organizations are working towards the top of their organizations and think that their case for narrow spans is stronger than for those working at the bottom. I often argue the reverse – that those people lower down need more coaching and hence narrower spans.

I also advise caution about just making changes to layers and spans. These are important and costs savings can be significant. However, most of the benefits are value for money, not added or created value. (Remember that hierarchy tends not to be as big an issue as hierarchical thinking.) Reducing layers also results in major disruption as some managers will lose their jobs and many people's reporting relationships will change. Therefore, I tend to leave changing layers until I am doing something more fundamental in an organization. For example, if I was changing people's roles or redesigning business processes then I might use this opportunity to reduce the number of layers too. I would generally avoid reducing layers without there being the existing necessity to disrupt the organization created by one of these bigger opportunities.

Grades

Grades are not normally considered to be part of an organization model, or as a way to develop a more effective or social organization. They should be. If grades are out of alignment with organizational layers it is not a huge issue but it certainly does not make things any easier. For example, a manager at grade 5 will find things much simpler if all those working for them are at grade 4 rather than some being at grade 4 and some at grade 3, or some at grade 5 (ie the same grade as the manager).

This is part of the reason why many organizations are moving to broader branding. For example, I designed an approach at EY that was based on just four bands, informally called learning, doing, managing and leading. We still had the traditional time-based grades of junior trainee, senior trainee, senior etc, but what was going to be important was the changes in bands. For example, these would be the points at which we would run assessment and development centres to control promotions and develop the new skills required at a new level. We also saw this as another way to reduce hierarchical thinking and ensure that team members were making their best possible contributions, regardless of their position in the hierarchy. Elliott Jaques recommends something similar, which is to have three grades within each strata. The important changes are the ones in strata but the more frequent changes in grade provide an ongoing sense of progression for individuals within these bands as well.

Many organizations will use proprietary grading or job evaluation systems to identify their grades. Companies that do not have anything like this can use systems such as Ram Charan's leadership pipeline to provide clear grading levels (Charan, Drotter and Noel, 2011). This suggests that the key changes are between managing oneself, managing others, managing managers, managing functional managers, managing business managers, managing group managers and managing enterprise managers. This would obviously be impacted by self-management or even just a more social leadership approach).

However, in achieving some alignment between layers and grades I would once again put layers first as the more important element in an organization, ie I would get the layers broadly right and then worry about grades. Job titles also follow on from both layers and grades, although these can also depend upon customer requirements and employee expectations. (Some organizations have internal and external titles so external title inflation does not put pressure on the grading system.)

Grading and job titles are also important from a social organization perspective. Grades and titles provide clarity, which helps people to work together easily, but too many grades or hierarchical titles – or too much focus on them – will also emphasize status differences and could reduce people's propensity to collaborate.

Careers

Careers also need to fit in with the rest of the organization, at least as long as being able to retain and progress people in a business is important. Companies often make changes to their organizations but forget about the consequence for careers. HR transformation is a good example. The three-legged stool of HR business partners, centres of excellence and service centres can make sense for HR delivery and impact but often leaves HR professionals unsure about their career development within an organization. Large businesses therefore often insert additional roles into the model, eg junior business advisor reporting to a business partner and partnering with less senior-level clients, not because it is needed by the model but to provide a progression route for HR staff.

One of the main trends within career management includes supporting lateral, and sometimes downwards, as well as upwards progression. Deloitte suggests people should think about navigating a corporate lattice, that echoes the network view of an organization, rather than a career ladder, which comes from a functional perspective. Careers should then include making moves across groups, business units and geographies etc (Benko and Andersen, 2010).

However, a smaller trend, though I would suggest this one is more important, is the move towards dual career streams, in which technical specialists, for example, are enabled to progress to the top of an organization and earn a large salary without having to become a people manager. The way that so many organizations in most sectors take technical specialists and force them to become people managers is a huge waste – they lose a great technical expert, gain a poor manager, and demotivate this poor manager's direct reports and potentially all of the people reporting indirectly to them too. Changing this is therefore, for many companies, one of the greatest opportunities for using the organizational architecture to create value.

Groups and links

The first element reviewed in this chapter was the design of individual roles – the final element in the OPM concerns the design of groups. The first issue to consider here is the extent of groupiness within an organization. Functions, projects, communities and networks can all be managed in more or less groupy ways. Some issues or domains also lend themselves to being dealt with either by individuals or through groups. However, different organizations will also lean more towards one or the other. People in very groupy organizations will spend much of their time in groups. Hierarchies can be arranged so that groups report into groups, as is done at Zappos. And HR processes can be directed mainly at group level – see my suggestions on this in Chapter 11.

Once the extent of groupiness has been agreed, organization designers can then start to map out the design of key groups. All of the groups considered part of the formal organization need to be fully mapped out using the ideas in this section. Informal groups can benefit from good design as well but this tends to be left to the individuals sponsoring or organizing these groups.

Design starts by ensuring that all groups have a clear purpose – a business need or a domain that people are passionate to come together around to have a positive impact. This purpose should be more suitable for achieving through a group than by allocating to an individual. As discussed in Chapter 4, group work can be hugely beneficial but there are costs and limitations in this too. Sometimes individuals can do things better than a group.

Design proceeds by selecting the group type (simple groupings, teams, communities and networks) to be used. Where groups form part of the organization structure this will often be defined by the particular organization form, which is suggested using the prioritization of core elements in the OPM. However, there are always plenty of other groups, of all different types, and both formal and informal, operating in most organizations too.

The selection of group types for groups that are not part of the organization structure can be assisted by arranging the four types – simple groupings, teams, communities and networks – in a 2 x 2 grid where the vertical axis is about an internal/external orientation and the horizontal axis is about a task or people focus. A task focus often requires extrinsic motivation whereas a human focus opens up opportunities for intrinsic motivation. I call this grid the orientation/motivation model (OMM), shown in Figure 9.1 (remember that the OPM deals with prioritization and the OMM motivation):

- Simple forms and communities are both inwardly oriented – within a function or domain and a group of people associated with this.

- Horizontal forms and networks are both externally oriented – on the outputs and customers of a project or on the other people who would help a network to grow.

- Simple and horizontal forms coordinate tasks but tend not to bring people together so well.

- Communities and networks help people to come together and relate with each other but they tend not to connect people to tasks so effectively.

Figure 9.1 The orientation/motivation model

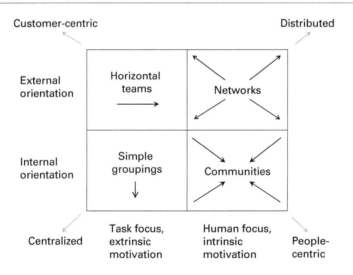

In Figure 9.1 the arrows indicate the main direction of interest. Functions manage downwards, horizontal organizations across a process or project, networks extend outwards and communities look inside themselves, though not too much or they become cliques. Knowledge flows in the opposite way, so up the organization in functions and outside-in from customers and other stakeholders in horizontal teams. Networks are great for accessing and bringing together information, but communities – due to their stronger ties – are better at distributing it (within a small group).

This way of presenting the four structures/groups is somewhat similar to the TIMN model (Ronfeldt, 1996), the competing values model (Cameron *et al*, 2007) and the organizational behaviour model (Hellriegel and Slocum, 2010).

A slightly different presentation of the same grid helps explain the main functions and benefits that can be achieved using the different group types. This is provided as Figure 9.2:

- Simple groupings enable coordination of work through professional focus.

- Horizontal teams enable collaboration through focused teaming.

- Communities enable what might be best described as cultivation, supporting desires around passion, practice and care for other community members.

- Networks enable cooperation around interests and commitments.

Figure 9.2 Comparing group types according to benefits provided

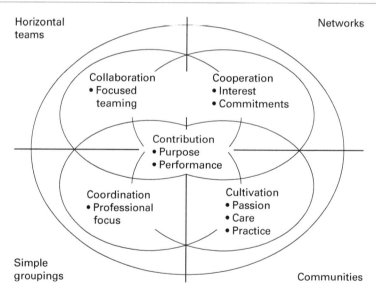

The use of coordination, collaboration and cooperation was discussed in Chapter 5. The idea of cultivation comes from General McChrystal's and Etienne Wenger's gardening metaphors referenced in Chapter 8. An alternative word to cultivation might be 'carefrontation', which is a mash-up of care and confrontation. I like the way that CIMB Bank in Malaysia used to describe this aspect of their organization – that there is a need to have disagreements and encourage debates, but these should always be conducted professionally and with due care for other peoples' feelings and emotions (Ingham, 2011). This combination is fairly core to what communities need to do. They need to confront ideas and each other to develop the best possible perspectives about a domain, and to help people achieve their best potential, but to do so with love, care and concern. Neither word applies perfectly but at least they mean that each cell in the model begins with the letter C (this approach seemed to work for McKinsey!).

At the centre of the re-presented OMM, or '5C' model, in Figure 9.2 is an area of contribution that can really be performed by any of the types of group, ie simple groupings, horizontal teams, communities or networks of purpose or performance, or potentially a combination of these. A good example is Valve's temporary, emergent cabals, described in its well-known employee handbook (Valve, 2012). Cabals are emergent and voluntary and so correspond to communities. However, once established they are serious project delivery vehicles and start to sound a lot more like traditional project teams.

Groups can be chosen using either version of this model (Figure 9.1 or 9.2) by identifying which of internal/external orientation and intrinsic/extrinsic motivation are most important to the success of the group and then selecting the most appropriate type. The choices indicated by the tool will generally also link to the structures generated by prioritizing the core elements in the OPM, as described in Chapter 6. So, for example, a work-focused organization would generally be expected to include a high proportion of project teams as opposed to other groups, and also for at least some of these project teams to be formalized within the organization structure.

Once the appropriate group type has been selected, group roles need to be designed. These may include:

- Sponsor or champion: providing a group with higher-level sponsorship, resources and advice, although they do not usually play a role within the group itself.

- Leader: taking overall accountability for the group's outputs, guiding its activities and directing group members as appropriate (applies particularly to project managers).

- Knowledge specialist: bringing in knowledge from outside the group, curating this and the group's knowledge, reviewing and approving group member contributions, and ensuring the knowledge is used to help the group achieve its aims.

- Subject-matter experts: providing particular technical advice or inputs into the group's work.

- Group coordinator: administering the group's activities, scheduling meetings and organizing its resources.

- Facilitator, coach or mentor: helping group members to work together, ensuring group members are included in group workings and supporting the communication between them (applies particularly to community managers, see Chapter 12).

Other roles may be required in certain groups or can be pulled in from the rest of the organization. This includes advisors on organization design and development or on the use of particular IT tools. Other roles such as liaison officers may be needed to share knowledge across groups working within the organization. This means that the roles element in the OPM needs to take account of these group roles as well as the roles required to perform the actual work of the groups and individuals working in the organization.

A final requirement for design of a group is to ensure an appropriate number of people are included within the group, taking into account the amount of work or other activities it needs to do within a particular time frame as well as the roles to be performed. All of the Dunbar numbers are relevant to this as there is a need to keep group size below about 15 (horizontal teams), 50 or 150 (communities and functional groupings) and 500 or 1,500 (networks) – as above these sorts of sizes the relevant social bonds break down. Amazon is a good example of an organization that aims to keep groups small, in this case to avoid the groupthink prevalent in larger teams. They do this through the 'two pizza' rule, which suggests that a team is too big if two pizzas cannot feed the entire group (Brandt, 2011). Rob Sutton suggests that hospitals can work effectively by dividing into pods of just six people (Sutton and Rao, 2014).

In EY we often had several hundred people in each office. We therefore divided these groups into smaller 'stables' each including less than 150 people. For us, the key objective was to keep down the number of managers who had to work together, aiming for a group of about six to eight managers, which equated to a group of 100–150 people around them. We believed that this small subgroup of managers would be able to work together more effectively, sharing resources, challenging each other or doing whatever else was required to enable the overall performance of the stable. However, in many organizations managing the number of connections will be more complicated than this because people participate in many different groups and therefore have multiple types of connection.

Another interesting example is the Japanese electronics supplier Kyocera, which uses its own approach to organization called 'amoeba management'. This divides the organization into small units, or amoebas, containing 3–100 people. These act as independent profit-and-loss centres directly linked to their respective markets (Inamori, 2012).

In addition to the above requirements, organization designers also need to think about the links and coordination mechanisms between different groups and individuals that are required to enable the organization to work and also for people to remain connected. These links can include structures, processes, meetings and less formal bridging relationships. Examples include:

- Tools like RACI analysis and handshake meetings, which are both frequently used within matrix structures. Handshake meetings are where the managers of two or more dimensions come together and agree how they are going to work across the matrix.

- Double-hatting and job rotation arrangements to help people working in different roles/jobs remember the challenges experienced by other people working in the organization. A good example is HR business partners and centres of excellence, which can often fall out with each other without one of these approaches, particularly if there is a poorly shared sense of purpose.

- Governance meetings such as the ones used within Holacracy®, described in Chapter 7.

- Voting, crowdsourcing or social communication technologies to provide collective intelligence across a group or the whole organization.

A good case example of a well-linked organization was BP under John Brown and their use of peer assists/peer challenges. This model created peer groups consisting of up to 12 businesses operating in the same area across BP's 150 business units. The challenge process made the top two businesses in a peer group responsible for the bottom two units. Half of all executives' bonuses were also made conditional on the performance of these lower-performing businesses. Meanwhile the peer-assist process provided time for people in the different businesses within a peer group to help each other. This change in organization structure, together with the two additional processes, made BP a much more integrated if very complicated company. (Peer groups were disbanded by BP's next CEO Tony Hayward before the Deepwater Horizon oil spill in 2010.)

Social organization designers may also want to consider opportunities for collective intelligence within organizational groups or potentially across a whole organization. I will pass over crowdsourcing approaches and prediction markets etc as these are not based upon social relationships. However, collective intelligence can also include facilitated conversations across an organization. These conversations can be enabled by organizational networks, large-scale facilitated events such as unconferences (see Chapter 12) or the use of social technologies (see Chapter 13).

A good example of a company using these types of links is GM. As part of GM2020, an initiative to create a collaborative workplace, the company has identified a need for links between the simple, operational parts and the networked, entrepreneurial areas of the organization. GM calls this an adaptive space (Arena and Uhl-Bien, 2016). Actions to bring people together over this space include summits of network brokers, 'co:labs' (hackathons), design-thinking-based catalyst camps and creative exchanges operating a bit like market bazaars. Much of this has taken place in GM's Innovation Xchange, which is a workspace purposely designed for entrepreneurial thinking. GM also includes networking thinking in its leadership development programme. One of the other ideas coming out of the initiative has been to encourage people to 'find a friend' to talk about their ideas with, rather then thinking they always have to consult a manager.

Organization forms and maverick organizations

Having considered all of the HR and other enablers that are part of an overall organization, other than the workplace, it will now be possible for organization designers to articulate the whole organization form. Describing an organization's form at the level of detail suggested by the OPM helps ensure an organization design has been thought through sufficiently clearly and that all the different elements are appropriately integrated and aligned with the intended outcomes of the organization.

One of the additional benefits of the OPM is that it can be used to review maverick organizations and explain what is really going on and why it is that these rather strange organizations work. Other commentators often fuse together different aspects of these organizations in order to demonstrate a particular point. They therefore miss a lot of the important detail that makes a model work. Buurtzorg and Zappos may both be 'teal' (Laloux, 2015), and Amazon and Morning Star may both be podular (Gray and Vander Wal, 2014) but, actually, they all have very different organization forms. Understanding these differences is important as not doing so may mean models are applied to needs and organizations they are not suited to – Zappos and Holacracy® is a perfect example.

The case study below reviews the complete organization form for yet another maverick organization, Spotify, and explains that what really makes this company special is its creation of social capital.

CASE STUDY Putting it all together at Spotify

Spotify is a Swedish music-streaming company employing over 600 people. The company's engineering and product organization provides a great demonstration of most of what I have been explaining in this part of the book. I also like using the example because the company has itself communicated its own organization so clearly, particularly in a video titled 'Spotify's Engineering Culture' (Kniberg, 2014). I recommend you view how the company articulates its own organization and then review how the OPM helps categorize this, enabling you to compare it to other organizations, and to consider aspects of the design for your own company.

Spotify does not have any specific organization principles but you will be able to see how its organization design flows out of its 'four value mantras', which describe how things are done in the Spotify way. These mantras are: think it, build it, ship it, tweak it (the four stages of agile product development, requiring agile, autonomous teams); give it everything you've got (through shared responsibility for continuous improvement); play fair (including trust, transparency and servant leadership); and go big or go home (which is about innovation, learning and fast failure).

Spotify's core elements

- Work: IT systems development performed in an agile way, though not using scrum. Downplaying the role of rules and standards and instead providing autonomy for work to be tackled in different ways, also minimizing handoffs. This approach would seem to extend to organizational processes too.

- Infrastructure: a lightweight, self-service model with different groups enabling and supporting each other.

- People: smart people but without big egos. Highly motivated employees who come to work to change the world together through music (94 per cent of whom report satisfaction in their employment).

- Connections: autonomous working does not stop lots of help, support and recognition taking place between people.

Spotify's structure

- Spotify believes community (and therefore people) is more important than structure. They incorporate communities (or 'guilds') into their structure. Plus even their project teams ('squads') sound very community-like (with one product leader suggesting their squad was like a group of volunteers working on something they are super-passionate about). However, I think what makes the organization structure special is the clever way these groups are connected through a loosely coupled network. This would suggest that the highest-priority core element for the company is actually the connections between its people.

- Spotify's network can be drawn as a three-dimensional matrix, as in Figure 9.3. However, a matrix, and especially a 3D one, is probably too formal and heavy-duty for Spotify and it is noticeable that they do not present their organization in the traditional but rather clunky and box-like way I have shown it. In fact they talk about aiming for a minimum viable organization. So I think it might be more appropriate to consider their organization as a meld.

Figure 9.3 Spotify's 3D matrix

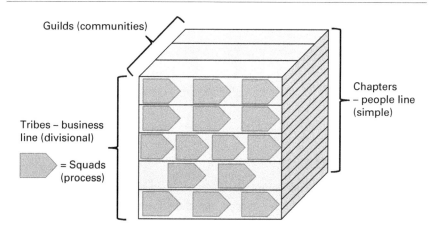

The structure includes:

- Squads (cross-functional project teams) of 6–12 people undertaking end-to-end development processes and ensuring product delivery and quality for one or more systems.

- Tribes (divisions) focusing on different product areas and including 40–150 people working in different squads.

- Chapters (simple groupings acting like resource pools for projects) organized by competency areas. These exist within tribes (ie people can keep the same people manager if they move between squads but not if they move across tribes). It is in these groups that people management processes take place.
- Guilds (communities of interest) allowing people to come together voluntarily and to be kept informed through mailings and unconferences. These groups cross across tribes and chapters.

Spotify's enablers

Spotify's organizational enablers:

- Workspace: not commented on.
- Workplace (see Chapter 10): optimized for collaboration, eg open yet closed off, adjustable desks, whiteboards, huddle rooms, presumably a few Spotify Connect speakers.
- Workstyles: informal communications. Spotify also has very people-centric HR policies linked to their Swedish heritage, eg their parental leave policy provides six months' paid leave, which can be taken flexibly, even in the United States (although the company video I reference above does not mention this).

Spotify's HR enablers:

- Roles: there is distributed decision making within and across the squads. Role allocations are supported through the use of 10 per cent innovation time, hack days and hack weeks.
- Reporting arrangements: servant leaders explain what they want and why, but are not involved in doing the work. Autonomous teams have 'aligned autonomy' for how they deliver this and how to work together.
- Grades: not commented on.
- Careers: not commented on; though at the time of writing, the web page on Spotify's engineering culture which I referenced earlier (Kniberg, 2014) linked to an interesting article on it (Goldsmith, 2016).
- Groups and links: a team-based organization, balancing individual accountability with collective responsibility, emphasizing trust over control, and using links such as peer code reviews to cross-pollinate between teams (also avoiding the need for scrums of scrums).

Spotify's other enablers:

- Leadership roles include chapter leads, product owners and agile coaches as well as technical and design leads, system owners and a chief architect. For critical systems the system-owner role is performed by two people – one from development and one from operations, combining the advantages of their separate perspectives.

Summary

Spotify is a very people-focused company but to me it competes on organization and especially social capital. I am sure the company's people are very talented and they are clearly very motivated, but there is nothing in Spotify's information to suggest that the company's human capital provides any differentiation compared to other technology companies. Instead of this, Spotify differentiates itself through its organizational architecture. Based upon the above analysis using the OPM I would describe Spotify's organization form as a loosely coupled and informal network of cross-functional project teams and communities of interest. This form and aligned architecture enable people to be more successful, creating organization capital. In particular, the organization form meets Spotify's objectives of allowing squads to be autonomous, but not suboptimized: 'Building products at Spotify should be like being part of a jazz band: although each musician is autonomous and plays a different instrument, they should all listen to each other and focus on the whole song.'

The design also creates trust and community between its people and this would last even without its current organizational architecture, which is why I suggest that the company competes on social capital too.

Summary and additional comments

1 Use of the OPM's HR enablers helps create organizations that fit with our natural tendencies to tribe and also maximize their ability to meet business needs. We can provide the right type of group, of the right size, balancing bonding and bridging, and with appropriate rather than excessive levels of hierarchy.

2 To avoid status threats, hierarchy should not be prominent but just needs to work effectively in the background. A poorly managed performance appraisal might trigger a status threat response, whereas simply having

work assigned by a manager might not. (Ideally the person would be involved in selecting that assignment to avoid a threat response being triggered by lack of autonomy instead.) Status differences can also be reduced by developing work styles emphasizing equality.

3 People have predicted the death of hierarchies for 50 years already (Leavitt, 2004). However, there is little sign of them going away. With good design they do not need to.

4 Good design involves careful selection of the elements in the OPM. These do not always need to be brought together in what can be rather standardized ways. For example, networks do not always need to be heterarchical. One reason I like referring to maverick organizations is that these companies often show how OPM elements can be combined together in creative, unusual ways.

References

Arena, MJ and Uhl-Bien, M (2016) Complexity leadership theory: shifting from human capital to social capital, *People + Strategy*, **39** (2), Spring

Benko, C and Andersen, M (2010) *The Corporate Lattice: Achieving high performance in the changing world of work*, Harvard Business School Press, Boston

Boyd, S (2015a) [accessed 6 March 2017] A Manifesto for a New Way of Work, *Work Futures*, 18 January [Online] https://workfutures.io/a-manifesto-for-a-new-way-of-work-139e1b3c1a4f#.vmbzivtkg

Boyd, S (2015b) [accessed 6 March 2017] Imagining a Corporation in 2050, *Backchannel*, 24 June [Online] https://backchannel.com/what-will-a-corporation-look-like-in-2050-281978852fc4#.yoxjdrmlm

Brandt, C (2011) [accessed 12 January 2017] Birth of a Salesman, *Wall Street Journal* [Online] http://www.wsj.com/news/articles/SB10001424052970203914 304576627102996831200

Cameron, KS, Quinn, RE, DeGraff, J and Thakor, AV (2007) *Competing Values Leadership: Creating value in organizations (new horizons in management)*, Edward Elgar Publishing, London

Charan, R, Drotter, S and Noel, J (2011) *The Leadership Pipeline: How to build the leadership powered company*, John Wiley & Sons, New York

Compagne, O (2014) [accessed 12 January 2017] Holacracy vs. Hierarchy vs. Flat Orgs, *HolacracyOne*, 18 March [Online] https://blog.holacracy.org/holacracy-vs-hierarchy-vs-flat-orgs-d1545d5dffa7#.s5kgwjjjd

Culbert, SA (2010) *Get Rid of the Performance Review!*, Business Plus, New York

Endenburg, G (1988) *Sociocracy: The organization of decision-making*, Eburon, Delft, The Netherlands

Fairtlough, G (2005) *The Three Ways of Getting Things Done: Hierarchy, heterarchy and responsible autonomy in organizations*, Triarchy Press, Bridport

Goldsmith, K (2016) [accessed 12 January 2017] Building a Technical Career Path at Spotify, *Spotify Labs*, 8 February [Online] https://labs.spotify.com/2016/02/08/technical-career-path/

Gray, D and Vander Wal, T (2014) *Connected Company*, O'Reilly Media, California

Hamel, G (2011) First, let's fire all the managers, *Harvard Business Review*, December

Hellriegel, D and Slocum, JW (2010) *Organizational Behavior*, South Western Educational Publishing, Cincinnati

Inamori, K (2012) *Amoeba Management: The dynamic management system for rapid market response*, Productivity Press, New York

Ingham, J (2011) [accessed 12 January 2017] Innovative Asian People Strategies, *Strategic HCM*, 1 October [Online] http://strategic-hcm.blogspot.co.uk/2011/10/innovative-asian-people-strategies.html

Jaques, E (2006) *Requisite Organization: A total system for effective managerial organization and managerial leadership for the 21st century*, 2nd rev edn, Gower Publishing, London

Johansen, B (2007) *Get There Early: Sensing the future to compete in the present*, Berrett-Koehler Publishers

Kniberg, H (2014) [accessed 12 January 2017] Spotify Engineering Culture (Part 1), *Spotify Labs*, 27 May [Online] https://labs.spotify.com/2014/03/27/spotify-engineering-culture-part-1/

Laloux, F (2015) *Reinventing Organizations: A guide to creating organizations inspired by the next stage of human consciousness*, Nelson Parker, Brussels

Leavitt, HJ (2004) *Top Down: Why hierarchies are here to stay and how to manage them more effectively*, Harvard Business School Press, Boston

McDowell, T, Agarwal, D, Miller, D, Okamoto, T and Page, T (2016) [accessed 12 January 2017] Organizational Design: The rise of teams, *Deloitte University Press* [Online] https://dupress.deloitte.com/dup-us-en/focus/human-capital-trends/2016/organizational-models-network-of-teams.html

Pflaeging, N, Vollmer, L, Hermann, S and Carvalho, V (2012) [accessed 6 March 2017] Organize for Complexity, *BetaCodex Network Associates*, White paper 12 and 13 [Online] http://www.betacodex.org/sites/default/files/paper/3/betacodex-organizeforcomplexity.pdf

Ronfeldt, D (1996) [accessed 6 March 2017] Tribes, Institutions, Markets, Networks: A Framework About Societal Evolution, *RAND* [Online] http://www.rand.org/content/dam/rand/pubs/papers/2005/P7967.pdf

Sutton, RI and Rao, H (2014) *Scaling Up Excellence: Getting to more without settling for less*, Crown Business, New York

Valve (2012) [accessed 12 January 2017] Handbook For New Employees, *Valve Corporation* [Online] http://www.valvesoftware.com/company/Valve_Handbook_LowRes.pdf

Designing the   10
workplace

Introduction

Chapter 10 is the last remaining chapter in this part of the book and deals with the workplace, the last remaining element in the OPM. This single organizational enabler could potentially have been included within a small section in Chapter 9 on enabling the organization. However, I am putting workplace design into a chapter of its own as I think it deserves deeper treatment. Workplace design provides a major opportunity for HR and others focused on people and organizational management. Just as with the rest of the organizational architecture, the workplace's most direct link is to organization capital and, in particular, to what is sometimes called spatial capital.

In many ways the workplace can have a greater impact on organization capital than any of the other enablers in the OPM. Ben Waber, a visiting scientist at MIT who conducts analytics using sociometers (explained in Chapter 13), suggests that changing the organization chart but not the seating will have little effect. However, 'if I keep the org chart the same but change where you sit, it is going to massively change everything' (Feintzeig, 2013). This means that workplace and organization design disciplines should be closely linked to one another. Unfortunately, this often tends not to be the case. Both disciplines are generally organized into two different functions – HR and property/corporate real estate/facilities management – and without coordinating links, the two groups can easily become disconnected.

The workplace also supports human and especially social capital. In particular, it has a huge impact on engagement and employer branding. It will also generally provide the main physical signal of an organization's values. However, sociologist Kristin Sailer reports that only 11–15 per cent of staff strongly agree that their workplace reflects their company's values. In addition, most stakeholders have no idea about how space represents what a company stands for (Sailer, Pomeroy and Haslem, 2015). Sailer and colleagues suggest that these companies are failing to connect the workplace with their values. I think they often are, it is just that many organizations' values are as bland, neutral and faceless as their workplaces – see Chapter 5 for ideas on improving these.

The workplace has an even stronger link with the social behaviours between people working in the organization. This is demonstrated via a relationship known as the Allen curve. This suggests that the likelihood of any two people communicating with each is four times higher if they are sitting 6 feet away from each other than if they are 60 feet apart (Allen, 1977). Waber and Magnolia (2014) have found that interactions between workplace neighbours account for 40–60 per cent of all of their communications. There is only a 5–10 per cent chance of employees interacting with someone even just two rows away. People seated more than 75 feet away from each other, particularly if they are on different floors, are unlikely to ever talk at all. Seating arrangements have a powerful influence on communication patterns so social organization architects need to include or be linked to workplace architects and designers even more closely than are the rest of HR.

Workplace design also provides lots of possibilities for innovative, creating-value activities, though property owners often have more opportunities than occupiers as the latter have limited control over their buildings. This chapter will review these opportunities and why it makes sense to integrate them within organization design. The chapter also looks at changes in organization form and how this relates to changes in the workplace. It ends with a summary of Part 2.

New places for working

Changes in the nature of work, in people's requirements and expectations, and in the range and power of technology are having major impacts on when, where and how people work. A lot of people no longer need to be stationed in one place all day. Even if they do, a lot of knowledge workers no longer need a big desk with a big PC and a monitor attached to a big printer together with a phone, fax, photocopier, stacks of paper, filing cabinet etc. A lot of people just need a portable device, good Wi-Fi and perhaps an additional mobile phone or headset.

This means that for some of the time at least, many people can work from a range of different locations. This includes their home, coffee bars and outside in a park, as well as in hotels, airports and even their cars. Some people use regular 'third places' and others base themselves in different and repurposed locations every day. I have written this book at the British

Library, at the kitchen table, on a step machine at a sit/stand desk and sitting on a sunroom sofa when, infrequently, the sun has been shining. I have used these multiple locations, in part at least, to give me a change in scene during the course of a day. I have not really used my home 'office' room at all, even though 15 years ago having this room was a key reason for buying my current house.

A further opportunity has been provided by the rise of co-working spaces. Some companies let their people use these spaces in preference to travelling in to their main office every day. Some firms are setting up smaller satellite locations arranged around the peripheries of major cities to allow their staff to co-work with others in the same firm. Some firms are also co-locating with co-working spaces to make it easier for their own staff to connect with different roles, skills and workstyles, making it easier to bring more diverse insights into the organization. For example, Amazon's Seattle campus includes a whole floor devoted to co-working.

Zappos's CEO Tony Hseih took this idea to a new level by investing $350 million of his own money in the downtown project around the company's head office in Las Vegas (Sachs, 2017). This space involves nearly 200 stakeholders including Zapponians, area residents, start-ups, independent workers and others. The success of the project has been measured through the 3Cs – collisions, co-learning and connectedness. Hseih suggests that return on collisions, or the number of probable interactions per hour per acre, is a more important outcome than return on investment (ROI).

Changes inside offices

As with HR, workforce design has evolved upwards through the levels in the value triangle. Its traditional focus has been on reducing cost and providing other value-for-money benefits, and more recently on helping add value to existing business needs. These objectives have led to the introduction of monolithic, open-space cube farms. Whilst not necessarily a problem, the amount of ongoing distraction inherent in this environment, together with a lack of choice and autonomy, can lead to lower effectiveness, productivity and innovation (Tidd, 2016). These distractions, which Basecamp founder Jason Fried suggests focus mainly on managers and meetings (M&Ms), are one of the main reasons that many people prefer to work at home or somewhere elsewhere in preference to the office (Fried, 2010).

Companies have also been reducing the number of seats, together with the amount of space assigned to each person, and therefore the floor space they need, in order to save costs. This has led to the introduction of hot desking, in which a certain number of people share a smaller number of work stations. Similar to and only slightly better than this is hotelling, where people make advance reservations for unassigned seating. However, given the opportunities for workplace design to impact human, organization and social capital, companies are now realizing that there are opportunities for creating value too. This is leading to a new focus on people and the ways they can do their best work.

This all means that today's workplaces need to do very different things than in the past. First, they need to play a part in contributing to an organization's differentiated capabilities, acting as a physical embodiment of its purpose and values. People also need to be able to work in a human way, having fun whilst – and in order to be – productive. This suggests the use of flexible workspaces rather than hotelling or hot desking.

Second, offices need to be much more attuned to people factors. A good example is noise. An adding-value approach to noise was to ignore it. A creating-value approach understands the impact it can have and seeks to remove or mitigate it. This goes back to understanding our brains. Nigel Oseland suggests that noise is unwanted sound. Therefore, it is about our environment but it is also about us and our interpretation. In fact, 25 per cent of noise concerns the actual sound and 41 per cent relates to psychological factors (Oseland and Hodsman, 2015). A good example is a dripping tap, which we can find annoying even though we interpret the similar sound of rain falling from leaves as calming and relaxing.

Dealing with this requires people to have alternative spaces to work in, and more privacy, including control over their personal information and stimulation (Congdon, Flynn and Redman, 2014). Working with Congdon's colleagues at Steelcase, Susan Cain, author of *Quiet* (Cain, 2012), developed four principles for designing quiet workspaces. These are control over the environment, sensory balance, psychological safety and permission to be alone. The last of these is about the freedom to focus and innovate without interruption – including the choice not to collaborate (Steelcase, 2014).

This requires a level of balance, between open and closed, quiet and high energy etc. It is this balance that keeps people engaged with the workplace and stops it becoming airspace (Chayka, 2016), the nowhere office (Tokumitsu and Mol, 2016) or anywhereist (Boyd, 2016). Facebook's 1 million square foot open-plan campus (Frearson, 2015) may just be too massive and open (Newport, 2016) despite the range of small meeting rooms and other spaces. Given this, it is a worry that choice, even if only perceived choice, is on the decline (McLaurin, 2017).

Third, organizations are right to recognize that workplaces do not need to accommodate everyone at the same time. People will generally not all be in the office together, eg some of them may work at customer sites a proportion of the time. However, there may be a need to accommodate customers, suppliers, contingent and gig workers and others in an organization's offices too. When people are in the office their focus is often less on doing work tasks and more on interacting, collaborating and cooperating with other people. Many people prefer to do work that is not collaborative at home. Therefore, even when people are in the office they will generally be working at their desks less than half of the time.

As knowledge working develops into relationship working a growing need is to be with the people that these relationships are with. The difficulty in this is that most often people have different types of relationships with people based in different places and who come together into different groups and in different ways. A workplace that works for one of these groups/needs probably will not work that well for another. This means organizations need to understand the trade-offs involved in the selection of different options and to prioritize the one that best meets the overall needs. This is, of course, exactly what organizations need to do to design the other elements of their architectures too. They therefore need to follow the process described in Chapters 5 and 9 and select the best workplace architectures based upon which of the core elements have the highest-priority needs. If there are multiple priorities this may result in a melded workplace that tries to respond to multiple requirements, perhaps through synchronized group times and lunch hours etc. For example, everyone could sit together within functions in the morning and then scatter into other spaces to network in the afternoon.

Repurposing the workplace

People generally do not need to be chained to their desks all day. They may not need desks at all. Instead of this, they need a range of spaces that help them to work and connect in different ways. This does not mean increasing the amount of space – it may mean not needing so much. For example, a functional grouping may benefit from more break-out space but can also find it useful to move their desks closer together to create more opportunities of synergies arising through chance and overheard conversations. Doing this creates at least some of the space for their new break-out areas.

Figure 10.1   Opportunities for social workplace design

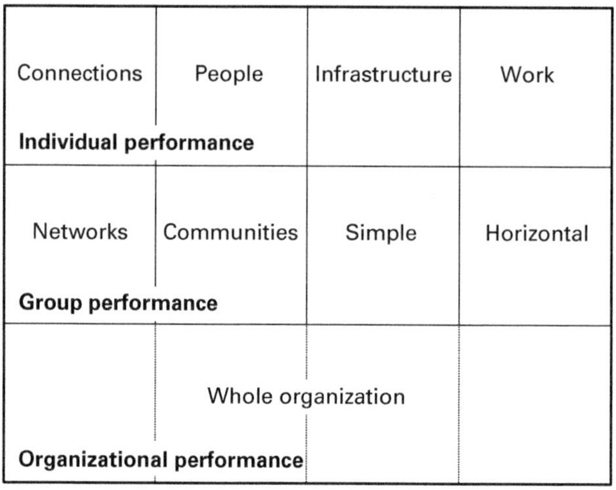

Connections	People	Infrastructure	Work
Individual performance			
Networks	Communities	Simple	Horizontal
Group performance			
	Whole organization		
Organizational performance			

Opportunities can be reviewed most easily by considering the different levels that people work at, ie on their own, in groups, and sometimes together with everyone else from the whole office or organization (sometimes referred to as me, us and we). These levels also need to be combined with the core elements of the organization, which influence how people work in the workplace. Putting these two dimensions together provides the opportunities shown in Figure 10.1. The top row in Figure 10.1 is about the need for people to be able to do work requiring concentration and focus, or speaking on the phone, on their own. Doing this requires certain support in terms of infrastructure, doing work, forming communities and participating in networks. The second row refers to the need for people to do other work in groups, recognizing that different types of groups have different needs. The third row is about the need to work together with everyone in a whole organization. Further detail on some of the specific options available within each of the cells in Figure 10.1 is provided below:

- Individual spaces:
  - Work-based spaces:
    - ability to do different types of work in different ways (activity-based working);
    - eg quiet booths for individual focus, pods for phone calls etc.

– Infrastructure-based spaces:

- air quality and temperature people can control, ideally by opening a window;
- good acoustics, eg white/pink noise or other sound-masking/sound-scaping systems;
- natural light to support circadian rhythms;
- good technology support, eg audio and video conferencing, and including power and Wi-Fi;
- access to kitchens, bathrooms, printers etc.

– People-based spaces:

- a human rather than just an economic amount of personal space, which people can influence and make it feel like their own;
- sufficient shared space to move around to meet emotional state and personal needs, which may change over the course of a day;
- personal or shared private spaces – sit-stand desks and ergonomic furniture;
- areas with a cosy, human feel, including comfortable soft seating for people to put their feet up;
- quiet reflection rooms, eg a library environment with books etc to show a need for calm and to provide opportunities for research;
- art – painting, photographs etc;
- music, interaction and humour, eg using musical strings as a screen or replacing carpet with astroturf;
- well-being support, eg break areas, fitness, massage, meditation etc;
- recovery areas, eg sleep pods;
- food – healthy eating;
- biophilic design elements – plants and other elements of the outdoors;
- outdoor working spaces – 'beer gardens', lawns, green roofs;
- a base to leave work and personal items – papers, wallet/purse, gym bag, shoes etc.

– Connections-based spaces:

- social play spaces, eg fussball, table tennis, games stations;
- densely occupied neighbourhoods to encourage serendipity;

- pods for one-to-one meetings, spaces for small group (two to five people) meetings;
- social dimension – local neighbourhoods people can belong to plus communal activities/destinations between adjoining group areas where resources are pooled to stimulate chance meetings and conversations, eg micro kitchens.

- Group spaces:
  - Horizontal teams (need team members to be together the bulk of the time, attending daily stand-up meetings etc, or be similarly connected via technology):
    - project rooms and information/status tracking, eg daily stand-up boards;
    - touch-screen team walls;
    - oval or rectangular team tables;
    - break-out spaces and meeting rooms for subgroups or concentrating;
    - agile, reconfigurable workplaces.
  - Simple groupings (for people who need to be connected but will often be working independently or in small groups and therefore do not need to be with each other all the time):
    - team spaces – not necessarily desks and almost certainly not based on grids of cubicles;
    - access to quiet areas, small group and team meeting rooms;
    - informal spaces to meet and write up/display on a wall.
  - Community spaces (for people who need to meet, socialize, discuss and work on issues together on a regular but infrequent basis):
    - huddle areas and other relaxed, comfortable meeting spaces;
    - supporting personal choice in meeting locations.
  - Network spaces (to enable people to come together as a crowd in order to be able to share, debate and work on issues):
    - creative spaces in blues and greens with low lighting levels to support innovation;
    - advanced collaboration spaces with tools and resources for collaboration and cooperation;

- multiple informal opportunities to get together and talk;
- plentiful whiteboards.

- Whole organization spaces:
  - Whole organization – work:
    - bringing the outside in – highlighting customers, products, services etc;
    - spaces for hackathons.
  - Whole organization – infrastructure:
    - visual knowledge sharing and communication systems, eg display screens;
    - areas for whole company/location briefings and meetings.
  - Whole organization – people:
    - areas for unconferences and social events etc.
  - Whole organization – connections:
    - encouraging transparency and working out loud via few walls and windows plus whiteboards etc;
    - layouts that promote movement and multiple opportunities for spontaneous encounters bridging structural holes;
    - open spaces, streets, courtyards and restaurants with round tables seating 10–12, all providing the opportunity for people to congregate, encouraging serendipitous chance collisions, informal interaction and enjoyable relaxed collaboration;
    - escalators versus lifts; staircases to get employees walking.

Organizations may need all or just some of these alternative arrangements, depending largely on their values (fussball tables will not work everywhere and the use of slides needs to be strictly limited to Silicon Valley!) plus the prioritization given to the four core elements in the OPM. A social organization, prioritizing connections, will probably want to provide creative and other informal meeting spaces. It may not need to have many project rooms. However, it will still want to use a range of spaces to support diverse personal characteristics, different working styles and various types of relationships. So it is about balance, but an unequal balance, reflecting what the organization sees as its priorities.

After having made this prioritization, social organization architects then need to undertake strategic design of office layouts to ensure the right groups sit with or near each other. A common approach is to put public areas where people congregate in the centre of an office to draw together people from different parts of the building. For example, animation studio Pixar works as a loosely structured community-based organization run by creative artists and it encourages everyone – from the janitors to the auditors – to submit ideas. Creativity is supported through collaborative opinion sessions and daily reviews where people show their unfinished work to help others input into this. The studio's building is designed to encourage interaction too. Its centre is a large atrium that contains a cafeteria, meeting rooms, bathrooms and mailboxes. Because everyone has strong reasons to go there multiple times every day this arrangement results in many valuable chance encounters (Catmull, 2008).

This approach is supported by zoning different areas of the office for different or mixed purposes, creating separate neighbourhoods. These areas can be identified using distinct styles, colours and visual cues. For example, a space for quiet concentration can be identified by rows of books rather than by labelling it as a library. This helps provide a sense of local identity plus movement between neighbourhoods. Areas can be further separated by plants or other screening, creating appropriate visual privacy whilst maintaining a level of transparency. Tall buildings, most common in urban areas, can use high-level bridges to connect over atria and also build roof terraces. Out-of-town offices can develop offices that feel a little like campuses, with streets offering access to different facilities. A common objective is to increase collisions, often by promoting functional inconvenience – making people take indirect paths to their destinations.

A special issue concerns whether functions should sit with their directors or whether these executives should sit together as a team. On one side of this argument there is the example of former New York Mayor Michael Bloomberg's 'bullpen'. He moved officials out of their marble offices and gathered them around him, sitting at standard-sized desks in an open space created in the historic speakers' hall (Barbaro, 2013) as a symbol of transparency and open communication. Bloomberg also uses the same approach at his financial information firm, Bloomberg LP. An example on the opposite side of things comes from marketing software vendor HubSpot. This company's staff switch seats every three months. After adding some structure to these changes the firm tried grouping its executives together in one part of the office too. The executives liked this arrangement but employees felt that it created too much separation (Feintzeig, 2013).

If executives are placed together it helps social cohesion to avoid obvious status differences. According to Gensler's UK workplace survey, 89 per cent of senior leaders have private offices, compared to just 23 per cent at lower levels of the organization (Tidd *et al*, 2016). Regardless of the logic for such divisions this is often perceived as one rule for the bosses and another for everyone else. This makes it more difficult for those people who are supposed to be leading their organizations to do so.

CASE STUDY Sharing accommodation at Airbnb

Airbnb is a good example of a company that has developed a collaborative workspace without resorting to open-plan cubicles and hotelling. Its spaces aim to create privacy without diminishing visibility, using long sightlines to help create a sense of community. As an example, the Portland office (Bittermann, 2014) includes:

- Belong everywhere: this is shared space (not anonymous space) and consists of a mixture of individual, team and social spaces. The approach emphasizes free desking to connect people to a variety of spaces across the office, so belonging is not associated with a single desk.
- High-contrast spaces depending on needs, eg on-demand/quick-access quiet spaces and noisier collaboration spaces allowing individuals to choose a location based on their current needs.
- Team hubs acting as shared resources for teams and which are flanked by communal tables and lounge seating. These spaces are the default area for team leads and others who need to stick together.
- Duck-in spaces for one, two or three people, providing acoustic privacy.
- Monitor zones for those who want to plug in.
- Large, medium and small meeting rooms.

Workplace mobility is supported by a digital workflow and storage solutions for tools and personal belongings. Power and data is distributed throughout, so a lounge chair is just as much a workspace as a communal table. Landing/standing desks provide a standing workspace plus room to charge a laptop and store coats and shoes/work slippers that people can get changed into after cycling into work.

Airbnb's ground control team act as community managers, creating a memorable experience for people by aligning workspace operations, eg provision of food and massages etc, with the company's core values. For example, there is only one choice of food at each meal, which helps people feel like they are eating together. Ground control use internal communications, employee celebrations, recognition and meet-ups to support the company's values and keep them top of mind.

Offices are designed by in-house architects and designers together with the people who will be working in them. This includes observations of existing behaviours, brainstorming of people's future needs, and surveys on their work preferences.

Designing for complexity

An important feature of many social workplaces is the way they are designed to encourage serendipitous connections. Google provides a good example of this, arranging 'magnets' or attractors, eg micro kitchens around neighbourhoods to stimulate chance conversations. Its restaurants provide free, healthy food and the conversations people have while they stand in line waiting to be served are seen as major enablers for innovation.

A further important aspect of workplace design is enabling people to co-design their own workspaces. Involving people is useful in the design of other elements in the organizational architecture too; however, it is even more important here. Research by Steelcase suggests there is a close connection between workplace control and engagement. In their survey 88 per cent of highly engaged employees suggest they can choose where to work in the office whereas only 14 per cent of highly disengaged staff say this is the case (Congdon, 2016). This applies particularly strongly to the people-oriented aspects of the workplace, eg the community and networking spaces where usage is optional and discretionary.

Some organizations move groups or individual people around at regular intervals to increase organizational cohesion or respond to individual preferences. However, moving people around the office can make them feel there is a lack of autonomy and control. Increasingly therefore, organizations will enable people to base themselves where they want to work, even if just for part of the day.

This means that although I include the workplace as part of the organizational architecture because it is part of the context we work within, it can be useful to see this as a way to develop an organizational society (see Chapter 12) as well. From this perspective, the workplace is something people can use to develop their relationships rather than just part of the context or environment they work within.

Making ongoing changes to the workplace is another good way to keep people engaged in the different spaces that are provided. This becomes even more important in those organizations that do try to match their work-places to the rest of their organization architectures. This implies that each restructure needs to be supported by changes in the workplace too. For both of these reasons it is useful to build flexible, reconfigurable workspaces that can respond easily to change.

CASE STUDY Developing the workplace at KLM

My favourite example of using an organization development perspective for workplace design comes from KLM Passenger Services at Schiphol Airport. The airline needed to implement a huge IT system which required developing a more agile organization. This was enabled by transforming a traditional and rather boring workplace into one that oozes innovation, transparency and hospitality. This new workplace was created following an intervention with the management team based on the idea of a *kgotla*. This is a Botswanan term for a meeting place where people get to really see and hear each other (Waddell, 2010). It starts with the chief (CEO) sharing their dream, after which everyone can add their voice. The chief observes, listens and asks questions and becomes aware of the real issues within the organization, as seen by the collective. Everyone shares their truth on the issue and the chief finally takes a decision based on all the inputs.

Following this intervention, KLM revisited its workplace principles and agreed it needed to get rid of silos, keep its people's relationships and improve togetherness. That required getting rid of the directors' offices – all executives now sit amongst their teams in the shared space. This includes open desk spaces and small meeting rooms called cockpits, organized around an open, flexible layout, co-creation square that can be used by all KLM staff. The design also features an 'oval office', which is a circle of comfortable seats facing a round table; another set of soft chairs acting as a boardroom; a no-rules coffee area and gardens. The choice of office colour was based on Dutch polders and tulip fields (Yapparov, 2014).

Summary and additional comments

1 The workplace provides what is probably the most obvious and certainly the most physical way that people experience the organization. It is therefore very important in ensuring organizational effectiveness and in building a social organization. Continuing to manage HR and organization design separately to property and facilities is no longer tenable.

2 The issue is that if we do not manage the workplace it is not necessarily going to evolve in an effective way. As described in Chapter 4 we evolved to live in tribes, not in huge cities or cramped offices. Living on top of each other has led to the development of social norms in which we tend to ignore each other, even when sitting next to each other. This is a shame as it means we deprive our social brains of what could make them much happier. However, in general it is not particularly damaging, eg when this happens on a train during the morning commute. But it is dangerous when it happens in the workplace. We need to find ways to get people to act differently.

3 Doing this requires designing appropriate organizations, including the right teams of the right size. It also requires appropriately designed workplaces. These requirements also need to be linked to other elements of the organization that we have not yet explored, ie the organizational society as well as the organizational architecture. A particular issue is that, even when working in collaborative settings, people will not collaborate unless they trust their colleagues. These requirements in the organizational society will be reviewed in Part 3.

Summary of Part 2 – Changes in organization form

People often talk about organizations moving 'from hierarchies to networks'. In my view, this is not quite what has been happening. And just as it is important to understand the organization forms used by maverick organizations, so it is important to understand that the change in form that everyone seems to think has been happening is not really what has been going on.

This is partly because hierarchies and networks are not equivalent concepts. As we know, networks are a major organizational archetype. Hierarchy is simply an aspect of organizational reporting arrangements. Also, when people complain about hierarchy they are not usually referring to there being problems in having different levels of importance or even in organizing based upon a tree structure. Plus, as suggested by CCL's data, reviewed in Chapter 6, hierarchical boundaries are usually much less significant than vertical boundaries between different groups. In any case, as suggested in Chapter 9, the main problem associated with hierarchy is not hierarchical structure but hierarchical thinking. Therefore I do not think there is a deep desire to move away from hierarchy. It is also not as if there is an overwhelming desire to work within a heterarchy – indeed many people would struggle to define this term.

It is true that a lot of organizations have been focusing on delayering their organizations. However, most large-scale restructures involving this have actually focused on bigger opportunities, such as changing organization form, rather than just delayering. Different organizational forms will have different levels of hierarchy – simple/functional forms have the most hierarchy and other forms, particularly communities and networks, have less. A consequence of increasing use of networks is therefore a reduction in hierarchy. But this has not been the reason for, or the main aspect of, the change. I find that, in general, people are really referring to a reduction in bureaucracy and the lack of agility inherent in a simple functional structure. The change they are talking about is therefore actually a move from centralized to decentralized and distributed networks.

However, even this move is really a result of two other changes. I can explain this best by applying the orientation/motivation model, used in Chapter 9 for analysing groups, to the analysis of organization structures, as shown in Figure 10.2.

Figure 10.2   Changes in organization forms

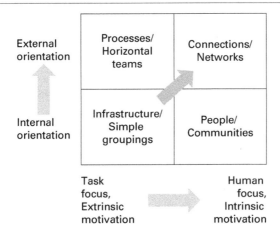

This presentation of the model suggests that there have been two independent shifts. These are from the bottom to the top of the model, ie from an internal to an external orientation, and from the left-hand to the right-hand side of the model, ie from a task to a human focus. The move away from simple, centralized groupings towards distributed networks is simply a result of the two other moves described above.

The first shift has been from an internal orientation to an external one. This has been caused by the need for greater agility and has moved organizations from the bottom to the top of the grid. Simple and community organizations are relatively static and stable. They are best used for exploiting existing opportunities for work and existing connections between people. The objective of doing this is often to improve efficiency. Horizontal and network-based companies are more changeable. These work well for exploring new opportunities and developing new connections between people. Their objectives tend to focus on effectiveness, efficacy and generating new energy.

The second shift has been from a task focus to human focus. Increased people-centricity, described in Chapter 3, has moved organizations from the left- to the right-hand side of the matrix. This may surprise some people as you could argue that digital technology is giving more focus to tasks. For example, as explained in Chapter 8, organizations can now use digital platforms to ask individual people to bid for individual pieces of work. However, digital can help people to connect in a more human way too. For me, digital supports either side of the above model. This is a bit like the move away from lifetime employment described in Chapter 2. This can be taken to suggest an increasing focus on task, eg through tours of duty, or it can be seen to reinforce the existing need to focus on people, eg career partnerships.

It is this change that is behind the move from horizontal project teams to greater use of networks. For example, I spent some time with an electronic components manufacturer that was switching from a capability of innovation to one of speed to market. The reason for this was that they felt that open innovation had reduced the potential impact of their internal innovation capability. When innovation was key they had an innovation process. However, they did not believe that speed to market could be supported by a process. Every new innovation would be different and this would mean that a process could not cope. Instead of this, they looked at reforming groups of people with the required strength of relationship, meaning that when needed these people could come together as a team and immediately start work. In terms of group development stages (Tuckman and Jensen, 1977), these latent networks would have already been through the forming and storming stages (although these do not strictly apply as people were not yet working in a group) and would therefore be capable of moving straight into performing.

This sort of change has introduced interesting new organizational challenges. The more mechanistic, task-focused horizontal structures on the left-hand side of the grid in Figure 10.2 can be managed by rules, process, job descriptions and tight governance. But the more organic, people-focused organizations on the right-hand side can only be influenced though the use of values and principles, with people aligning with these and creating new forms of behaviour through social calibration.

I like the way that Bjarte Bogsnes (2016) compares the difference between task- and people-focused organizations to that between traffic lights, which impose structure and order on a road junction, and roundabouts, which rely much more on unstructured self-organization. Traffic lights implement a simple rules-based system which is regulated centrally. Roundabouts just assume that people have a shared purpose in wanting the traffic to flow well; they apply one general principle, which is normally that drivers should give way to others already on the roundabout. In both cases, these rules and principles should be cascaded from a company's organization principles, as described in Chapter 5.

The rules used in task-focused organizations are more specific, and also tend to be articulated more formally, than principles, especially when self-organization is involved. You can see this in the way that Zappos has to use a detailed constitution and formal organizational governance processes, whilst Buurtzorg shapes its organization through a short list of ground rules and locally developed processes. However, my favourite example of a mechanistic rules-based organization is investment firm Bridgewater, which runs according to 210 detailed principles and suggests that teams should work as a machine designed to achieve their goals (Feloni, 2014).

The use of principles in people-focused organizations is often supported by high levels of investment in areas like trust and transparency (see Chapter 12). However it is still difficult to achieve the same levels of adoption or compliance as in a rules-based, task-focused organization. This limitation provides further constraints on the use of community and network structures.

You see this in workplace design too. For example, spaces for functional departments can generally impose rules on etiquette, ie around noise levels. However, rules will generally not work in shared spaces. Here, broader principles emerge from the actions of individuals. Designers can facilitate their identification, for example, by getting people together to ask them what the principles are and should be. However, even then some people will probably ignore these suggestions.

This difficulty applies to other people-focused activities too. For example, the same problems are often found with social learning activities such as action learning. Whilst this can provide one of the most effective forms of learning, the common finding is that it does not work that well. Sets may work for a couple of sessions, whilst they are facilitated, but when the group is left to run its own sessions a few people fail to attend and the conversation is less valuable, and then the set very soon peters out. Making all these people-centric structures and activities work requires organizations to be much more serious about their purpose, values, norms etc.

As noted previously, the two separate shifts along the two axes of the OMM work together to produce a broader movement from centralized to decentralized and partially distributed networks. This is the change described in Brafman and Beckstrom's book, *The Starfish and the Spider* (2006): spiders are centralized with behaviours being determined in their heads – if the head is cut off the spider dies. Starfish are decentralized with major organs replicated throughout each arm – there is no head and this means that if the starfish is cut in half it just produces two starfish.

The shift is also linked to one from a simple to a more complex world, which is in itself caused partly by a more external orientation and more intrinsic focus. For example, Cynthia Kurtz's confluence/tetrahedron model (Kurtz, 2010), developed with Dave Snowden based on his cynefin model (Kurtz, 2003), suggests that centralization works well in a simple/known environment, and that centralized and distributed networks can work well together in a complicated environment, but that in emergent, complex environments it is distributed networks that thrive.

John Hagel and John Seely Brown suggest that the traditional control mindset cannot cope in this increasingly interdependent environment. Control seeks to preserve stability and predictability whereas what is needed is flexibility. We therefore need a new mindset built on trust. This focuses on establishing shared expectations rather than specifying in detail the actions that must be performed (Hagel and Brown, 2002).

This links to the change from command and control to 'coordinate and cultivate' described by Tom Malone in his writing on the future of work (Malone, 2004). His suggestion is that new decentralized organizations, including internal markets, democracies and loose hierarchies, can combine the benefits provided by the scale and knowledge efficiencies of large organizations with the freedom, flexibility and human values of smaller ones. Malone also notes that decentralized organizations are affected by the paradoxes of standards and of power. The first of these paradoxes suggests that decentralization often requires standards for interaction. Rigid standards in one part of a system can enable increased flexibility in other parts of the system. I notice this best when designing unconferences. These need to feel unplanned and spontaneous but they require a lot of planning and structuring to make their unstructured approach work effectively. The second paradox is that the best way to gain power is to give it away. People tend to resist when others try to micromanage them, and even if they capitulate they will lack the intrinsic motivation that would come with more autonomy.

A similar shift is behind changes in the workplace too. Originally, industrialized workplaces were created to bring tasks together in close proximity, but even more importantly, to facilitate control over the people doing them. This created gigantic spaces filled with standardized workspaces, emphasizing hierarchy and order. As described within this chapter, today's offices emphasize natural groups, social relations and spontaneous, serendipitous social encounter. This has created a 'portable worksphere' and nomadic working styles (Gou, 2017).

Increasing interest in social organizations has also reinforced and will continue to support the above change. Therefore, whilst the most important need for any particular business remains the design of a best-fit organization, the direction of travel is clearly towards network-based structures. As an example, an increasing number of companies are making a distinction between exploitation of current business opportunities and exploration of new ones. Some suggest splitting their organizations to focus separately on these two things. However, the above analysis suggests the need may just be for a new set of project teams and networks operating on top of existing functions, divisions and communities. Social organization designers should expect to make more use of new, melded, network-based organization forms like this in the future.

References

Allen, TJ (1977) *Managing the Flow of Technology*, MIT Press, Massachusetts

Barbaro, M (2013) [accessed 12 January 2017] The Bullpen Bloomberg Built: Candidates Debate Its Future, *New York Times* [Online] http://www.nytimes.com/2013/03/23/nyregion/bloombergs-bullpen-candidates-debate-its-future.html

Bittermann, J (2014) [accessed 12 January 2017] Airbnb's Portland Office Offers a Diverse Range of Working Environments, *Designboom*, 21 December [Online] http://www.designboom.com/architecture/airbnb-portland-office-customer-experience-12-21-2014/

Bogsnes, B (2016) *Implementing Beyond Budgeting: Unlocking the performance potential*, John Wiley & Sons, New York

Boyd, S (2016) [accessed 12 January 2017] Ism's, Work Futures, 21 September [Online] https://workfutures.io/isms-b55c8ba809d8#.51w2xohnw

Brafman, O and Beckstrom, RA (2006) *The Starfish and the Spider: The unstoppable power of leaderless organizations*, Portfolio, New York

Cain, S (2012) *Quiet: The power of introverts in a world that can't stop talking*, Crown, New York

Catmull, E (2008) How Pixar fosters collective creativity, *Harvard Business Review*, September

Chayka, K (2016) [accessed 12 January 2017] Welcome to Airspace, *The Verge*, 3 August [Online] http://www.theverge.com/2016/8/3/12325104/airbnb-aesthetic-global-minimalism-startup-gentrification

Congdon, C (2016) [accessed 12 January 2017] Why Employee Engagement Matters, *Steelcase*, 2 March [Online] https://www.steelcase.com/blog/why-employee-engagement-matters/

Congdon, C, Flynn, D and Redman, M (2014) Balancing 'we' and 'me': the best collaborative spaces also support solitude, *Harvard Business Review*, October

Feintzeig, R (2013) [accessed 12 January 2017] The New Science of Who Sits Where at Work, *Wall Street Journal* [Online] http://www.wsj.com/articles/SB10001424052702304441404579123230310600884

Feloni, R (2014) [accessed 12 January 2017] Billionaire Investor Ray Dalio's Top 20 Management Principles, *Business Insider*, 5 November [Online] http://uk.businessinsider.com/ray-dalios-bridgewater-management-principles-2014-11

Frearson, A (2015) [accessed 12 January 2017] Facebook Moves Into California Campus Designed by Frank Gehry, *Dezeen*, 31 March [Online] https://www.dezeen.com/2015/03/31/facebook-moves-into-campus-frank-gehry-silicon-valley-california/

Fried, J (2010) [accessed 12 January 2017] Why Work Doesn't Happen at Work, TED, October [Online] http://www.ted.com/talks/jason_fried_why_work_doesn_t_happen_at_work/transcript?language=en#t-489738

Gou, Z (2017) Workplace design revolution: the inside-out urbanism, in *Design Innovations for Contemporary Interiors and Civic Art*, ed L Crespi, IGI Global, Pennsylvania

Hagel, J III and Brown, JS (2002) [accessed 12 January 2017] Control vs Trust – Mastering a Different Management Approach, working paper [Online] http://www.johnseelybrown.com/paper_control.pdf

Kurtz, C (2003) The new dynamics of strategy: sense-making in a complex and complicated world, *IBM Systems Journal*, **42** (3), pp 462–83

Kurtz, C (2010) [accessed 12 January 2017] Confluence, Story Colored Glasses, 22 June [Online] http://www.storycoloredglasses.com/2010/06/confluence.html

Malone, T (2004) *The Future of Work: How the new order of business will shape your organization, your management style, and your life*, Harvard Business Review Press, Boston

McLaurin, JP (2017) [accessed 12 January 2017] The Surprising Truth About Choice, *Gensler On Work*, 17 January [Online] http://www.gensleron.com/work/2017/1/17/the-surprising-truth-about-choice.html

Newport, C (2016) [accessed 12 January 2017] Is Facebook's Massive Open Office Scaring Away Developers?, *Study Hacks Blog*, 9 October [Online] http://calnewport.com/blog/2016/10/09/is-facebooks-massive-open-office-scaring-away-developers/

Oseland, N and Hodsman, P (2015) [accessed 12 January 2017] Planning
for Psychoacoustics: A Psychological Approach to Resolving Office Noise
Distraction, *Workplace Unlimited*, April [Online] http://workplaceunlimited.
com/Ecophon%20Psychoacoustics%20v4.5.pdf

Sachs, A (2017) [accessed 12 January 2017] Zappos's CEO is Helping Revitalize
Downtown Las Vegas. He Took Me On a Whirlwind Tour, *Washington Post*,
19 January [Online] https://www.washingtonpost.com/lifestyle/travel/zapposs-
ceo-is-helping-revitalize-downtown-las-vegas-he-took-me-on-a-whirlwind-tour/
2017/01/19/b1e62e2e-d8f4-11e6-9a36-1d296534b31e_story.html

Sailer, K, Pomeroy, R and Haslem, R (2015) Office design: facilities management
insights from an evidence based design practice, *Work & Place*, 5, pp 6–9

Steelcase (2014) [accessed 12 January 2017] The Quiet Ones, *360 Magazine*, 68,
12 November [Online] https://www.steelcase.com/insights/articles/quiet-ones/

Tidd, P (2016) [accessed 12 January 2017] An Inconvenient Truth for the UK
Workplace?, *Gensler On Work*, 28 July [Online] http://www.gensleron.com/
work/2016/7/28/an-inconvenient-truth-for-the-uk-workplace.html

Tidd, P, Clay, J, Sigler, A, Tvergaard, A, Ekundayo, S and Agarwal, A (2016) UK
Workplace Survey, *Gensler* [Online] http://www.gensler.com/research-insight/
research/u-k-workplace-survey-2016

Tokumitsu, M and Mol, J (2016) Life at the Nowhere Office, *New Republic*, 6
September [Online] https://newrepublic.com/article/136558/life-nowhere-office

Tuckman, B and Jensen, M (1977) Stages of small group development, *Group and
Organizational Studies*, 2, pp 419–27

Waber, B and Magnolia, J (2014) Workspaces that move people, *Harvard Business
Review*, October

Waddell, A (2010) [accessed 15 March 2017] Kgotla (Botswana Public Assembly),
Participedia, 7 December [Online] http://participedia.net/en/methods/kgotla-
public-assembly

Yapparov, G (2014) Cool Offices: KLM's Schiphol Airport Offices, The
Netherlands, *So You Know Better*, 7 June [Online] http://soyouknowbetter.
com/2014/06/07/cool-offices-klms-schiphol-airport-offices-the-netherlands/

PART THREE
Tending an organizational society

Recruiting, managing and developing people

11

Introduction

Part 3 focuses on applying the people and organizational approaches from what we usually refer to as HR and organization development (when defined by activities versus outcomes) to the social organization. In particular it focuses on creating an organizational society that will enable an organization to optimize the benefits provided by its social architecture. This is about creating an environment where people experience less stress and lower levels of cortisol and in which they are able to connect together to optimize levels of serotonin and oxytocin.

Because developing an organizational society focuses on relationships we cannot continue to ignore complexity in the way we did in Part 2. Therefore, whilst we designed and built an organizational architecture we need to think about tending and cultivating an organizational society.

Chapter 11 starts off this part of the book with a review of the role of people management in a social organization. There are two sides to this. The first is based on a fairly traditional approach to HR, which recruits and develops individuals who will be able to play a useful role in an organizational society. The second is to lift these same HR practices up to a group level, adjusting them appropriately for this new focus in order to create better connections and relationships. As social network analyst and consultant Valdis Krebs explains, each person in a network affects and is influenced by the other people in it. In such a connected system we can no longer focus on the performance of individuals, we must concern ourselves with system outcomes and the performance of the connected whole (Krebs, 2007).

This is not even a particularly new requirement. For example, the first article I have seen that criticized HR for focusing on individuals rather than their role within social networks dates back to the 1990s (Brass, 1995).

Just a few years later, Krebs suggested that social capital would provide the killer app for HR going into the 21st century (Krebs, 2000). Then in 2005 the former CEO of Cargill described how he had focused on creating social capital during his tenure there. He suggested that some of the highest-impact activities they had used were apprenticeships, networking forums and making a long-term commitment to people, eg by avoiding laying off people during downturns (MacMillan, 2006).

We might call these activities social HR, though that term is often applied to HR activities using social media. Some of this book's social HR activities do use social technologies, which are explored further in Chapter 13 – however, many do not. They are social because they focus on groups of people rather than individuals, and because they therefore contribute towards the accumulation of social capital.

To me, this is a much more useful way to think about social recruiting, social learning, social recognition etc. Social should not just refer to transforming these processes by using social media, nor even just making them more group-based, but should focus on rebuilding them to contribute to social outcomes. However, it is also worth noting that this opportunity to create social capital is the main reason why using social media and more social approaches is so useful. These can make HR approaches more efficient and effective but can also create competitive advantage through the creation of social outcomes.

I can illustrate this best using the example of social learning. This often works better than traditional, formal learning, regardless of whether it is based on social media or face-to-face social approaches. These approaches could include action learning or open space events (unconferences/bar camps) – see Chapter 12. It can be more efficient to bring people together to share and co-create knowledge, particularly through an online community, than to pay for an external trainer and get everyone to attend a course. It can also be more effective, particularly for social, as opposed to Cartesian, knowledge.

This distinction comes from John Seely Brown who notes that Cartesian knowledge, which is about content and facts, can best be learnt through Cartesian sage-on-a-stage training. Social knowledge, which is about how things are done, particularly through other people, can best be learnt through interaction with other people, ie social learning (Brown and Adler, 2008). A lot of this is fairly obvious, for example at EY it was clear that for our auditors to pass their accountancy exams they needed to attend lots of lectures and read lots of textbooks (Cartesian knowledge/learning) whereas a lot of our leadership-focused learning was provided in management development centres (social knowledge/learning). However, we still get things mixed up and waste social learning opportunities doing Cartesian things.

One idea I like for changing this is Jane Hart's suggestion of the flipped webinar (partly based on the flipped classroom idea) in which information is sent out before a webinar and this valuable time spent online with other people is used for conversation about people's reactions to the material that has already been distributed (Hart, 2011).

However, as already explained, the greatest opportunity for this sort of activity is the creation of social outcomes. For example, social learning can lead to organizational learning and even the creation of the learning organization (Senge, 1993). This is an organization that is able to learn deeper, better, faster than its competitors and is another of Dave Ulrich's favourite examples of organizational capability delivering competitive advantage (see more on the learning organization later in this chapter).

The point relates to all areas within HR and is reinforced in Figure 11.1. Individually focused activities usually only create human capital. Social activities usually create human capital too, and can sometimes do so more efficiently and more effectively than their individually focused counterparts. And they create social capital as well. This social capital is probably worth at least as much as, if not more than, the human capital. Therefore social activities create at least twice the value of individually oriented ones.

Figure 11.1   Impact of individual and group-oriented activities on human and social capital

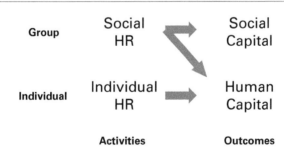

Making HR processes social also has a further benefit, which is that by being social, activities become more easily anchored into the norms and conversations of the organization. They therefore create social capital (as above) but they also contribute directly to social capital too. For example, a number of organizations talk about having a 'performance culture' but the only one of these I have experienced where I felt this to be true was where performance management was social. This meant that people talked about it with each other. The ongoing discussion made managing performance seem important and ensured that people thought about it. Where performance management is limited to a conversation between a manager and those reporting to them it is never going to become anchored in this way and therefore does not feel so important within the organization.

In this chapter, each of the two types of opportunity described above are reviewed for recruitment, onboarding, performance management, reward and recognition, learning and development, communication, career management, exit and alumni management, employee relations and talent management.

Recruitment

Recruitment can provide social organizations with the critical resource of people who know how to and wish to collaborate. This is particularly important since collaborative skills are some of the hardest for people to develop. It is for this reason that Cisco recruits a lot of its engineers via gaming conferences. Gamers learn to be great collaborators by leading and engaging in guilds of virtual and unpaid volunteers. It is more effective to recruit these people and then to train them in computer networking equipment than to take people skilled in the technical products and train them in collaboration skills.

In Chapter 5, I noted that team intelligence depends more on the emotional intelligence (EQ) of individual team members than it does their individual IQs. So, in a social organization, it may be even more important to select for EQ than it is normally. One useful approach to doing this is to recruit more women, who tend to have higher levels of EQ. Another idea is provided by Margaret Heffernan who suggests she always asks a particular question during recruitment, which is 'who helped you get here?' If someone cannot answer that question Heffernan advises not to hire them, as no one gets anywhere on their own (Jacobs, 2016). I also like Southwest Airlines' example of asking candidates to read out a statement in front of a group. Candidates might think they are being tested for confidence or clarity in speaking but actually Southwest is watching the other candidates to see if they applaud the person who has just spoken (Hansen, 2009).

As well as recruiting people for their propensity to collaborate, companies can also recruit people based upon their existing networks of contacts, because they believe these networks will be useful in the future. An example is recruiting people into social media jobs that could be supported by checking candidates' social media usage, perhaps by using a rating system such as Klout (klout.com).

Another useful approach is involving the group that a person is going to be working with in that person's recruitment. Doing this helps ensure this person will help raise the performance of the group as a whole – essential when the purpose of the activity is providing an effective group rather than just effective individuals. It also helps ensure the group will take responsibility for the success of the new joiner. This approach is used within teams at Whole Food Stores and is described later in this chapter. It is also used to provide networks of contacts for new joiners at Goldman Sachs, explained below.

Recruiting can also extend beyond just finding someone to do a job and instead focusing on filling structural holes within a network. For example, people from different areas of an organization could be involved in a person's selection to help ensure that a new joiner is well placed to bridge across these networks.

Potentially even better than any of these opportunities might be recruiting an intact team into an organization, as sometimes happens in sectors such as banking and technology, or which can be the purpose/result of merger and acquisition transactions, ie aqui-hiring. The opportunity may also become more significant with growth of autonomous teams of employees and of gig-economy flash teams.

Diversity is another important aspect of social organizations, which is heavily dependent on recruitment to provide the right people (though their retention is very important too). The key need here is often to translate words into action, eg by avoiding moral credentializing in which organizations develop diverse shortlists but still predominantly select white men, particularly at senior levels. Development sessions focusing on unconscious bias such as Google's (Feloni, 2016) or Facebook's (Lapowsky, 2015) courses, both of which are available publicly, can help. We can also make bias play to our own interests. We know that people recruit in their own image, so if we want collaborative people we should ask brokers, boundary spanners and energizers to lead our hiring.

However, whilst these actions may make us more aware of other people's biases they often fail to understand our own (Comaford, 2016). Getting a hiring manager to take assessments such as Harvard's Implicit tests (https://implicit.harvard.edu/) may therefore be more useful. Yet the best solution is often to nudge people's behaviours in the right direction. Blind recruitment – removing people's names as well as other potentially socially exclusive factors such as the universities they attended – is a good example of this. However, it is still important to note that whilst increasing diversity is useful to increase performance, greater diversity also makes teams more difficult to manage (Gratton, 2007).

One further important point on recruitment for social capital is that the link also works the other way around. This can be seen most easily in employee referrals, which generally result in higher-performing recruits than many other resourcing methods. This is not because people working in an organization will necessarily have friends who are particularly good at doing jobs their organizations need people for, though the 'small world' theory (from Chapter 4) would suggest this may be true too. But the even more important factor is the way someone referring a successful candidate will be likely to coach and mentor the new person after they have joined. It is the increase in social capital resulting from this recruitment approach that makes it so effective.

CASE STUDY Social recruiting at Goldman Sachs

To join this company at a senior level you will probably have had around 25 interviews (Gratton, 2007). There are three reasons for the approach. The first is that Goldman is pre-eminent in its sector and this approach to recruitment demonstrates this status. The second is that Goldman wants to ensure it has the best possible people and human capital and the long process helps ensure that it gets them. The process is designed to be an effective funnel where one manager passes information and further questions to the next, meaning that it is very unlikely indeed for someone to get into the firm unless they are extremely talented. I understand the process does not always work quite that well but that is at least the intent.

But the third and main reason Goldman puts this effort into hiring is that they believe in the importance of social capital. The 25 interviews ensure that new starters have a network of about this number of senior people who know them and can ensure they will be successful. Goldman is different to other investment banks not just in its pre-eminence but also in its communitarianism. Goldman feels quite like a family – which is probably a good thing given that new recruits are unlikely to see much of their existing family again (Zarya, 2016)! In fact Goldman's sense of community is so strong that it is not easy to be successful without a network of senior-level relationships. This need for people to be well networked is so important that it is worth the cost of the 25 interviews, and of course, presumably the potential 24 interviews for some people who still do not get in. The cost of these additional interviews could be saved by having the interviews take place during onboarding rather than selection. However, that would still not be enough. The real benefit of the actual approach is not just that 25 senior leaders know the new starters – it is also that they share a sense of responsibility for them being there.

It might also be worth noting that another unique attribute of Goldman Sachs is that it is a very secretive firm and the data above is a bit out of date, in fact it is from before the global financial crisis and Goldman is now a very different firm. However, if you check interview reviews for VP-level jobs and above on Glassdoor, the interviewees all say they had around 25 interviews. Plus, I had an ex-Goldman employee on one of my workshops a few weeks ago and she had 23 interviews when she joined Goldman a few years after the crash – and she was in HR. And a client told me that when one of her staff left to join Goldman he got called by most of the 25 people he had met at that firm within the following 24 hours of accepting his new job. So the approach above is still current and it is not even just bankers who have to go through it. Having 25 interviews is absolutely not best practice but it is a great best-fit approach for a firm like Goldman Sachs that competes on the relationships between its people.

Onboarding

The halo/horns effect suggests that people will make their minds up about a new employer early on their first day. Therefore their induction/onboarding process needs to be fun and participative – not boring or top down. In addition, the information people need in a new organization is mainly social, not Cartesian, so it makes sense to dispense with the heavy induction packs and first-day talk-and-chalk courses and do something more fun and social. My favourite example of this is Telus's 90-day collaboration scavenger hunt, which uses the company's social networks to provide people with induction information (Morgan, 2012).

How about bringing people in on their first day and asking them to work in small groups to identify what they need to know? A facilitator can help them to integrate these requirements into a single comprehensive list. People can then split into other groups, each taking some of these requirements and then going to find things out. One group goes to see the chief executive, another researches things on the enterprise social network etc. After a few days, people get back together and present to each other what they have found out. This works in a similar way to an unconference, with people taking charge of what they need to know and learning socially, meaning that their learning becomes more relevant and fun and is therefore more likely to be acquired and retained.

Valdis Krebs suggests that in the new social world, HR's focus on hiring must now become to hire and wire – to recruit the best people with the best network and then to integrate them into the organization (Krebs, 2008). Induction or onboarding is a great opportunity to provide this integration. A particularly good opportunity is to use boundary spanners as mentors. They can introduce a new starter into different groups and help to develop them as effective brokers too. (Broking and boundary spanning were defined in the section on social networks in Chapter 4.)

Social network analyst Rob Cross suggests using a pull- versus push-based approach that shows people how a new joiner can be useful to them. This works better than getting the new joiner to focus on building a network or promoting the new joiner's skills to other people. It is about morphing the new joiner's expertise to what people care about and building energy in the relationship by giving contacts something useful early on. Contacts made during induction can be retained as weak ties for use when they are needed.

Performance management

Performance management is going through a profound transformation, becoming more regular and informal, often supported by abolishing appraisals and ratings. These create unnecessary status differences so their removal is a positive move for the development of more social organizations. I also like the shift towards giving people responsibility for their own performance management, enabling them to get feedback when they want it, against the competencies they are interested in, from the people they want feedback from.

However, these changes now need to be extended in order for performance management to become social too. CEB has found that 65 per cent of enterprise contributors do not receive the highest performance ratings. In addition, 67 per cent of those who do receive the highest ratings are not enterprise contributors (CEB Corporate Leadership Council, 2012). This suggests we are failing to recognize the people who drive the social organization.

Objectives can be made more social by supplementing the traditional vertical cascade with horizontal objectives in which people agree between themselves how they are going to support each other. Objectives can also focus specifically on collaborating with other people, or this can be picked up through lists of competencies or behaviours. This opportunity is not used that often in many organizations. For example, CEB's research has found that 83 per cent of employee performance reviews focus on individual task performance versus network performance (CEB Corporate Leadership Council, 2012).

It is also useful for people's objectives to be shared across teams or a whole organization, eg by putting these objectives on the organization's intranet. Doing this can avoid duplication or omission of work within people's objectives and helps people to optimize their relationships by thinking about how they can support the others they are connected to or are meeting for the first time.

Objectives can also be shared by multiple people. The traditional view of organizations has been that accountability can only ever be placed on one person. However, the increasingly social nature of work and organizations is starting to challenge this, with a number of organizations experimenting with shared accountabilities.

Reviews can also be extended to include performance in different roles, eg within networks and communities as well as in functions or on projects. One way of doing this is to include crowdsourced feedback, ie allowing anyone in a company to provide feedback on anyone else (as in HCL in Chapter 3). This also reduces both bias and the likelihood that that an appraisee will enter into a threat state due to status differentials with their manager (Rock, Davis and Jones, 2014). Most importantly though, it helps ensure people think about their relationships with others. This is often enabled by online technology but does not always need to be.

For example, at EY we developed a team debrief process in 1997, well before the availability of any social technologies. All we did was to put up flipchart pages around a project room, each with a heading relating to an attribute of effective teaming. We got all team members to write a couple of positives and a couple of negatives for each team attribute using different Post-it notes and to paste these on the flip pages. Pairs of team members then took a flip page and made sense of the comments on the Post-it notes. We then went round the room reviewing each of the attributes until we had a complete view of the team's performance.

The second stage of the process was to do a similar thing for individuals. So we put up more flip pages but this time headed by the name of a team member. People then did the same thing with Post-it notes but this time for each other person. Each team member then took their own flip page, made sense of the comments and fed back to the whole team only what they felt comfortable in disclosing. However, we found the level of disclosure in these sessions improved quickly as people got used to the debrief process. The idea was that when someone had an individual review with their manager/coach they would informally feed in the reviews they had gained from the debriefs in the different teams they had been working on. Although this was an informal requirement we felt confident we would know if someone was getting very different feedback in the debriefs from the information they disclosed to their manager. I facilitated a lot of these sessions and felt they all went really well.

Some organizations generate similar peer-to-peer feedback through the use of surveys, which are collated together and people then come back together to listen to the results. This is useful too, although I think the group conversation is probably more useful when it can be done. In fact, in the ideal world social performance management just becomes part of the ongoing social conversation within an organization.

CASE STUDY Managing for a growth mindset at Microsoft

Along with its functional organization design, one of the approaches used by Microsoft to mitigate the trade-offs involved in its selection of a capability in talent has been an emphasis on a growth mindset, referred to in Chapter 3. This mindset is being reinforced through performance management.

Changes have included abolishing ratings and stack ranking. These were seen to be too rigid and were not motivating – or were motivating the wrong sort of behaviour. This included increasing competition between people rather than encouraging them to work together to beat the company's competitors (Warren, 2013). The company's approach to ranking employees had even been compared to the Roman Empire's practice of decimating underperforming legions by culling every tenth soldier (Bevan, 2014).

The firm has now replaced these annual reviews with a more agile and organic system based on regular 'connects' throughout the year. These focus on helping people to understand the impact they are having on others in their team and elsewhere. People are now very clearly focused on and rewarded for collaboration (Ritchie, 2016). In fact, I was speaking at an event at Microsoft's London HQ recently where one of the company's staff suggested they could achieve about 70 per cent of their potential rewards through meeting their own objectives – the rest would come from exhibiting a growth mindset.

Recognition

Recognition is another great process to use as part of a social architecture and to cultivate an organizational society, especially as this has always been a social process. Modern social recognition enables everyone in an organization to both give and receive feedback, on an ongoing basis, against important requirements such as the organization's values. Therefore as long as these values include something like collaboration then recognition becomes a social process that encourages other social processes. People in many national cultures enjoy participating in recognition as it provides status and acts as a social reward. It is therefore an easy process to engage people with, stimulating the social nature of an organization. Some organizations are even using it as a partial replacement for performance management, which people tend not to enjoy so much. But if people are receiving lots of recognition it must mean they are exhibiting some aspects of good performance too.

Reward

Reward practices also need to support the development of people's social relationships. This means they need to support status, relatedness and fairness. They also need to be designed with care as, from a social perspective at least, misaligned or inappropriate reward can often do more harm than good. For example, behavioural sciences professor Samuel Bowles has found evidence in 51 experimental studies that rewards which emphasize self-interest can backfire. This is because of the crowding out – or overjustification – effect, in which extrinsic motivators take the place of ethical and generous motives (Bowles, 2016). Lynn Stout has also found that pay for performance promotes selfishness and supresses prosocial behaviour (Stout, 2014). CEB has found that paying people for their contributions to others reduces enterprise contribution, ie their willingness to help other people, by 25 per cent (Kropp, 2014). If performance management can encourage competitive behaviour then inappropriate variable reward can do this very thoroughly indeed (Ingham, 2015).

Social organizations also benefit from having pay differentials that are less than those that have developed during the 'war for (individual) talent' over the last two decades. Some organizations suggest that their high performers are worth several tens or even several hundreds of times as much as their low performers. The result of this is that pay differentials, in Anglo-Saxon national cultures at least, have increased substantially. These differentials make no sense in social organizations, particularly when these companies need everyone to act as leaders and their structures to be more heterarchical. These trends should be bringing people's pay levels closer together rather than having them torn further apart.

The suggestion that these differentials now need to be reduced does not negate our increasing understanding of a growing gap between the contribution of high and low performers (O'Boyle and Aguinis, 2012). However, it also recognizes that this difference is often the result of relationships with, and the support of, other people, as well as often a large amount of luck. This has a particularly significant role given the amount of bias involved in selection and career progression processes. Also, a growth versus fixed mindset would suggest paying rewards for performance improvements rather than for existing high levels of performance.

It is increasingly recognized that the main reason pay inequality is increasing is because there are growing performance differences between firms (Song *et al*, 2015). However, even if inequality is mainly outside the control of an individual firm, from the perspective of the social organization, it is important that internal inequality is tackled too.

As well as reducing pay differentials, I would expect to see the use of bonuses, benefits and share schemes being extended beyond executives so that all staff are rewarded in similar ways, even if the proportion of these rewards varies according to position. Currently just 19 per cent of UK directors can take a 'birthday holiday' but only 4 per cent of non-managers get to do so. Additionally, 47 per cent of directors can attend team-building experiences, whereas only 5 per cent of non-managers receive this benefit (Frith, 2016). This differential also acts to segregate different groups of staff, horizontally and vertically.

Supporting the above, social organizations also need to increase reward transparency. Most organizations encourage people to keep their reward secret as people tend to judge the worth of other people by focusing on what they can see people doing rather than the real challenges in a job, which tend to be less tangible. This means that pay levels can be hard to justify. However, we are living and working in a world where people are easily able to share information with each other and, more importantly, there is a greater expectation that things will be shared. Given this increasing level of transparency, trying to maintain secrecy around reward or anything else is increasingly unsustainable.

Transparency is also increasing externally as well as internally, particularly through systems such as Glassdoor's Know Your Worth and LinkedIn's salary tool, as well as increasing amounts of legislation around external equal pay reporting. I was involved in some of Glassdoor's research on reward transparency, which showed that women believe this would help moves towards equal pay (Sanghani, 2015). In any case, pay transparency tends not to be a major issue in countries where all or some of the salaries are made public. Also, business leaders and HR professionals already know and accept people's salaries and there is no good reason to think HR can handle this information but that other people cannot.

One of the main businesses promoting transparency is Buffer, which emphasizes how this breeds trust and leads to better teamwork. Supporting its 'open salaries' approach, the company has published how it calculates salaries, bonuses and equity payments. It also lists the amounts that all its staff receive (Gascoigne and Widrich, 2015). Transparency should apply to the design of reward programmes too. Engagement in these programmes depends on both procedural and distributive justice. It is difficult for people to trust that they are getting paid appropriately if they have not been informed, and ideally involved, in the creation of a programme.

As well as the above changes, social organizations may also need to move towards paying teams and other groups rather than just individuals. This is a difficult shift to make work and involves high risks. For example, it can increase competition between teams, just as it reduces this within teams. Linked to this, research on cases where team-based reward has been used, particularly where this has involved knowledge workers, tends not to be that favourable. However, the results of team-based reward will obviously depend on how it is used and, in many of the cases that have been reviewed, team rewards had not been designed that well. The main problem seems to be that communication has been left too late. Garbers and Konradt's recent meta-analysis of 30 different studies of team rewards also suggests that team rewards work best for smaller teams and mixed-gender teams. It also notes the importance of distributing rewards equitably rather than just equally between team members (Garbers and Konradt, 2013).

The best suggestion I have heard to make team-based reward work is to reward a team for the performance of the individuals and divide this reward between the individuals according to their contributions to the team. This ensures individuals focus on collaboration not competition within the team but also that they and the whole team are focused on helping increase the individual performance of each person. This should help avoid any tendency towards social loafing.

Some companies use gamification mechanics and, in particular, virtual currencies. These game elements can be used to help people measure their progress and achievement against their colleagues. They can then be converted into real rewards at a later point. Doing this can potentially provide greater motivation but without the same cost to the employer. Innovation systems are often based upon this mechanic.

One good example of this approach is the viral pay approach used by IGN. This company shares a proportion of its profits with employees through the use of $1 tokens, which can then be distributed throughout the workforce according to the wishes of each employee. Although distributions are kept secret the company does publish the amount received by the most successful employees, as a way of inspiring other employees (Boyd, 2011). However, it is important to remember that these programmes must be used appropriately to improve motivation, productivity and performance. Used inappropriately, these game elements can lead to unhealthy competition and dysfunctional behaviours. In addition, it is important that gamification does not crowd out people's intrinsic motivation to perform in their roles.

Probably the best thing that social organizations can do is to pay people what they are worth and then focus on more important things. This approach can be supported by prosocial rewards in which money is paid as an appreciation of performance, but is donated to charity, or to another person in the organization.

CASE STUDY Competing on love at Whole Food Stores

Whole Food Stores use an alternative approach to team- and individual-based reward. This company's desired organizational capability is love – a deep emotional regard for other people. As CEO John Mackey suggests, 'Love is not something that is commonly explored in business. But it's time for love to come out of the closet. For competitive advantage…' (Mlabvideo, 2010).

This approach means that Whole Foods treats people as ends in themselves, not as means to an end. The first way it does this is through high levels of autonomy and transparency. Responsibility for key operating decisions, including both stocking and staffing, is delegated to small self-managing teams within local stores. This is supported by open sharing of operating, financial and salary information. This means that teams can control their own staffing levels, deciding when necessary on whether to recruit another person or simply to take home a bonus and work that bit harder themselves. It also helps consistency as everyone can see what is happening in other stores. And it acts to motivate people to develop and take on new roles, as they can see which jobs come with more reward.

People are also given a say in the choice of people who will be working in their team. New associates are temporarily assigned to a particular team, but at the end of their probation period team members vote on whether they should continue to work there. These decisions are based on whether a new joiner can make a cost-effective addition to the performance of the team. If not, regardless of the individual's skills and engagement etc, then it is a case of 'it's not you, it's us' but there is no point in the person being in the team.

Base pay is paid individually but gainsharing payments are based upon the team. Whole Foods has also set a salary cap so that no executive will earn over 19 times the average employee pay. Over 90 per cent of stock options have been granted to non-executives.

Learning and development

Collaboration is currently not something people generally do well. CEB suggest that whilst 57 per cent of people display high levels of individual task performance only 20 per cent demonstrate effective network performance (CEB Corporate Leadership Council, 2012). The development of collaboration skills appears to be difficult too. Social cognitive neuroscientist Kevin Ochsner suggests that social skills are the least trainable area of leadership skills (Neuroleadership Institute, 2015). Improving this situation starts with helping people to become more aware of the need to develop their social skills.

The content that people need to understand starts with the social brain, including social threats and rewards, ingroups and outgroups, relatedness and empathy etc (from Chapter 4). Emotional intelligence can provide a useful framework for this, including the development of mindfulness to increase self-awareness of one's own emotional state and potential biases. Social awareness requires people to use their capabilities for empathy to listen to and seek to really understand other people. Social management, or influencing, depends on developing effective relationships – see Chapter 12.

People also need to understand the role of social networks and the effectiveness of their own personal network, either through a traditional stakeholder analysis, or a more modern analysis of their ego network, ie the network of relationships around them. They also need to understand the roles of bonding and bridging and that developing large networks is not always useful. Instead of this, people should be thinking about developing connections to other people they do not currently have access to, especially where these links act across boundaries. One of the benefits of helping people to develop their own networks in this way is that this enables them to reduce connections to people who do not reciprocate prosocially and hence this makes an overall network more cooperative (Rand, Arbesman and Christakis, 2011).

The next important skill area focuses on being able to communicate, collaborate, cooperate and cultivate relationships within today's social world. This needs people to develop their reputations and personal brands and to develop relationships ahead of particular needs. This may require understanding of digital technologies to be able to use social and other tools effectively. People should also seek to understand complexity and develop skills in navigating paradox, one of Dave Ulrich's new HR competencies (Ulrich *et al*, 2017).

People also need to understand how to balance social and other activities so that they do not become excessively overloaded. It is important to remember that our social brains love relating with people and can tend to do this excessively if we do not manage them. Even overinvestment in empathy can have negative consequences for people (Waytz, 2017).

It is also important to manage demands for support from other people. Rob Cross suggests that managers often spend over 90 per cent of their working hours in meetings, on the phone and responding to e-mail (Feintzeig, 2016). Much of this is about poor organization design and poor management, especially hierarchical or silo thinking. However, avoiding this collaborative overload also demands that individual people be generous without being selfless (Grant and Rebele, 2017), reducing excessive demands through robust calendar management and other tactics. Doing this helps free people up to engage in social activities which will have a positive payoff – an approach Heidi Gardner calls smart collaboration (Gardner, 2017).

Useful resources to support these development needs include Lynda Gratton's book *Glow* (2009), which discusses cooperative mindsets, crossboundary networking and energizing other people. I also recommend Jason Lauritsen and Joe Gerstandt's book *Social Gravity* (2012), which reviews investing in and being open to connections, authenticity, meaning, karma and staying in touch.

Social organizations can also focus on developing groups and networks rather than just individuals. This can start with reviewing the skills that are required across a group and ensuring that missing skills are acquired by someone in the group. However, it should not always be necessary for each person in a group to learn all the required skills. Similarly, connections outside a group can be shared by the people included within it. Ideally, new skills and new connections will be allocated to team members rather than a team manager who will generally be most likely to suffer from collaborative overload.

Team development sessions can include activities such as Frederick Miner's winter survival exercise to show the value of groups. This generally finds that the best person in a group will make a better decision than the whole group, but that the group makes a better decision than the average person. As it is not generally possible to identify the best decision maker for a certain requirement this latter point does lead to an improvement in decisions (Miner, 1984).

Development activities can utilize individual and organizational networks, for example by encouraging people to develop personal learning networks, and to get involved in delivering training to each other. This encourages people to think prosocially, which means learning takes place more deeply, in the social brain. New habits are also easier to take on board when they are developed socially.

Organizations can also develop learning into a capability called the learning organization. This capability is about being able to learn faster, smarter or deeper than a company's competitors. It describes an organization in which the whole workforce learns together rather than leaving this to individuals or small teams. The problem with these more traditional approaches is that when someone brings a new idea or skill into a business the rest of the organization often rejects it. If the whole organization participates in a learning experience then the new insights are much more likely to gain traction. This means that the organization can easily respond to the things happening around it. This saves it the need to inject a big mechanistic shock, such as bringing in a new chief executive every few years when it becomes evident that the organization has fallen behind changes in the business environment.

The concept is well explained in Peter Senge's book *The Fifth Discipline*, which was a provocative book that gained a lot of interest when it was first published in 1990 but failed to get implemented in many businesses. There is a suspicion that the idea was simply communicated too far ahead of its time – that with the technology available in 1990 it was simply too difficult to make organizational learning work. These days, with the capabilities provided by social media, it is a lot easier to achieve this.

Career and alumni management

In their book on social capital, Laurence Prusak and Don Cohen argue that social companies need to promote from within and demonstrate a real commitment to retention (Cohen and Prusak, 2001). This book was written some time ago and you could argue that the finding no longer applies. However, the reason the two authors suggest retention is important is that 'relationships only happen, and trust can only flourish, when people know each other' – and this still applies. I therefore suggest that social organizations still need to focus on retention when they can.

This means that companies still need to invest in people's careers. However, these days this needs to be about creating free movement for people rather than trying to control career moves as in a chess game. This is about helping people to create brands and get recognized, ensuring that managers can advertise forthcoming jobs and skill needs, and creating opportunities for people to move around and take on projects, secondments and other types of assignment. When people leave, their previous employer can keep in touch with them, partly to add to their external relationship capital, and partly to attract them back later on.

Talent management

As soon as we recognize the social nature of organizations, traditional definitions of talent start to seem less appropriate. For example, Harvard professor Boris Groysberg tracked analysts moving between investment banks and found the correlation between those identified as stars in one firm and the next was very low. It appears that what made the star analysts so special was not actually anything about them but was to do with the network of people they had around them (Groysberg, 2012).

This means that as well as updating their HR processes, social organizations also need to think differently about talent and talent management. Existing talent groups need to be complemented by social talent who are the people who can create the right networks, eg CEB's enterprise contributors. Social network analysis can also be used to identify people acting in particularly important social roles (see Chapter 13). Organizations generally identify less than half of these social influencers in current lists of talent (Cross and Thomas, 2009).

It is also important that social talent management processes are not divisive. I recommend an approach I call talent slicing, in which instead of talent being defined in a static way it is reinterpreted dynamically, say every few years, in order to look at different aspects of performance and potential. This means that over time lots of different people will be treated as talent, avoiding the potential for ingroups and outgroups to be created.

Organizations may also want to think even more innovatively about talent management and focus on talented groups rather than talented individuals.

Summary and additional comments

1 Social organizations need to tailor their HR and management processes to create social capital. This will generally be by either focusing on people with particular social skills or social networks, or by shifting focus to improving the performance of groups.

2 Just as the definition of human capital is being expanded to take in people not working as employees, so social capital also needs to take account of much broader numbers and types of relationships. This means that social, as well as traditional, HR processes need to be broadened out to apply to contingent and gig economy workers too.

References

Bevan, S (2014) Performance improvement plans and the culture of fear, *HR Magazine*, 8 April

Bowles, S (2016) *The Moral Economy: Why good incentives are no substitute for good citizens*, Yale University Press, New Haven

Boyd, EB (2011) [accessed 6 March 2017] At IGN, Employees Use a 'Viral Pay' System to Determine Each Others' Bonuses, *Fast Company*, 16 December [Online] https://www.fastcompany.com/1801532/ign-employees-use-viral-pay-system-determine-each-others-bonuses

Brass, DJ (1995) A social network perspective on human resource management, *Research in Personnel and Human Resources Management*, ed GR Ferris, vol. 13, pp 39–79, Emerald Group Publishing, Bingley

Brown, JS and Adler, R (2008) Minds on fire: open education, the long tail, and learning 2.0, *EDUCAUSE Review*, **43** (1), pp 16–21

CEB Corporate Leadership Council (2012) [accessed 6 March 2017] Driving Breakthrough Performance in the New Work Environment, *CEB* [Online] https://www.cebglobal.com/content/dam/cebglobal/us/EN/top-insights/executive-guidance/pdfs/eg2013ann-breakthrough-performance-in-the-new-work-environment.pdf

Cohen, D and Prusak, L (2001) *In Good Company: How social capital makes organizations work*, Harvard Business School Press, Boston

Comaford, C (2016) [accessed 6 March 2017] How to Work with Unconscious Bias in Your Organization, *Forbes*, 26 June [Online] http://www.forbes.com/sites/christinecomaford/2016/06/25/how-leaders-bust-unconscious-biases-in-business/#751a6091437d

Cross, R and Thomas, RJ (2009) *Driving Results Through Social Networks: How top organisations leverage networks for performance and growth*, Jossey Bass, San Francisco

Feintzeig, R (2016) [accessed 6 March 2017] So Busy at Work, No Time to Do the Job, *Wall Street Journal*, 28 June [Online] http://www.wsj.com/articles/so-busy-at-work-no-time-to-do-the-job-1467130588

Feloni, R (2016) [accessed 6 March 2017] Here's the Presentation Google Gives Employees on How to Spot Unconscious Bias at Work, *Business Insider*,

11 February [Online] http://uk.businessinsider.com/google-unconscious-bias-training-presentation-2015-12

Frith, B (2016) [accessed 6 March 2017] Senior Staff Receive More Benefits Than Junior Employees, *HR Magazine*, 6 September [Online] http://www.hrmagazine. co.uk/article-details/senior-staff-receive-more-benefits-than-junior-employees/ 334011/

Garbers, Y and Konradt, U (2013) The effect of financial incentives on performance: a quantitative review of individual and team-based financial incentives, *Journal of Occupational and Organisational Psychology*, **87**, pp 102–37

Gardner, HK (2017) *Smart Collaboration: How professionals and their firms succeed by breaking down silos*, Harvard Business Review Press, Boston

Gascoigne, J and Widrich, L (2015) [accessed 6 March 2017] Introducing the New Buffer Salary Formula, Calculate-Your-Salary App and the Whole Team's New Salaries, *Buffer Open*, 24 November [Online] https://open.buffer.com/ transparent-salaries/

Grant, A and Rebele, R (2017) [accessed 6 March 2017] Beat Generosity Burnout, *Harvard Business Review* [Online] https://hbr.org/cover-story/2017/01/beat-generosity-burnout

Gratton, L (2007) *Hot Spots: Why some companies buzz with energy and innovation – and others don't*, Financial Times Prentice Hall, Harlow

Gratton, L (2009) *Glow: How you can radiate energy, innovation and success*, Financial Times Prentice Hall, Harlow

Groysberg, B (2012) *Chasing Stars: The myth of talent and the portability of performance*, Princeton University Press, New Jersey

Hansen, M (2009) *Collaboration: How leaders avoid the traps, create unity, and reap big results*, Harvard Business Press, Boston

Hart, J (2011) [accessed 6 March 2017] The Flipped (or Social) Webinar, *Centre for Learning & Performance Technologies*, 9 December [Online] http://www. c4lpt.co.uk/blog/2011/12/09/the-flipped-webinar/

Ingham, J (2015) Transforming reward into a strategic contributor to talent management, in *Talent Management Handbook*, ed T Bickham, ASTD Press, New Jersey

Jacobs, K (2016) [accessed 16 April 2017] Organisations must build social capital to deal with complexity, *HR Magazine*, 10 November [Online] http://www. hrmagazine.co.uk/hr-most-influential/profile/organisations-must-build-social-capital-to-deal-with-complexity

Krebs, V (2000) Working in the connected world: social capital – the killerapp for HR in the 21st century, *IHRIM Journal*, June, pp 89–91

Krebs, V (2007) Managing the 21st century organisation, *IHRIM Journal*, **XI** (4), pp 2–8

Krebs, V (2009) Social capital: the key to success for the 21st century organisation, *IHRIM Journal*, **XII** (5), pp 38–42

Kropp, B (2014) [accessed 12 January 2017] When Employees are Paid to Help Each Other, They Are Less Likely to Lean In: A Performance Paradox, *CEB*,

16 July [Online] https://www.cebglobal.com/blogs/when-employees-are-paid-to-help-each-other-theyre-less-likely-to-lean-in-a-performance-paradox/

Lapowsky, I (2015) [accessed 6 March 2017] Facebook Publishes its Managing Bias Course for All, *Wired*, 28 July [Online] www.wired.com/2015/07/facebook-managing-bias-course

Lauritsen, J and Gerstandt, J (2012) *Social Gravity: Harnessing the natural laws of relationships*, Talent Anarchy Productions, Oregon

MacMillan, W (2006) *The Power of Social Capital*, Harvard Business Review Press, Boston

Miner, FC (1984) Group versus individual decision making: an investigation of performance measures, decision strategies, and process losses/gains, *Organizational Behavior and Human Performance*, **33**, pp 112–24

Mlabvideo (2010) [accessed 12 January 2017] John Mackey: What's Love Got To Do With It?, *Management Innovation Exchange* [Online] https://www.youtube.com/watch?v=ED1R2zqdtCg

Morgan, J (2012) *The Collaborative Organization: A strategic guide to solving your internal business challenges using emerging social and collaborative tools*, McGraw Hill Professional, New York

Neuroleadership Institute (2015) [accessed 6 March 2017] Pick Stars Early and Transition Them Better, *Neuroleadership Summit* [Online] https://summit.neuroleadership.com/pick-stars-early-and-transition-them-better/

O'Boyle, E Jr and Aguinis, H (2012) The best and the rest: revisiting the norm of normality of individual performance, *Personnel Psychology*, **65**, pp 79–119

Rand, DG, Arbesman, S and Christakis, NA (2011) Dynamic social networks promote cooperation in experiments with humans, *PNAS*, 29 November, **108** (48), pp 19193–8

Ritchie, J (2016) Transforming a company: how Microsoft's new employee performance system supports its business and cultural transformation, *WorldatWork Journal*, Second quarter

Rock, D, Davis, J and Jones, B (2014) [accessed 6 March 2017] Kill Your Performance Ratings, *Strategy + Business*, **76**, 8 August [Online] http://www.strategy-business.com/article/00275?gko=c442b

Sanghani, R (2015) [accessed 6 March 2017] Women Want Bosses to Reveal Colleagues' Salaries to 'Level the Playing Field', *The Telegraph*, 18 February [Online] http://www.telegraph.co.uk/women/womens-business/11419941/Women-want-bosses-to-reveal-colleagues-salaries.html

Senge, PM (1993) *The Fifth Discipline: The art and practice of the learning organization*, Random House Business, London

Song, J, Price, DJ, Guvenen, F, Bloom, N and Wachter, TV (2015) Firming up inequality, NBER Working Paper No. 21199, May

Stout, LA (2014) [accessed 6 March 2017] Killing Conscience: The Unintended Behavioral Consequences of 'Pay For Performance', *Journal of Corporation Law*, **39** (1) [Online] https://ssrn.com/abstract=2407096

Ulrich, D, Kryscynski, D, Brockbank, W and Ulrich, M (2017) *Victory Through Organization: Why the war for talent is failing your company and what you can do about it*, McGraw Hill Education, London

Warren, T (2013) [accessed 6 March 2017] Microsoft Axes its Controversial Employee-Ranking System, *The Verge*, 12 November [Online] http://www.theverge.com/2013/11/12/5094864/microsoft-kills-stack-ranking-internal-structure

Waytz, A (2017) The limits of empathy, *Harvard Business Review*, January–February

Zarya, V (2016) [accessed 6 March 2017] Goldman Sachs Wants You to Know That Its Employees Have Lives, *Fortune Careers*, 11 January [Online] http://fortune.com/2016/01/08/goldman-sachs-work-life/

Facilitating dyads, triads, groups and organization effectiveness

12

Introduction

Well-designed organizations and people management processes are important but having people who want to and are able to collaborate, cooperate and cultivate their capabilities and relationships is even more critical. This is what I call an organizational society. Developing it requires people to have a strong sense of being part of a community and a broader society. This spirit, attitude and linked behaviour can be encouraged by various organization development interventions operating at different levels in an organization.

These are:

- individuals;
- pairs or dyads;
- triads;
- groups;
- intergroup;
- whole organizations.

Before I review the above I will also describe the development of trust that is essential in a social organization.

Developing trust

From a social, as opposed to organizational, perspective the most important factor in creating and maintaining a social organization is trust, the extent to which someone believes that another person means what they say and will act in the first person's best interest. When there is trust in a relationship, someone will allow themselves to be vulnerable to the actions of another. This enables them to engage in broader exchanges together rather than seeing every instance of sharing or cooperation as a transaction.

Trust exists at different levels in an organization, from dyadic trust with one other person, to group-based trust (as psychological safety) to a general level of trust in a whole organization. First off, the quality of a dyadic relationship can be seen to depend on trust plus an additional factor, which is someone's perceived competence, ie whether they have the ability to follow through on their commitments.

At EY, we used a model developed for us by Malcolm Parks, now a professor in interpersonal communication at the University of Washington, who later wrote up some of his research, though not this model, in a book on personal relationships (Parks, 2006). The model was developed for use in consulting sales but I have also used it for internal relationship development, including, in particular, for HR business partners. This model, provided as Figure 12.1, suggests that competence development underpins the formation of personal trust.

Figure 12.1   Developing collaborative relationships

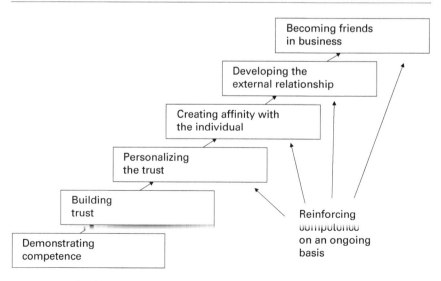

The way I explain the model is that it starts with demonstrating competence. Without this, it is very difficult to get anyone to want to work with you. So if someone asks you to do something, you do it, successfully, a few times, and people start to trust you to do that one thing. Building trust is about showing competence in a number of different tasks. Once you have done this you start to be trusted as a business partner, or whatever, rather than just for doing specific things. Personalizing the trust is about carrying on delivering competently until you start being trusted as an individual rather than just someone acting in your job. From this point on, continuing to develop a relationship switches to the personal relationship. Creating affinity is about making sure that working together is seen as enjoyable – so it is not just that someone expects a good solution, they also look forward to discussing the problem with you. Developing the external relationship is about adding in an external context, broadening out the agenda and extending it into different situations. For example, this perhaps used to be about playing golf together whereas nowadays it might be about responding to some of their tweets. It is an important step for business partners wanting to become business players/allies. This relates to the ability to talk about customers, the financials etc, as I discussed in Chapter 1. Doing this requires developing the external relationship first, as otherwise a business partner may just not be seen as credible when they seek to move on to the business agenda. Becoming friends in business is the point at which affinity becomes the main attribute of the relationship and it is at this point that the two people will stay in contact when one of them leaves the business they have been working in.

The reason I like using this model with business partners, and also line managers, is that very often people do not want to be friends in business with their internal clients or the people they are managing. I suggest to business partners that there are two aspects to their role. There is the HR side, which may require some sense of separation, though I think that is reducing. But then, on the business partnering side, the role is all about relationships. On this side of the job description, business partners who do not want to be friends in business are deliberately restraining their own effectiveness.

More recently, a rather different idea about trust has become popular. This alternative has been promoted by social psychology professor Amy Cuddy, famous for the 'Wonder Woman' pose. Referring to an example of the halo/horns effect, she notes that people make quick decisions about each other when they first meet. These decisions are mostly concerned with whether a person can be trusted, which is about the warmth of the relationship, and whether they can be respected, which is about competence. She suggests that most people believe competence is the more important of these factors in a work relationship. However, in fact, we have evolved to place trustworthiness as the most critical requirement. Cuddy also suggests that placing people into ingroups or outgroups depends on both warmth and competence so that people seen as being cold and competent will be placed within an outgroup, but so will someone seen as warm but incompetent (Cuddy, 2015).

Professors Tiziana Casciaro and Miguel Lobo call these two groups competent jerks and lovable fools. Their research shows that when people need help completing complex projects they turn to likability over ability. People say they would favour competence but in practice they spend time with the people they like (Casciaro and Lobo, 2005). This seems to support Cuddy's emphasis on warmth too. However, the research conducted by Casciaro focused on fairly loose cooperation, including survey items such as: we interact at work; I go to this person for help and advice; and I go to a person to help me think out of the box etc. These points all relate to working with people when there is no need to do so.

I have not done, or seen, any research on this but I propose a reason for the differences between the Parks model and Casciaro/Cuddy's research could be that the former focuses on collaborative, and the latter on cooperative, relationships. As noted earlier, I have used the Parks model mainly with professional services teams. This is the same environment described by Heidi Gardner in her book on collaboration, in which she suggests that competence trust is perceived as a bigger barrier than interpersonal trust (Gardner, 2017). This might just be about more people saying they favour competence when, once again, they act differently to this in practice. However, I believe there is something beyond this too.

I link the primacy of warmth or competence to the motivation dimension in the opportunity motivation matrix (see Figure 9.1) On the task-focused/externally motivated (left-hand) side of this model, where people have to work with each other to get things done, the first thing people look to is competence. On the people-focused/internally motivated (right-hand) side, where investment of time in cooperation or cultivation is discretionary, it is warmth that is a more important factor. I suggest that in these environments it might be more appropriate to see the top three steps in the Parks model acting in parallel to the first three steps, rather than after these in series.

Developing person-like-yourself relationships

Even in task-focused groups, competence only gets people so far. Great relationships still depend on warmth, or trustworthiness. There is also reason to believe this attribute is becoming even more central to relationships. This is based on the Edelman Trust Barometer, which for more than a decade has catalogued a decline in trust around the world. It also suggests that the greatest falls in trust have been associated with roles providing power and authority – including politicians, lawyers, newspaper editors, bankers etc. This trend is known as the death of deference and it applies within businesses and other organizations too. However, there is a type of relationship that has seen an upswing in trust just as significant as the general fall. This is what Edelman calls a person like yourself (PLY), which broadly relates to someone with whom you have a shared social identity – someone in an ingroup rather than an outgroup.

In the 2017 results, a PLY is now the joint most credible source of information about a company, along with technical and academic experts, with 60 per cent of people rating these PLYs as extremely or very credible. This is a much higher level of trust than is placed in CEOs, with just 37 per cent seeing them as similarly credible (Edelman, 2017).

This switch is having a profound effect on organizations. For example, take the case of corporate communications. Many companies used to rely on monthly or quarterly glossy magazines to communicate with their people. The front cover often featured a smiling picture of the chief executive and would be followed inside with a message asking everyone to pull together to meet some challenges. This approach used to work 10 or 20 years ago. Nowadays few companies use this approach and, where they do, it generally does not work – few people read the magazines and those who do reject the messages.

Instead of this, smart internal communication professionals walk around the office with their mobile phones. If they see the CEO approaching they take out their devices and ask the CEO to respond to a quick question. They then go back to their desk and upload the video to their internal YouTube-type channel, and the video will go viral – everyone in the company will view it. The interesting thing for me is that the message is often the same one that would previously have been included in the glossy magazine. But because it is in real time, unscripted and not so professionally produced, and because it therefore seems more authentic, it works in a way that a glossy magazine does not. In fact, it presents the CEO as a PLY. It works even better if, now and again, the communication practitioner suggests there is nothing that important going on in the business and instead asks the CEO to tell people about their weekend fishing trip or whatever they have been doing.

Of course, if the CEO is paid 129 times as much as you are then you are very unlikely to see them as a PLY and you are less likely to trust them as a result. Organizations might therefore be much better off with a less well paid CEO, even if this person creates less dazzling business strategies.

At least this way, people will be more committed to supporting the strategies they do come up with. After all, a well-implemented average strategy is much better than an amazing one that is left on the shelf! This is the reason that Whole Food Stores limits the reward of its CEO to just 19 times that of its average employee.

This shift makes being a friend in business even more important than it used to be. Therefore, whilst I suggest that task-focused work still depends most strongly on demonstrating competence, taking those first moves towards establishing personal trust are now more critical and will probably benefit from being taken earlier than perhaps they used to be. For people-focused work, warmth may now be the single most important factor.

In either case, creating a PLY-based relationship is key. The good news is that this is something that can often be achieved quite easily. This is because we often place people in an ingroup based on their similarity or familiarity, as well as whether they reciprocate our positive responses to them. So if we identify similarities we create relatedness between us. This is not about cloning – two people as different as people can possibly be can still identify things they have in common. These can be really simple things – for example that they come from the same town, have read the same book, have been to the same place on holiday, follow the same sports team, have a similar taste in music etc.

This effect has been validated by neuroscience as well. Jan van Bavel has found that when we observe people in pain, our brains indicate greater social pain when those people are from the same ethnic group as us. However, this effect can be moderated by identifying a common group membership that they share (Bavel and Cunningham, 2013).

Once this new connection has been identified, this provides the basis to both be seen as, and to see the other person as, a PLY. That opens the door to trust, cooperation, prosocial behaviour and more powerful learning. Building on the points made in Chapter 11 it is possible to learn from someone without trusting them. But it is easier to learn with someone, co-creating new meanings together, when trust-based relationships exist. This is why disclosure, and therefore tools such as Joseph Luft and Harry Ingham's Johari window (Handy, 2000), are so useful. (It is also why, in 'About the author', I told you that I have a cat.)

Falling in love with your colleagues

There are a number of other important attributes linked to trust that support the social organization, and which I could review as well, including altruism, authenticity, care, compassion, honesty, reciprocity, respect, vulnerability etc. However, instead of that I will turn to the attribute that perhaps best describes the type of mojo (Chapter 5) that the social organization is, or at least could be, about. Love. This is a concept that, as John Mackey suggests (in Chapter 11), seems out of place in a business environment. In fact around 10 years ago I commented on a blog post to say I did not think love had any place in business (Henkes, 2007). Lynda Gratton suggests that at the start of her 'Hot Spots' research she thought even the idea of management being about creating friendships was rather extreme (Gratton, 2007)!

Also, when I mention love to HR people, most of them suggest they have too much of that going on at work already! But of course I am not talking about *that*. Love is about having a deep emotional regard for other people. It is about going beyond the job description to help someone, even if at your own expense. It is the opposite to the petty politics and turf warfare that mark so many organizations today.

Some businesses are in fact already talking about love in connection with their customers. For example, Saatchi & Saatchi uses the concept of 'lovemarks' to refer to brands that connect through intimate relationships rather than functional issues. Lovemarks are defined based upon two dimensions – love and respect. These link back once again to the ideas of warmth/trust and competence/respect. An earlier version of the idea was called trustmarks but this did not tap deep enough into human emotion. Former CEO Kevin Roberts notes that he always sensed scepticism and discomfort when mentioning 'the L word' but believes it is important to fix on the fundamentals of human nature (Roberts, 2006). I think we now have the opportunity to push back against the same type of limitation within our organizations too.

Psychology professor and marital stability expert John Gottman suggests couples need five times as many positive interactions between themselves as there are negative (Lisitsa, 2012a). There have also been suggestions that a three-to-one ratio applies at work, but the research behind that was flawed. Still, Gottman's analysis seems sound, particularly as it enables him to predict, to high levels of accuracy, which couples will get divorced. Dave Ulrich uses Gottman's ideas on 'love maps' (Lisitsa, 2012b) – your knowledge about your partner's life – and notes that 'whilst it may be awkward to talk about HR's love maps, the same logic applies' (Ulrich, 2015).

Falling in love with your colleagues is about understanding what matters to them and doing your utmost to deliver against this. It is about trust on steroids. The concept is awkward, and it is probably unrealistic to suggest implementing it. However, if it was possible for people to love their colleagues, I do not think you would need any of the other ideas described in this book at all.

Developing individuals

This chapter is about developing connections and relationships rather than recruiting for and developing skills, which was addressed in Chapter 11. However, there is still something about helping people connect with themselves that I think belongs here too. This is about helping people to understand and share their dreams. One of my favourite books is *The Dream Manager* (Kelly, 2007), which describes the role of a dream coach in a fictional company. I used to think there were no real examples of this until I discovered it in – yes, of course – Zappos. Their Wishez programme picked an employee at random every month and the Wishez coach then worked to make their dreams come true (Zappos Family, 2011).

Developing pairs (dyads)

The simplest type of organizational group is based on a dyadic relationship, which involves a pair of people sharing their thoughts, emotions and behaviours. Of particular importance is the vertical dyad linkage of a hierarchical reporting (or leader–member exchange – LMX) relationship. This is where a lot of coaching and other development activities are focused.

Much of this development focuses on the use of psychometric and other tools, particularly those focused on the relationships between people such as FIRO-B, TMS, SDI, MSCEIT etc. Another way of making these tools more social is to use them as a standard across an organization. For example, at one point Microsoft seemed to be putting all of its people through the MBTI psychometric test. People turned up for meetings with coffee mugs that identified their own MBTI style and people were therefore able to moderate their communication to the type of the other person. Three-hundred-and-sixty-degree feedback also has a role in this type of development activity.

Many development activities can be very simple but highly effective. A good example is the use of randomized coffee trials (Gurteen, 2014), used to connect people and give them time to talk over a coffee, creating new, weak, dyadic relationships.

Developing triads

Although more development activity focuses on pairs, it is trios – or triads – that are the most fundamental units in establishing networks. This is because adding an extra person to a former dyad impacts the way people are perceived and creates different group interactions. This qualitatively changes the nature of the relationships. For example, if I dislike the new person in a triad then I will like the other person more, as they are now my favourite. If I like the new person better then I will become less close to the other person.

Based upon the idea that a friend of my friend usually becomes my friend, triads of strong ties tend towards triadic closure, so a triad with only two strong ties is a 'forbidden triad'. The result of this is that each person in a triad can take responsibility for the relationship between the other two people. This means triads are more complex and exist at a super-personal level in the way that dyads do not.

For example, a triad member can escape blame for something they have not done by shifting responsibility to the group. In a dyad they only deal with one other person so this cannot be done. A person can also be constrained by a coalition of the other two people, providing the group with an ability to act for the collective. Triads tend to last longer than dyads because someone can stabilize the group when the relationship between the other two breaks down. However, triads involve less emotional support than in a dyad as people are more cautious about expressing how they feel about someone.

The patterns created by these triadic interactions influence how a whole network or organization will work. They can also inform systems-based coaching to improve relationships within small, often executive, groups, such as the golden triangle of the CEO, CFO and CHRO. The book *Coach and Couch* provides a nice example of coaching for a triad of CEO, CIO and COO (De Vries *et al*, 2015).

Developing groups

Within groups, trust manifests itself as psychological safety. According to Amy Edmondson, this is about having a sense of confidence that the work environment is conducive to taking interpersonal risks. In psychologically safe environments, 'people believe that if they make a mistake others will not penalize or think less of them for it. They also believe that others will not resent or penalize them for asking for help, information or feedback' (Edmondson, 2002).

Psychological safety is not quite the same thing as trust as it is more about the shorter term, about yourself rather than another person, and is something that is shared across a group. However, the concepts are clearly quite similar. Safety also has links to social sensitivity and conversational turn-taking, which have also been found to be enablers for team performance (see Chapter 5). Psychological safety is particularly critical for group learning, which is growing in importance given that teams are forming and reforming at an increasing rate. This leads to seeing teaming as a dynamic activity rather than a traditional, bounded group structure (Edmondson, 2010).

Google's Project Aristotle, which reviewed 180 teams over a period of several years (Duhigg, 2016), identified psychological safety as the most important dynamic informing the success of these groups (Rozovsky, 2015) – sales teams with high psychological safety overperformed by 17 per cent and ones with low safety underperformed by 19 per cent. Google recommends developing safety by creating an environment in which people can speak freely, letting team members own the process for creating new team norms, and showing an interest in team dynamics (BetterWorks, 2016).

Other potential development actions include team building, transition planning, confrontation meetings, mediation, role analysis and negotiation – including RACI/responsibility charting, work design (eg GE Workout/General Motors GoFast processes), appreciative inquiry (AI) and action learning. There are also tools such as Belbin and TMS, and a couple of team competency instruments, such as the Aston Team Performance Inventory.

Groups can also be improved by developing their internal and external networks, eg by creating bonding and broking relationships. Rob Cross suggests four inflection points that help network effectiveness. These are managing the centre of the network to avoid overloading connectors; leveraging the periphery of the network to ensure inclusion more quickly; bridging organizational silos to ensure effective collaboration at key network intersections (eg across functional lines or physical distance); and building energy and enthusiasm to create agility more easily (Cross, 2010). This activity can also be supported through the use of social network analysis – see Chapter 13.

Social organization designers can also support the design of group processes and practices such as Zappos's governance process (Chapter 7) and Morning Star's agreement process (Chapter 8). Another good example is Southwest Airlines' conflict management process. This is used when people have not been able to resolve conflicts themselves. This process focuses on an information-gathering meeting, which is only completed when a solution has been agreed. People are expected to do whatever they need to do, including baring their souls, to make this happen. As well as managing the conflict the process's goals are to maintain or develop people's self-esteem and mutual respect. However, if the conflict cannot be resolved it probably means that both people do not belong in the company (Gittell, 2005).

An important aspect of managing these social processes is arranging a common cadence across the organization or group, eg by having a team meeting at the same time every week. Another, possibly even more important requirement is ensuring that meetings are structured and managed effectively to minimize their time and optimize their benefits.

It can also be useful to get involved in facilitating the creation and managing the life cycle of groups. I have already referred to the well-known Tuckman model of team development in Chapter 10, however, there are also alternatives for other types of groups. As an example, communities can be seen to develop through initiation, potential, coalescing, discovery, maturing, growing up, stewardship and transformation stages (Gee and Hanwell, 2014). Part of developing a group involves creating PLY relationships between group members. Jan van Bavel's research shows that, as long as others feel similar to us, people will cooperate even when only recently connected. This suggests that one of the most important group behaviours is allocating time to talk about matters not directly connected to projects or other tasks (Haas and Mordenden, 2016).

Networks and communities are harder to maintain than teams as they do not have the same focus on meeting short-term business objectives. Facilitation is therefore even more important. Community management is thus an increasingly critical role for both HR and social organization designers.

All of the interventions listed above also apply to virtual groups, which have the same sorts of needs, but in which both development and effective performance are more difficult. These groups have to work even harder to ensure spontaneous communication, eg by structuring it as part of regular formal communication (Neeley, 2014). They also have to rely even more on technology (see Chapter 13).

Developing intergroup/cross-boundary relationships

Promoting cooperation and collaboration across groups and networks can involve increasing intergroup contact, implementing super-ordinate goals, developing common ingroup identity and/or finding a common enemy, exchanging team members and resolving intergroup conflict. It can also involve developing more or better bridging ties between the networks.

These actions are important as two of the key needs for the social organization are to replace hierarchical thinking with less vertically oriented intrapreneurial thinking, and especially to replace silo thinking with more horizontally oriented collaborative thinking.

Part 2 of the book provided suggestions for changes to organizational architecture that can make the effects of vertical boundaries between groups and horizontal layers between hierarchies less pronounced. However, silo and hierarchical thinking are mainly about people, their relationships and organizational norms. Therefore, actions such as exchanging team members are likely to play a significant role in social organization designers' plans.

Developing a whole organization

Developing the whole organization often involves large-scale facilitated techniques such as real-time strategic change, search conferences, future search, open space technique (unconferences and bar camps) and world cafe sessions. My favourite events are the unconferences I have mentioned previously (eg for 'Connecting HR' in Chapter 8). These are somewhat like conferences, but un! The un part is that there are no speakers, no presentations, no formality etc. Instead, a group of people get together and decide what they are going to talk about. They then spend the rest of the day talking about it. Because all of the sessions are heterarchical and people are discussing what they have suggested is important, the events always have lots of passion and energy. They are great for social communication, learning and planning, as well as relationship/organizational society development.

All the above approaches work best when designed for a particular organization and set of circumstances and needs. For example, the last time I facilitated an unconference we wanted there to be some actions to take away at the end of the day. However, we did not want to do a traditional debrief as this would result in taking back control from the group. We resolved this by combining an unconference with use of fishbowl technique (Hamlin, 2006) in which people shared and amplified the actions they were going to take.

Inclusion is another requirement that can be usefully tackled at the whole organization level. One way of supporting this is to increase people's contact with others who are different from them, eg through mentoring by boundary spanners. This helps us become more open and accepting of people's differences. Inclusion is important in ensuring the maximum contribution to social capital and to business performance. People also need to be able to see themselves as full members of the whole organization group, reinforced by individual PLY relationships between group members. This is possibly one of the most critical needs in developing a social organization.

Many social and prosocial behaviours are limited and constrained by people asking themselves 'what's in it for me?' (WIIFM). Often people will not see enough return to proceed with a particular desirable action. Even if they do, asking themselves this question can reduce the authenticity of their response. WIIFM is never going to go away, nor is it desirable that it should. However, cooperation and cultivation will never be performed optimally if that is all there is. WIIFM therefore needs to be supplemented by 'what's in it for us?' (WIIFU). This emerges from inclusion and a deep sense of shared social identity, supported by high levels of generalized organizational trust. One organization that has managed to develop a WIIFU approach is ARM. I think the people there really do think about each other first, and the impact of doing this is seen in the company's results (Ingham, 2011).

Generalized organizational trust is based in part upon the average levels of trust experienced in dyadic relationships, plus the psychological safety in groups, which a particular individual experiences. However, it also depends upon their perspectives of the organization and its employer brand, the conversations they have had about this, and other supporting evidence such as a company's Glassdoor ratings.

This means that it is helpful to reinforce the experience people are having of the organization. One way of doing this is through stories. These resonate with our social brains and ripple through social networks. They therefore act to stimulate learning, retention and communication. Pictures (even models, sometimes) can play a similar role. I also like to use metaphors as I find these connect deeply with people. I have already suggested metaphors for the four types of structure from the OPM/OMM:

- Simple structures as Roman legions (suggested for Microsoft in Chapter 7).

- Horizontal structures as pro sports teams (used by Netflix in Chapter 5).

- Community structures as families (used by Union Industries in Chapter 6).

- Network structures as jazz bands (used by Spotify in Chapter 9).

More generally, many organizations would benefit from developing the quality of the conversations between their people. People create meaning through the language they use and the topics they discuss. Social organization designers need to pay attention to the language used in the organization, including the deletions, distortions or generalizations that are used and the stories that are told. Techniques like discourse analysis can be included in an organization's measurement approaches too (see Chapter 13).

CASE STUDY Telling individual and team stories at Visa Europe

I attended an event at Visa Europe some years ago to hear about the way the company was creating an environment in which people do not feel they are 'being done to', but are 'doing it for themselves' and 'making ownership and accountability personal'. They had developed a new inspirational dream 'to be the world's most trusted company' and a new shared spirit that would make them different to other organizations by being competitive yet collaborative, trusted and a multicultural family.

We discussed a programme that supported these objectives and involved individuals and teams in identifying and developing stories to understand what the opportunities were, and to help them do more of what they wanted. Phase 1 was about the individual – and participation in this phase of the programme was made voluntary in order to create a different dynamic from the past. The phase consisted of plenary introduction sessions; small group sessions of just six to eight people, which were facilitated by an inspirational player – someone who had 'been there and got the T-shirt'; and development and communication of a personal values story. Having identified this story, individuals considered its implications by asking themselves three questions:

- Given you are this person and these are your skills and talents, what can you bring to this organization?
- How does this link? (Are you doing what you wanted to do when you grow up?)
- Are you in the right job and the right organization?

This would then lead on to an action plan. I heard one participant in the programme describing his story, which explored his 'home me' and his 'CV me'. He explained that once he had identified his talents from this story and discussed this with his group, his 'CV me' became the 'real me' – the distinction was removed: 'I'm now more passionate and enthusiastic for everything I do in life, directed to what I'm good at and would like to do anyway.'

This phase of the programme was focused on developing human capital but it started to develop social capital too, via people sharing their values stories within the team.

Phase 2 was all about social capital and focused on whole teams. The phase involved a team being facilitated to consider its alignment in terms of its purpose and its customers' dreams and nightmares:

- The team as a whole considers what they want to achieve.
- They then get in some customers to describe what keeps them awake at night.
- The team discusses what it wants to achieve for its customers.

The team would also look at its values, realigning its purpose based on the customer input that had been received. It would then move on to consider the implications of this, including barriers and challenges for action planning.

In terms of results, people had generally been very positive about the programmes. However, disbelievers were tolerated as long as they did the job they were expected to do. And some people had left the organization. Engagement, customer satisfaction and other statistics had gone up but the chief executive had said that the most important indicator was the stories people were telling and what he was seeing in the organization.

Summary and additional comments

1 Trust, love and psychological safety help create environments that our social brains experience as providing low/fair status differentials, related-ness and fairness. This helps individuals, teams and whole organizations to communicate, collaborate, cooperate and cultivate their relationships.

2 Actions concerning organizational societies have more potential to do damage than those concerned with the organizational architecture. Non-expert social organization designers should therefore take care in using any of the practices suggested in this chapter.

3 Developing an organizational society mainly depends on encouraging high-quality conversations between individuals, and within and between work groups (simple groupings, horizontal teams, communities and networks). Other groups may also have a role in developing the social organization. In particular, there is potential for unions and works councils etc to provide a very helpful, supportive role in tending an organizational society.

References

Bavel, JV and Cunningham, W (2013) [accessed 6 March 2017] When 'They' Become Part of 'Us', 'They' Don't All Look Alike, *Society for Personality and Social Psychology Connections*, 25 February [Online] https://spsptalks. wordpress.com/2013/02/25/socialidandpersonmemory/

BetterWorks (2016) [accessed 6 March 2017] Goal Summit 2016: The Science Behind Effective Teams at Google, 9 May [Online] https://www.youtube.com/watch?v=0K5Sr8MIcnU

Casciaro, T and Lobo, MS (2005) Competent fools, lovable jerks, and the formation of social networks, *Harvard Business Review*, June

Cross, R (2010) Improving leadership effectiveness through personal network analysis and development, in *The Organizational Network Fieldbook: Best practices, techniques and exercises to drive organisational innovation and performance*, pp 264–81, ed RL Cross, J Singer, S Colella, RJ Thomas and Y Silverstone, Jossey Bass, San Francisco

Cuddy, A (2015) *Presence: Bringing your boldest self to your biggest challenges*, Orion Publishing, London

De Vries, MFRK, Koroto, K, Florent-Treacy, E and Rook, C (2015) *Coach and Couch: The psychology of making better leaders*, Palgrave Macmillan, Basingstoke

Duhigg, C (2016) [accessed 6 March 2017] What Google Learned From its Quest to Build the Perfect Team, *New York Times Magazine*, 25 February [Online] https://www.nytimes.com/2016/02/28/magazine/what-google-learned-from-its-quest-to-build-the-perfect-team.html

Edelman (2017) [accessed 6 March 2017] 2017 Edelman Trust Barometer Reveals Global Implosion of Trust, 15 January [Online] http://www.edelman.com/news/2017-edelman-trust-barometer-reveals-global-implosion/

Edmondson, AC (2002) Managing the risk of learning: psychological safety in work teams, in *International Handbook of Organizational Teamwork*, ed M West, D Sjosvold and KG Smith, John Wiley & Sons, Chichester

Edmondson, AC (2010) *Teaming: How organizations learn, innovate, and compete in the knowledge economy*, Jossey Bass, San Francisco

Gardner, HK (2017) *Smart Collaboration: How professionals and their firms succeed by breaking down silos*, Harvard Business Review Press, Boston

Gee, I and Hanwell, M (2014) *The Workplace Community: A guide to releasing human potential and engaging employees*, Palgrave Macmillan, Basingstoke

Gittell, JH (2005) *The Southwest Airlines Way*, McGraw Hill Education, New York

Gratton, L (2007) *Hot Spots: Why some companies buzz with energy and innovation – and others don't*, Financial Times Prentice Hall, Harlow

Gurteen, D (2014) [accessed 6 March 2017] Randomised Coffee Trials [Online] http://www.gurteen.com/gurteen/gurteen.nsf/id/randomised-coffee-trials

Haas, M and Mordenden, M (2016) The secrets of great teamwork, *Harvard Business Review*, June

Hamlin, K (2006) [accessed 16 April 2017] Unconference Methods: Fish Bowl Dialogue [Blog] UnConference.net, 12/7 [Online] http://unconference.net/unconference-methods-fish-bowl-dialogue/

Handy, C (2000) *21 Ideas for Managers*, Jossey Bass, San Francisco

Henkes, M (2007) [accessed 6 March 2017] Employee Retention: Where is the Love?, *HR Zone*, 4 September [Online] http://www.hrzone.com/perform/people/employee-retention-where-is-the-love-by-matt-henkes

Ingham, J (2011) [accessed 16 March 2017] #CIPDSocial 11 Bill Parsons (ARM): Social Media and Why Business Needs to Take Notice, *Strategic HCM*, blog, 7 December [Online] http://strategic-hcm.blogspot.co.uk/2011/12/cipdsocial11-bill-parsons-arm-social.html

Kelly, M (2007) *The Dream Manager: Achieve results beyond your dreams by helping your employees fulfil theirs*, Hyperion, New York

Lisitsa, E (2012a) [accessed 6 March 2017] The Positive Perspective: Dr. Gottman's Magic Ratio!, *The Gottman Institute*, blog, 5 December [Online] https://www.gottman.com/blog/the-positive-perspective-dr-gottmans-magic-ratio/

Lisitsa, E (2012b) [accessed 6 March 2017] The Sound Relationship House: Build Love Maps, *The Gottman Institute*, blog, 7 November [Online] https://www.gottman.com/blog/the-sound-relationship-house-build-love-maps/

Neeley, T (2014) Communicate better with your global team, *Harvard Business Review*, 11 December

Parks, MR (2006) *Personal Relationships and Personal Networks*, Lawrence Erlbaum Associations, Mahwah

Roberts, K (2006) *Lovemarks: The future beyond brands*, PowerHouse Books, New York

Rozovsky, J (2015) [accessed 6 March 2017] The Five Keys to a Successful Google Team, 17 November [Online] https://rework.withgoogle.com/blog/five-keys-to-a-successful-google-team/

Ulrich, D (2015) [accessed 6 March 2017] The Future of HR is about Relationships, *People Management*, 2 (3) [Online] http://www2.cipd.co.uk/pm/peoplemanagement/b/weblog/archive/2015/03/24/the-future-of-hr-is-about-relationships.aspx

Zappos Family (2011) [accessed 6 March 2017] Zappos Wishez Program [Online] http://www.zappos.com/blogs/tag/zappos-wishez-program/

Using social technologies and analytics

13

Introduction

Social media is having a profound impact on many people's lives. It has also changed the way companies service their customers and market their products and services, as well as their job openings. Other than the operational benefits provided via search engine optimization etc, social media provides benefits in terms of better connections, relationships and conversations outside a firm, ie increasing relationship capital.

Social technologies help us to connect. They also help us to keep in contact with people we would otherwise lose touch with. And they help us to connect with others through our existing connections. For example, rather than the six degrees of separation referenced in Chapter 4, the average degrees between Facebook members has been calculated to be 3.57 (Bhagat *et al*, 2016).

One of my favourite social media apps is Swarm, which used to be part of Foursquare. Unlike most people who use it for its gamification elements – eg becoming the mayor of a particular place, often to gain offers and discounts – I use it for identifying and connecting with people. For example, at a conference I will log-in to Swarm and see who else has checked in there. They will generally have included a photo, or syndicated their check-in to Twitter, in which case I can find their photo there. Then I can walk around the conference hall looking for them – when I see someone I think is the person I can introduce myself and ask if they are who I think they are. This often produces an interesting reaction, but once I have explained that I found them on Swarm it produces a connection. In fact without really saying anything we have already become PLYs (people like yourselves, from Chapter 12) as we both use Swarm.

This ability to bring us together as PLYs means that we can also use social technologies to manage our relationships, although that is sometimes made harder than it should be (eg when LinkedIn decides to remove the ability to tag contacts' profiles). Interestingly, although social media has meant we can increase the number of our connections, it has not had much effect on the number of relationships we are able to maintain. For example, Robin Dunbar has found that the average number of Facebook friends is 155 (Dunbar, 2016).

We can also use social technologies to have conversations, both on completely open platforms such as Twitter and, increasingly, via more closed ones like Facebook and WhatsApp groups. Our social brains mean that we often find it easier to access information via conversation rather than more directly. For example, at one stage as social media was developing, a lot of people's favourite tool was their RSS reader, which provided a personalized real-time perspective on the social (and other) media world. Nowadays, a lot of people gain a similar input via Twitter. This provides much of the same information but it comes through the Twitter activity stream and so each input contains a name, photo and often the context of a relationship. The information referred to, or linked to, in the tweets is therefore socially and emotionally tagged, making it more interesting, relevant, and easier to process and learn from. This is the same reason why traditional intranets (where information goes to die) have lost ground to social knowledge management systems. The really interesting thing is that it is the 'noise' – ie the status updates about what people have been doing, which systems like Twitter get criticized for – that helps us to connect as PLYs and makes these systems so successful.

Increasingly, we are able to use social technologies within our organizations to gain similar benefits from people's connections, relationships and conversations internally too. There is also some evidence that having these internal online connections can make it easier to support external online connections with customers. For instance, one of my favourite examples of internal social applications was BestBuy's Twelpforce. This was canned in 2013 in response to the declining amount of conversation taking place on Twitter versus elsewhere. However, for a while it offered BestBuy a significant advantage and the company explained they were only able to operate it because of the collaborative environment they had built previously by using an internal enterprise social network called Blue Shirt Nation.

Social technologies also offer additional positive impacts by providing more opportunities for relatedness and also by developing organizational (as in not just online) social networks. It is certainly possible to use these systems to develop pure online relationships, but meeting face to face when possible is always really useful too. Unfortunately, the adoption of the tools within organizations has generally not been that successful. Social technology analyst Charlene Li has commented that the landscape is littered with failed technology deployments. Less than half of enterprise social networks are used regularly by a large proportion of employees (Li, 2015). I will explore the reasons for this lack of take-up in this chapter; however, one factor is lack of ambition in their use. For example, their main benefits are often reported to be reduced travel and photocopying expenses – these are worthwhile, but are absolutely only value-for-money benefits.

Getting more value out of the tools needs them to be linked very clearly to achieving social outcomes and also to be closely integrated with the other social activities addressed within this book. Li also notes that collaboration depends on trust, and that 'The tools themselves matter less than the ability of leaders to describe the intent and purpose of the tools. Simply putting a technology platform in place won't suffice – you must think through how the organization will change and how you will lead it into and through that change' (Li, 2015).

The tools can involve drawbacks too. As well as the social media risks that are well understood within HR, social technologies can contribute to the collaborative overload described in Chapter 11. Team chat systems seem to be a particular problem (Fried, 2016). Once again, this is about balance. Some organizations attempt to ensure people manage social tools in a better way but a more useful approach is to help individuals manage them for themselves. This is why understanding use of social tools needs to be part of a social organization's development programmes (see Chapter 11). Hopefully, the issue will become less significant with the development of better filtering and personal AI assistants such as IBM Watson's Workspace Moments.

We can also get carried away, using the tools to extreme, constantly seeking novelty, new information and especially social connections and exchanges. Sherry Turkle's research suggests that something as minor as having a mobile phone on the table in a meeting can negatively impact a conversation due to the ongoing threat of interruption (Turkle, 2015).

Excessive social-seeking behaviour also impacts our attention and ability to learn from our experiences. This is why neuroscientists often seem quite strongly against social media. I have often found that odd – since, for example, I often feel I learn most from the conferences I attend when I am busy blogging and tweeting. I spoke to social cognitive neuroscientist Matt Lieberman about this at one of the Neuroleadership Institute's summits and he suggested tweeting can be helpful for learning, even if it does impact on attention. When tweeting I am thinking about the people who are going to read my tweets. This turns on my social brain and means that I am learning socially as well as non-socially and this opens up deeper levels of learning – and I am still likely to attend to content that is most relevant for me.

So you are welcome to tweet about the final topics of this book that remain to be reviewed:

- digital HR and people management;
- digital technologies for the organizational society;
- social data-based analytics;
- social network analysis;
- return on connections, relationships and conversations.

Part 3 ends with encouragement to focus on liberating rather than controlling (people, data, technology etc).

Digital HR and people management

HR technology has progressed through the same sort of evolution as the rest of people management and workplace design, following the levels in the value triangle. In the 1990s and entering into the 2000s, HR technology was about value for money, making things easier by providing better administration. This level includes our systems of record, providing a single source of truth and core HR functionality, as well as data for the HR discipline. In the late 2000s we moved on to adding value, supporting the achievement of business objectives. Adding-value technology includes our systems of engagement, ie the automation of talent management processes, providing information for manager decision making and basic analytics. Because the focus of adding value is on the business we could use best practices, and be content with configuration rather than customization, which led to a shift towards cloud-based software as a service (SaaS).

Then, in the late 2010s, the focus became creating value – identifying new strategic opportunities through systems of productivity that allow people to do more for themselves. These systems include social collaboration and recognition; mobile apps, app stores and wearables; augmented and virtual reality; gamification/serious gaming; and sharing/gig economy platforms. All of these help create value by providing people throughout an organization with knowledge for their own productivity improvement. Because they are often designed to be used by everyone within an organization the user experience is key, meaning that unlike traditional HR systems, these new apps are designed for usability at least as much as they are for their functionality. Therefore they tend to be limited to point applications, which can be used to meet particular, best fit, needs.

It is all of the people-focused productivity systems listed above that I think are the basis for what might be called digital HR.

This extension of HR technology into all three levels of value has led to it having a very significant impact on the way people are managed and the benefits that can be obtained. It has also enabled HR's strategic role. This applies to the development of social capital just as much as it does to human capital, so digital HR is therefore a major driver of the social organization. Some social processes are only really feasible when using social or other digital tools.

This means that instead of HR or talent management systems, the new focus in HR technology is on point-of-performance apps, which enable people to achieve more, including by developing their connections, relationships and conversations. Examples available at the time of writing include:

- performance management apps, eg Workboard, BetterWorks, Impraise, Reflektive, Zugata, TruQu;
- reward, eg Bonusly;
- recognition, eg Globoforce, Achievers, WorkStars;
- learning, eg Coursera, Degreed, Udemy for Business;
- a range of social productivity apps such as OfficeVibe's FaceGame, Relationology, Universe of Emotions and Never Eat Alone/Lunch Roulette (Hewlett, 2013).

Rob Cross describes a nice idea from a dinner at the end of an offsite meeting. Each person was given an electronic name tag that was programmed with the person's existing network and requirements and was able to communicate with the other tags. If someone approached another person who was outside their network and had the requisite expertise the tag would flash a welcome greeting suggesting the topic they should discuss (Cross and Thomas, 2009).

PwC did something a bit simpler at one of their Partner conferences. They developed an app that integrated requirements from the business strategy, needs for geographic connection and an individual's own network to provide each person with a customized 'top 10 people to meet'. These people were identified with a photo and their table number to aid networking (ConnectedCommons, 2015)

There is huge potential in these and other similar digital tools. However, the main opportunity is the use of corporate social media.

Digital technologies for the organizational society

Corporate social media operates at a number of levels and in four main ways, which relate to the four types of group identified in the OMM. This is shown in Figure 13.1.

Figure 13.1   Opportunities for corporate social media

As demonstrated in Figure 13.1, internal social technologies operate in four zones:

- Zone 0 provides a base of effective, though not necessarily social, communication support. This includes instant messaging; audio, video and web conferencing, eg Cisco Webex; telepresence and social sharing, eg Box, Dropbox, Microsoft OneNote/Evernote Enterprise etc.

- Zone 1 enables social activity streaming, allowing people to update their status and see the status updates of others in a social news feed. Some systems also support automated updates (documents being added in

Sharepoint etc), file sharing, groups and other applications. These systems include Microsoft Yammer, Google's G Suite (includes Google+, Drive/Docs and Hangouts), Salesforce Chatter, Tibbr, Sitrion, Socialcast, Atos BlueKiwi etc.

- Zone 2 enables true social behaviours via activity streams plus a broader package of applications, including more extensive profiles plus blogs, pictures, videos etc and more portal-like functionality. Further differences between systems depend in part on which of the group types from the OPM they focus on, shown in Figure 13.1:

  - Social knowledge management systems provide simple, functionally based applications, including documenting knowledge to provide collective intelligence, sharing ideas and achievements and enabling other communications. The main example is Microsoft Sharepoint.

  - Social collaboration systems support horizontal project teams, including holding structured conversations around projects, aligning conversations with the flow of work and keeping in close contact with other team members, eg through messaging/chat. Examples include Slack, Microsoft Teams, Atlassian HipChat, Cisco Spark, SAP/SuccessFactors Jam and IBM Notes.

  - Social networking systems allow people to connect, develop relationships and have ongoing conversations with each other, including tagging people with skills and then finding people based on the skills they have been tagged with, ie expertise location, and exchanging ideas and comments across the whole organization. Examples include IBM Connections and Jive (which also does collaborations and communities well).

  - Social communities enable people to set up and participate in groups, helping them to develop their relationships. This is supported by community management functionality such as customized privacy settings. Examples include Salesforce Employee Communities, Microsoft Office 365 Groups, Telligent, Hoop.la and Workplace by Facebook.

- Zone 3 provides deeper functionality within more specialist areas that progress beyond typical business requirements. I have illustrated some of the most popular specialisms. Social intranets such as ThoughtFarmer, Interact Intranet, BroadVision Clearvale, Elium and Beezy provide more social knowledge management capabilities. Social project management systems such as Trello, Asana and Basecamp provide further advantages for teams. Social learning systems such as Saba offer social learning communities and broader learning capabilities. And social innovation systems such as Spigit and Innocentive@Work provide focused social networking capabilities.

The model does not work perfectly. For example, some systems offer capabilities in each of these areas. This applies particularly strongly to Microsoft, which is integrating OneNote, Sharepoint, Teams, Yammer Groups and Skype for Business together within Office 365. (In fact, the company's increasingly integrated products and integrated organization, described in Chapter 7, seem to offer further support for Conway's Law, referred to in Chapter 2. Traditional HR and talent management systems have also developed or acquired a range of social and other productivity systems, eg Oracle Social Network Cloud, PeopleFluent Socialtext.)

There are also other technologies that can be used. For example, in South Africa, due to challenges presented by the country's infrastructure, a client looked at using their EPOS system and internal radio station to provide a form of social networking. I am also not sure where to place things like holograms, augmented reality, video conferencing robots and socibots, or chatbots and the focus on conversational user experience (UX), which support communication in some organizations.

However, as you can see, each zone offers increased levels of functionality. Even zone 2 offers substantial capabilities, eg many organizations gain significant benefits from Yammer. Social capabilities here already outperform those of e-mail in many contexts, encouraging some companies to drop e-mail for corporate social media (Burkus, 2016).

Ten years ago I would have devoted a major part of this book to these tools and functionality. These days I do not feel the need to do that. The tools are now fairly well known and there are well-established cases for using them. In any event, the issues involved in their use are hardly ever about the technology but instead concern the human and social needs that the systems were designed to support. This is also one of the reasons for leaving social technologies to the last chapter of the book. Doing this also emphasizes that the shift to the social organization is brought about by sociological change, not just social media.

It is also the approach and behaviour that is important, not the technology – eg taking the case of Morning Star: this company launched its CLOU system without modern technology but has now moved the system online. This extends the system's utility, meaning that anyone can now review any of their colleague's commitments to check on the work the organization is undertaking or to plan how to interact with someone. It has also allowed other functionality to be added, eg the CLOU system now enables people to provide performance feedback on each other (Green, 2010). But the fact remains that the main idea of agreeing commitments remains fundamentally the same as it was before.

Digital technology as organization development

As identified above, the key to any of these systems is designing for the people who will be using them. Therefore, it is useful to treat their implementation as an organization development project, perhaps led by HR, even if the specific choice of technology is made by IT. Also, as with other organization development projects, these systems need to be developed in an ongoing, iterative manner, sensing how they are working and moving on to the next action to continue their development.

I also recommend the use of personas during these projects. These are summarized outlines of imagined people who represent and embody large or important segments of a target audience. They build upon common attributes within these audiences such as demographics, attitudes or behaviors that might influence the way these people use the system (Adlin and Pruitt, 2010).

Personas can help social organization designers and IT teams to think about the challenges and opportunities involved in introducing corporate social media systems to people in these different segments. Even more importantly, they help designers to keep focused on, and develop empathy for, the people who will be using the system, as well as the changes they are going through. Without doing this, it is very easy for the technology to become the focus of an implementation project.

A further approach I have used is to survey leaders and managers on the behaviours they want to develop within the organization, presenting choices between alternatives along a spectrum. For example, in one client, this included one spectrum outlining potential behaviours from controlling for effective decisions to liberating people for fast decisions. Another line ranged between allocating work to the right people based on grade, and allocating based on contribution. In another client, I discussed some particular moments of truth where these behaviours would be tested with the executive team. The agreed behaviours could then be used to create a freedom framework, charter or bill of rights for people working in the organization. This helps ensure people know what they are encouraged to do and what they are encouraged not to do. More importantly, it helps the managers to reinforce, rather than limit, the desired behaviours.

Social data-based analytics

Over the last 10 years, analytics has become an essential part of HR and people management. This is partly about the increasingly strategic nature of people management, ie the progression up the value triangle described in

Chapter 2. However, it is also down to new technology, which is allowing more people management activities to be automated, digitized and interrogated for patterns and correlations. This includes the substantial new capabilities provided by artificial intelligence and machine learning/cognitive computing. New visualization capabilities have also helped organizations to optimize the value of their analytics, gaining additional insight too. Some systems also enable changes to be made to the core data through the visualizations.

The supplementary benefit of introducing process automation technologies is that many of these produce streams of exhaust data that can be analysed to provide insight on the newly automated processes. These streams can sometimes be classified as big data. (The data in HR systems is neither big enough nor unstructured enough to be defined in this way.) Many technologies come with embedded analytics to help provide insight from this exhaust.

The easiest and potentially the best way of generating this type of insight is to use existing technologies that are already in place within the organization. However, if necessary, new technology can be implemented. Ideally this will provide value for the people providing their data so they have an incentive to use the technology. But sometimes a system that does not offer any benefits to individuals can be used. The next three sections review each of these opportunities in reverse: introducing new technology to provide data and analysis; introducing new enabling technology; and conducting analytics on existing technology.

Introducing new technology to provide data and analysis

A lot of analytics can only be performed by introducing new systems designed specifically to generate data to inform the analysis. This can be very useful for the individuals providing the information, as well as for the organization, but it is often necessary to extrinsically reward use of the technology too.

One good example is the use of radio frequency identification devices, and sometimes microchips, which can be injected under the skin and connect people into the internet of things. Sometimes of course, people also want to have, or already do have, somewhat similar devices. For example, people often wear Wi-Fi and Bluetooth-enabled health trackers (including digital watches) as they value the personal insights these devices can provide. This development is sometimes referred to as the 'quantified self'.

The most interesting research in this area has been conducted by Alex Pentland and Ben Waber at MIT using badge-like devices called sociometers, developed in collaboration with Hitachi, which brands the device as Hitachi Business Microscope.

The devices are worn on a lanyard around people's necks. They include various sensors, including infrared and wireless transceivers, an accelerometer and a microphone to monitor the interactions between people based on how they move and speak, where they are, and the conditions in the workplace such as the lighting and temperature levels. When two devices spend time in proximity to each other the system registers that a couple of people are in communication with each other. Sensors also pick up information on the quality of the conversation as indicated by the extent and frequency of nodding and hand gestures, and the way that people are speaking. This sort of technology can be used in many different contexts, eg to measure energy levels during a meeting to help the chair person keep it on track or to analyse an organization's social network.

CASE STUDY Socializing over lunch at Bank of America

Waber describes an interesting project for Bank of America that was designed to understand how differences in social interactions might have been leading to varying levels of performance between and within call centres. A number of teams in one of the call centres were given sociometers to wear, promoting some concerns about Big Brother-type surveillance. However, once the purpose of the study was explained, call-centre agents felt much happier. They had always felt that interactions with other people were important but had been unable to demonstrate the fact.

The sociometric data showed that team performance was linked to cohesive activity, ie chatting, between team members. Cohesiveness was not provided by formal meetings or conversations at people's desks but in the brief overlaps between people's lunch breaks. As a result of the research the bank aligned people's breaks, leading to an 18 per cent increase in cohesion, a large fall in employee turnover and a very significant cost saving (Waber, 2013).

Bank of America is an interesting case study, not just because of the use of the technology, but because it provides such a powerful illustration of the benefits of increased relatedness. In addition, it shows that this is the case even in a call-centre environment, which is typically run based on value-for-money principles, reducing human contact for the sake of increased efficiency. Yet even here it seems that social trumps human capital.

However, a slight concern is whether the study needed to take place. People seemed to know they would benefit from more interaction. A better, more organization development-focused approach might have been to talk to them about this, understand their needs, and experiment earlier with aligning schedules to fit the way people wanted to work. That is, could they just have been a bit more human/social without needing the data suggesting that being more human is a good idea?

Predicting team relationships at Saberr

The other common example of analytics using introduced technologies concerns data provided via surveys and questionnaires. As an example, Saberr provides a system called Base for predicting the effectiveness of relationships within teams. People complete a 15-minute multiple-choice survey thinking about themselves, ie their values, drivers or preferences and also, and in particular, their tolerances, eg whether they get upset by spelling mistakes. This focus on tolerances is based on earlier research into online dating, which found that the key to predicting relationships is whether someone is likely to find the other person irritating. Most people get on with most people but most of us also have trigger points that can separate us. When people push these buttons it will make it harder for us to have positive relationships. So it is helpful to feel similar to someone, as described in Chapters 4 and 12. But we can also get on with people if we have high tolerance for different types of people or just the things these other people value.

Saberr matches the information that has been provided on one person's acceptance of another and the other person's acceptance of them. It does this for each pairing and then looks at the broader and more complex dynamics that occur in triads and larger groups (outlined in Chapter 12). The system then generates reports for each individual and also the team as a whole, providing information on the predicted dynamics between team members. This includes the values they agree about in terms of having similar priorities and/or being tolerant of each other's views. And it also shows values they disagree with. Saberr recommends this is then given to the team as they have the most incentive to act on their problems. Everything is done online, allowing scoring and analysis to be completed in an agile, short-cycle way.

The system can be used in a variety of contexts. In recruitment or team resourcing it can be used to help identify which teams a candidate would fit best into, or to help teams select the individual who would be most likely to have the greatest fit. This meets an increasing need, given demands for faster teaming. In addition, people are increasingly unprepared to wait it out if they are not gelling with others in a team. For both reasons it is important to get team resourcing done right first time. The system would work best in a team focused on execution rather than innovation as it is then more useful to have higher homogeneity amongst team members.

The system can also be used to support team management and development. For example, Saberr profiled 60 people working on a number of sales desks in a recruitment company. These recruiters were all working and potentially competing with each other to place the same candidates into similar posts in different organizations. The analysis was then correlated with sales revenue to show that desks where recruiters had the best relationships with other recruiters performed better than other desks, with this difference accounting for about 30 per cent of the variation in sales performance. This gave the client the opportunity to help the lower-performing desks to model themselves on the higher performers.

This may be an increasing need as organizations become more people-centric. As explained in Chapter 10, the less rules there are the more important values and principles become. Therefore, if you do not have strong governance you need even better social cohesion. Alistair Shepherd, Saberr's co-founder, told me that the company is also developing a digital coaching tool for managers and team members. I like this idea as it would move focus away from fit, which is not always a good idea, to improving team effectiveness, regardless of the level of fit of the individuals. You might even be able to use the new system, or something similar, to improve diversity. For example, you could look to recruit people who do not fit, but have a broad tolerance for others who have a similar lack of fit.

Shepherd also suggested that as a group of people in any organization grows larger, their values quickly iron out to the values of an average human being. Therefore, to use Saberr's approach at an organizational level, Shepherd suggests using a network/team of teams approach. This would involve ensuring that at least one person from each team knows and has tolerating relationships with at least one person from other teams across the organization. It is not necessary, or helpful, for everyone to have the same values as everyone else.

Introducing new enabling technology

Sometimes it is possible to introduce new technology that generates data and insight whilst supporting people directly too. This makes it easier to ensure take-up of the system. A good example of doing this is implementing a social recognition system, which I included in my list of creating value HR technologies earlier in the chapter. As I explained in Chapter 11, recognition is a valuable and compelling social HR process that can lead to high levels of adoption. Therefore, some organizations introduce recognition systems before they move on to other corporate social media, believing (correctly) that if they can get their people to be social around recognition it will be easier to get them to be social over other aspects of work as well. However, the reason for raising recognition systems in this part of the chapter is that these also offer the benefit of extremely valuable exhaust data. This relates to who is giving and who is receiving the recognitions, helping identify talent; and what values or other criteria recognitions are based upon, assessing how well each value is lived.

CASE STUDY Analysing teams at Cisco

Another example of introducing new technology is provided by Cisco. Ashley Goodall, the company's head of leadership and team intelligence, suggests it always has at least 30,000 dynamic, transient teams doing work but not on the HR system. This means HR has no input on resourcing, coaching, assessing this element of people's value or compensating them based upon their full performance. In response to this, Cisco has developed a visualization system that helps them understand how many teams there are and helps team members to see their networks separate from the organizational hierarchy.

The system provides a team and team leader portal called Teamspace, which people can use to assess their strengths, find their teams and run an eight-item engagement pulse survey. Team leaders can use the system to judge team members' performance and, in return, gain a performance snapshot on their team. They also get to see performance patterns over time, supported by suggested priorities for team development. Goodall's team gains insight on everyone's performance, aggregated across the teams they have worked with during the previous year.

Cisco is also looking for correlations between this and other data to understand more about the performance of the teams and the careers of team members. One of the things they have done is to ask executives about which teams they would like to clone. They have then compared the questions in the engagement pulse survey to the high-performing teams, as identified by the executives. Goodall has identified that these best teams statistically outperform on six out of eight engagement items. The top three are whether other team members share their values, whether team members have their back (ie whether they are experiencing psychological safety) and whether they can use their strengths. Cisco is now looking at how they can amplify the teaming excellence found in these best teams, eg by selecting the right team leaders, and in the way they help intact teams.

The system has been designed to encourage weekly performance check-ins, firstly to increase engagement but also because real-time usage is needed to get real-time insight. And it offers valuable insight to team members and leaders so that people use it and the company is able to gain the data that it needs.

Conducting analytics on existing technology

The final, and potentially best, option is to introduce new analytics to build on existing technology and data streams. This can be the best solution because it does not require people to do anything new but simply generates new benefits based on something people are already doing. Analysing the nodes, links and semantics within these systems provides insight on people's connections, relationships and conversations respectively.

The most common example is to mine e-mail trails and corporate social media activity streams to analyse existing social networks. This type of social network analysis can be done on a batch or real-time basis and can work on a very large network. This approach can replace or supplement more traditional (though still not that extensively used) survey-based approaches. However, it will only relate to the types of relationship maintained within the e-mail or social media system, ie it will not include face-to-face relationships etc. A basic introduction to social network analysis is provided in the next section of this chapter.

The information being mined is the message meta-data (sender, receiver, time stamp etc) so the analysis focuses on connections and relationships rather than conversations. Example systems include TrustSphere, Polinode and Laurence Lock Lee's Optimice Swoop Analytics. Swoop uses data from Yammer and provides the sort of metrics you would get on an external social media platform. For individuals this includes the numbers of posts, replies, likes, mentions and response rates, an ego network visualization, their give/receive balance, proportion of two-way relationships (measuring reciprocity) and their network density (see next section). The enterprise dashboard provides an overview of users, two-way relationships, the pattern of cross-team collaboration activity per person, key players, influential people, response rate, hot topics, most active people and groups, and the most engaging posts.

VoloMetrix, which is now part of Microsoft, does analytics on Microsoft's Office Graph data set, which informs its Delve analysis tool. This provides people with analysis on how they have spent their time during the previous week, including hours spent on meetings, e-mail and focused activity, including time spent after hours. It also provides information on people's relationships, including key contacts and the connections they are losing touch with. This is data that most people have not seen or given much thought to and it helps them to think differently about how they spend their time.

One of VoloMetrix's clients was suffering the effects of excessive bureaucracy through procedures, checklists and status meetings. A project was established to free up front-line managers from managing up and status reporting so they could spend more time on the floor, helping junior colleagues. The researchers calculated and benchmarked an organization load index based on time spent in meetings and e-mails. This suggested the company could take back 10,000 hours of unproductive work, which would also reduce managerial redundancy and improve engagement. The solution was to provide information on where time was being spent, which created a feedback loop driving down time spent on meetings and e-mail by two hours per week over the next nine months. This contrasted to the time wasted by the control group who did not receive the reports, which got dramatically worse, increasing by 3.5 hours per week over the same period (ConnectedCommons, 2016). (This is an interesting example but it looks to me as if the target group were transferring their collaborative overload on to the control group. Given the complexity of today's work environments this sort of unintended consequence can often occur.)

Heidi Gardner provides another example for a professional services client where the time reporting system had been used to compare changes in employees' project-based networks with revenue and other business objectives. This demonstrated that more-collaborative employees consistently achieved better results (Gardner, 2017).

Internal social analysis can even be performed using people's external social media-based networks (Fire, Puzis and Elovici, 2013). External social networking can be analysed using Marc Smith's NodeXL.

Analysing conversations requires full access to e-mail or online social networking data so this may present privacy and confidentiality issues. Systems like UltiPro Perception (formerly Kanjoya) can provide sentiment analysis on the conversations taking place within an organization to provide a broad variety of insight. Systems operate at various levels of analysis, increasing in validity from dictionary-based systems to natural language/

semantic processing, to cognitive computing/machine learning. (You can try out IBM Watson's cognitive semantic analysis here: https://personality-insights-livedemo.mybluemix.net.)

Social network analysis (SNA)

Social network analysis (SNA) maps and measures the connections and relationships between people, both visually and mathematically. The approach emerged in sociology and anthropology but is also used within businesses where it is sometimes called organization network analysis. Experts/vendors include Rob Cross from Activate who uses UCINET analysis and NetDraw visualization software; and Valdis Krebs from Orgnet who uses his own InFlow system. Other tools include Maven7's OrgMapper, Syndio, Synapp, Innovisor and KeyNetiQ. I use several of these tools.

The traditional way of collecting data is through a survey. Questions should focus on whatever aspect of social capital are important in a particular organization. However, a particularly useful question is whether someone would like to spend more time with a person. This helps identify people at risk of collaborative overload. SNA visualizations are called sociograms and look a little like the network diagrams in Figure 4.1. They can also show the changes in organizational connections over time. Autodesk provides an interesting example of this type of dynamic visualization using their simple/hierarchical organization structure (Matejka, 2012). The mathematical analysis often uses algorithms to disentangle key messages from the considerable noise that exists in these data sets, especially when they have been generated from actual communication flows.

Rob Cross suggests that key organizational metrics are network density and cohesion. Important individual metrics are degree, betweenness and closeness centrality, plus measures of brokerage and boundary spanning (Cross and Parker, 2004). Density is a measure of overall network connectedness based on the percentage of possible ties. Cohesion is the average of the shortest paths required to reach all network members. Centrality metrics are focused on individuals but can provide insight on the whole network too. Degree centrality is the average number of connections per person in a network. Betweenness centrality is the extent to which a person brokers unconnected people. Closeness centrality is the extent to which a person has short path lengths to many other people.

For instance, groups or clusters within hub-and-spoke and multi-hub networks (networks A and B in Figure 4.1) will have high degree and betweenness centrality. Network hubs can also be identified by using individuals' clustering coefficients. This measures the connectivity around each person, ie whether their neighbours are also connected to each other, through the proportion of triads (defined in Chapter 12) that are closed. An area of high clustering indicates some form of subgroup within the network, eg one of Cisco's dynamic teams, or an informal community of practice.

Online networks often look slightly different to the above topologies. Most often they are core and periphery networks. These consist of three concentric rings. The centre is a densely connected core. The middle ring consists of loosely connected network fragments. The outer ring is made up of largely disconnected people who are often referred to as lurkers. Etienne Wenger calls these people legitimate peripheral participants (Lave and Wenger, 1991) and suggests they are vital to community effectiveness. People often move from the periphery to the network core. They can also provide a useful audience for people in the core.

The 90–9–1 rule (Nielsen, 2006) suggests that 90 per cent of online networks will be lurkers, 9 per cent will contribute some of the time, and 1 per cent will participate frequently. With effective community management etc, networks can do a lot better than this, but the rule is still a broadly accurate indication. This suggests that online communities need to be significantly larger than physical ones in order to get the mass of people they need to provide a sustainable core. Many online groups, which are often called communities, are really networks not communities but, as explained above, they do often have a community at the centre. The other reason for calling them communities is that this makes a group sound nice and human. However, it does not necessarily indicate any sense of community. For example, I moderate a Google+ community on Social HR (Social HR, 2017). I sometimes find interesting information shared within this group but it has absolutely no resemblance to a true community.

You can also look at this the other way around. Because many people are part of a large number of groups, including projects, communities and networks, they simply do not have time to contribute to many of these. They may be in 100 groups but only contribute actively to one, less so to a few others, and lurk in the majority. Groups that want to increase the numbers of active participants need to think about how they get more of these people to see the group as important enough to put more of their limited time into it.

Other metrics help identify key people within the network. Rob Cross notes that 3–5 per cent of people generally account for 20–25 per cent of networking connectivity so we need to be able to identify these people. They include:

- Hubs or central connectors who have high degree centrality which makes them highly influential.

- Pulsetakers who either have a small number of connections to central connectors or have established high closeness centrality in other ways. This gives them a finger on the pulse of the organization. They are very good at distinguishing weak signals from noise.

- Brokers who have high betweenness centrality. They hold the network together and control information flow.

- Boundary spanners who have similar metrics but visualizations will show their bridging is across network boundaries. They are critical for sharing information across disparate parts of the organization and can act as effective change agents. Boundary spanners are likely to be top performers within an organization.

- Energizers or charismatic connectors who are people who create energy through their connections and relationships. They can infect a large number of direct and indirect connections around them.

The people in these roles are an organization's social talent, ie from a social capital or social network-based perspective, these are the people who make the largest contributions to the performance and potential of the organizations they work within. However, Rob Cross suggests these people are only identified as talent, in the way we are currently defining and measuring it, about 25–40 per cent of the time.

Undertaking an SNA validates planned connections or reveals the emergent patterns of interaction in organizations, and enables their changes over time to be monitored and influenced. It is therefore a useful intervention to undertake. However, it is not always necessary to use an SNA to become a social organization. It is a bit like an engagement survey that can sometimes be used, even when everyone already understands why engagement is low, and no one has any intention to do anything differently when this fact is re-presented. Most organizations will face significant opportunities to improve social capital, which should be easily discernible without running an SNA survey.

Even if more insight is required, it may still not be appropriate to conduct an SNA. People tend to see these studies as more sensitive than engagement surveys. This can be a major barrier to their use, especially as initial levels of trust in an organization can often be quite low. SNA surveys also need a high response rate to generate sensible results. Plus there are alternatives. One option is to run a focus group. For smaller groups, there are organization development approaches that can be used such as group pictures (drawing a group) or group sculpting (physically moving people around a room). Another simple approach is mapping the communication flows during a group meeting.

The caveat, and it is a big caveat, is that if an organization is intending to make decisions about individual people based upon social insights they should conduct an SNA, or gain similar insights by using sociometers or the like. This is because subjective identification of social talent groups tends not to be that accurate. We should not just trust our intuition for this.

I would also think about running an SNA survey if there was a different but clear purpose for this. For example, I might well do a survey before changing the workplace design, holding a conflict resolution meeting, or introducing an enterprise social network. In these cases an SNA could be seen as part of an organization development process and would almost certainly be cost effective in terms of its impact on the next intervention in the process.

CASE STUDY Analysing social networks at Juniper Networks

Juniper's initial interest in social networks was triggered by a need to find out which people had been involved in a particular customer outage. The business executives provided Steven Rice, executive vice president of HR, with a list of 300 people they thought had been involved. He surveyed these people and identified that about 50 per cent were not part of the programme. However, the remaining 50 per cent identified over 700 more people who were also central to the programme. This provided over 900 people who were involved in serving the customer (Boudreau and Rice, 2015). An SNA survey on these 900 people identified 5 per cent of them who were connectors, brokers and boundary spanners and who accounted for around 20 per cent of all connections. When Rice looked at these people it became evident that they were not on any hi-po list, succession plan, compensation beauty list etc. This showed that Juniper's HR processes did not get to the heart of which people drove business performance. Rice therefore closed down these processes and introduced new, more social approaches across the organization (Roberts, 2014). He also maintained contact with the social talent group.

This came in useful following a major change in strategy. The executives wanted to understand how quickly they could mobilize the company around their new plan. A basic questionnaire survey showed that only 30 per cent of people understood the new approach. In response, over a three-week period, Rice broke down the social talent into smaller groups of about 10 people and had each group sit down with the CEO. These people were then told to go out, tell their friends about what they had heard, and get them excited. The next survey showed over 80 per cent of people understood and appreciated the shift in strategy.

One worry linked to the SNA data has been that the top 10 per cent connected people in the network experience 21 per cent lower engagement scores due to collaborative overload. This insight has given Juniper a much better understanding of some highly critical people at risk of attrition. The company therefore brought the network back together and created experiences to build the skills that the social talent needed to maintain their effectiveness more efficiently.

Calculating return on connections, relationships and conversations

Despite the amount of data and insight that can be developed around social activities and outcomes it can be very difficult to demonstrate that these are linked, or show how they impact changes in the rest of the business. There are two major problems. The first is that many activities linked to cultivating an organizational society tend to be intangible. This may not apply to the use of social technologies, but many other activities, particularly those relating to organization development, described in Chapter 12, can be very difficult to measure in an objective way. This difficulty also applies to the outcomes of social activities, ie the connections, relationships and conversations that are hoped will result.

Jay Cross and Jon Husband explain that because of these difficulties it is often not possible to calculate return on investment (ROI). They suggest a more appropriate measure for the network era is ROII, which is the return on investment in interaction (Cross and Husband, 2009). I also like Euan Semple's suggestion that rather than calculating the ROI of using social tools we should look at the ROI of not using them: 'What is the financial benefit of continuing to do things in inefficient ways when there are more effective alternatives available?' (Semple, 2012).

The second issue is about complexity. This means that even when it is possible to understand why things are as they are (descriptive analytics) it can still be impossible to predict how things will be in the future (predictive analytics): 'Although a complex system may, in retrospect, appear to be ordered and predictable, hindsight does not lead to foresight because the external conditions and systems constantly change' (Snowden and Bone, 2007). This means that measures and analytics provide limited help and, instead of this, organizations must probe – ie take the best action they can, then sense, and respond.

General McChrystal, who I mentioned in Chapter 8, refers to the near-perfect, real-time 'situational awareness' provided via feeds from unmanned arial vehicles and GPS monitoring etc. However, even despite all of this he still suggests that big data cannot save us: 'While this profusion of information proved of great value, it was never very useful for prediction... We have moved from data-poor but fairly predictable settings to data-rich, uncertain ones' (McChrystal *et al*, 2015).

This means that social business designers may need to satisfy themselves and their stakeholders with using qualitative and subjective measures and with seeking to understand relationships between social activities, social outcomes and business results, without being able to prove they exist. In this environment, analysis needs to be complemented by synthesis – the development of an understanding of the whole system. Return on connections, relationships and conversations also becomes a conversation rather than a number, informing a broader organization development approach.

Summary and additional comments

1 Social technologies and analytics offer new and exciting opportunities for developing social organizations. In the main, however, it is still important to focus on what a particular organization is trying to do. As described in Chapter 5, this should be about using best-fit social activities to develop appropriate social outcomes. Technology and data can enable these activities, they should not replace the thinking about what activities it makes sense to undertake. Doing otherwise would risk repeating the experience relating to early and excessive use of e-learning, which I described in Chapter 1.

2 There will be exceptions to the above. As described earlier, the human brain loves novelty and certain things can work just because they are new. This applies particularly well to shiny new technology. It is important that social organization designers keep abreast of new developments in technology, and if something is developed that may create even better social outcomes then I would encourage you/them to go ahead. Just be careful about how much time, effort and money you are investing – and engage in conversation about whether the return on connection exists.

Summary of Part 3 – Liberating vs controlling

Social organization designers sometimes see the use of social technology and the data it produces as an opportunity to deal with the intangibility and complexity of the social organization (referred to above). The increasing use of wearables is a good example of this. Organizations sometimes see their people walking round with Fitbits and Apple Watches and using the data these devices provide to help them do the right things more consistently. (I love being reminded to breathe every two hours, for example.) Or they read the case studies on the use of sociometers and think they need to benefit from these. So they call someone in and give people badges or whatever, and think they can use this data to make their people do the right things. This often does not work.

My best example on this comes from the *Daily Telegraph*. Their journalists came in one day to find strange black boxes fitted under their desks. People asked their managers what the boxes were for and were told they supported better environmental management. But the journalists checked the logo on the boxes and found out the firm in question focused on saving space by introducing hot desking etc. The workforce rebelled and the next day the black boxes had all been removed (Waterson, 2016). It was a crazy (though sadly very common) thing to do – especially with a group of journalists, whose jobs are all about investigating things!

The mistake that organizations like this are making is to use creating value technology in a value-for-money way. What I mean by this is that they are forgetting that wearables are about helping people do more for themselves (explained in the section on digital HR at the start of this chapter). To take the data from these wearables and treat it like data from the HR system of record makes no sense. The opportunity is not to use the data but to give the data back to their people to help them do the right thing for themselves. It is not the quantified organization that is important, but the quantified and enabled person!

More broadly, this is an extreme example of a mistake that is made about all of the actions associated with growing an organizational society, and some of those linked to the social architecture too (eg those relating to the workplace design). As mentioned in Chapter 2, social behaviours are discretionary and depend upon people being intrinsically motivated to adopt them. The cultivation of an organizational society, and therefore all the social activities described in Part 3 of the book, should be about liberating people, not controlling them.

This last statement marks the end of Part 3 and also the conclusion of the book. However, having completed it, you may want to turn back to the options identification process (Figure 5.1) in Chapter 5. This model/chapter will help you plan how to cultivate your organizational society, as well as to design a social architecture, in a way that will help you to create social capital and a new basis for competitive success.

References

Adlin, T and Pruitt, J (2010) *The Essential Persona Lifecycle: Your guide to building and using personas*, Morgan Kaufmann, San Francisco

Bhagat, S, Burke, M, Diuk, C, Filiz, IO and Edunov, S (2016) [accessed 6 March 2017] Facebook Research, Three and a Half Degrees of Separation, 4 February [Online] https://research.fb.com/three-and-a-half-degrees-of-separation/

Boudreau, J and Rice, S (2015) Bright, shiny objects and the future of HR, *Harvard Business Review*, July–August

Burkus, D (2016) [accessed 6 March 2017] Some Companies are Banning Email and Getting More Done, *Harvard Business Review*, 8 June [Online] https://hbr.org/2016/06/some-companies-are-banning-email-and-getting-more-done

ConnectedCommons (2015) [accessed 6 March 2017] Thought Leader Spotlight: Ted Graham, PwC, *ConnectedCommons* [Online] http://www.connectedcommons.com/451-2/

ConnectedCommons (2016) [accessed 6 March 2017] Reimagine Productivity With Organisation Analytics – Chantrelle Nielsen, *ConnectedCommons*, 1 June [Online] http://www.connectedcommons.com/506-2/

Cross, J and Husband, J (2009) [accessed 6 March 2017] Productivity in a Networked Era: Not Your Father's ROI, *Chief Learning Officer*, July [Online] http://www.internettime.com/2009/06/not-your-fathers-roi/

Cross, R and Parker, A (2004) *The Hidden Power of Social Networks: Understanding how work really gets done in organisations*, Harvard Business School Press, Boston

Cross, R and Thomas, RJ (2009) *Driving Results Through Social Networks: How top organisations leverage networks for performance and growth*, John Wiley & Sons, Chichester

Dunbar, RIM (2016) Do online social media cut through the constraints that limit the size of offline social networks?, *Royal Society Open Science,* 3 (1), 20 January

Fire, M, Puzis, R and Elovici, Y (2013) [accessed 6 March 2017] Organization Mining Using Online Social Networks, *Cornell University Library* (arXiv:1303.3741v2 [cs.SI]), 2 September [Online] https://arxiv.org/abs/1303.3741

Fried, J (2016) [accessed 6 March 2017] Is Group Chat Making You Sweat?, *Signal v. Noise*, 7 March [Online] https://m.signalvnoise.com/is-group-chat-making-you-sweat-744659addf7d#.84fky0dyx

Gardner, HK (2017) Getting your stars to collaborate, *Harvard Business Review*, January–February

Green, P (2010) [accessed 1 December 2017] The Colleague Letter of Understanding: Replacing Jobs With Commitments, *Management Innovation eXchange*, 15 April [Online] http://www.managementexchange.com/story/colleague-letter-understanding-replacing-jobs-commitments

Hewlett, SA (2013) [accessed 6 March 2017] A New Way to Network Inside Your Company, *Harvard Business Review*, 8 January [Online] https://hbr.org/2013/01/a-new-way-to-network-inside-yo

Lave, J and Wenger, E (1991) *Situated Learning: Legitimate peripheral participation*, Cambridge University Press, Cambridge

Li, C (2015) Why no one uses the corporate social network, *Harvard Business Review*, 7 April

Matejka, J (2012) [accessed 6 March 2017] OrgOrgChart: The Evolution of an Organization, *Autodesk Research*, 12 December [Online] https://www.autodeskresearch.com/projects/orgorgchart

McChrystal, S, Collins, T, Silverman, D and Fussell, C (2015) *Team of Teams: New rules of engagement for a complex world*, Penguin Books, London

Nielsen, J (2006) [accessed 6 March 2017] The 90–9–1 Rule for Participation Inequality in Social Media and Online Communities, *Nielsen Norman Group*, 12 October [Online] https://www.nngroup.com/articles/participation-inequality/

Roberts, B (2014) [accessed 6 March 2017] The Value of Social Network Analysis: Conducting a Social Network Analysis Can Help Companies to Reveal Their Unexpected Influencers, *Society for Human Resource Management*, 1 January [Online] https://www.shrm.org/hr-today/news/hr-magazine/pages/0114-social-network-analysis.aspx

Semple, E (2012) *Organisations Don't Tweet, People Do*, John Wiley & Sons, New York

Snowden, DJ and Bone, ME (2007), Providing a leader's framework for decision making, *Harvard Business Review*, November

Social HR (2017) [accessed 17 March 2017] Social HR, Google+ community [Online] https://plus.google.com/u/0/communities/106421696029286952798

Turkle, S (2015) *Reclaiming Conversation: The power of talk in a digital age*, Penguin Putnam, New York

Waber, B (2013) *People Analytics: How social sensing technology will transform business and what it tells us about the future of work*, Financial Times Prentice Hall, New Jersey

Waterson, J (2016) [accessed 6 March 2017] Daily Telegraph Installs Workplace Monitors on Journalists' Desks, *BuzzFeed News*, 11 January [Online] https://www.buzzfeed.com/jimwaterson/telegraph-workplace-sensors

INDEX